CHECKPOINT 300

Checkpoint 300

COLONIAL SPACE IN PALESTINE

Mark Griffiths

University of Minnesota Press
Minneapolis
London

Portions of chapter 1 are adapted from "Biopolitics and Checkpoint 300 in Occupied Palestine: Bodies, Affect, Discipline," *Political Geography* 65 (2018): 17–25, with permission from Elsevier. Portions of chapter 2 are adapted from "Women and Checkpoints in Palestine," *Security Dialogue* 52, no. 3 (2021): 249–65. Portions of chapter 3 are adapted from "Women's Lives beyond the Checkpoint in Palestine," *Antipode* 52, no. 4 (2020): 1104–21. Portions of chapter 5 are adapted from "A Relational Comparison: The Gendered Effects of Cross-Border Work in Palestine within a Global Frame," *Annals of the American Association of Geographers* 112, no. 6 (2022): 1761–76, copyright 2022 by American Association of Geographers, reprinted by permission of Taylor & Francis Ltd, https://www.tandfonline.com, on behalf of American Association of Geographers.

Published by the University of Minnesota Press
111 Third Avenue South, Suite 290
Minneapolis, MN 55401-2520
http://www.upress.umn.edu

ISBN 978-1-5179-1983-2 (hc)
ISBN 978-1-5179-1984-9 (pb)

A Cataloging-in-Publication record for this book is available from the Library of Congress.

Printed in the United States of America on acid-free paper

The University of Minnesota is an equal-opportunity educator and employer.

For Jean and Paul

Contents

Introduction. Corridors and Turnstiles: 1
Colonial Control in Palestine

1 The Punitive Commute: 19
   Disciplining Palestinian Labor

2 Women at the Checkpoint: 43
   The Colonial Production of Gender

3 Beyond the Checkpoint: 65
   Domestic Life in Palestine

4 An Urban Geography of Checkpoint 300   83
   and the Hebron Road

5 Producing Checkpoint Space: 119
   Global Flows of Ideas and Technologies

6 Re/making Colonial Space: 151
   Refusal, Adaptation, Survival

   Conclusion. Geographies for a   177
   Decolonized and Free Palestine

   Acknowledgments   191

   Notes   195

   Index   225

Introduction

Corridors and Turnstiles

COLONIAL CONTROL IN PALESTINE

Checkpoint 300 is between two of the most important centers of Palestinian life, Jerusalem and Bethlehem. Built into Israel's West Bank wall (the "separation barrier"), the checkpoint complex is itself an extraordinary organization of space: turnstiles and corridors corral and subordinate a colonized population for inspection and validation by soldiers and security staff. Crushing queues, unpredictable delays, and the always-pronounced threat of denial or detention have made crossing part of a punitive commute endured by thousands of West Bank Palestinians each day. Some can pass through as laborers using special work permits, others as students, hospital patients, or worshippers during religious holidays. Still others are excluded by Israel's strict permit system: many women, younger men, the blacklisted, and generally anyone without a sanctioned purpose to cross. Around Checkpoint 300, in a once vibrant part of northern Bethlehem, the residents and businesses that remain must endure the spacio-cidal effects of Israeli military control. As the wall carves out space for Israeli settlers on the other side, it reaches deep into a part of the city of cultural and economic significance, subjecting all Palestinian life in the area to intense surveillance and frequent explosions of military violence. Israeli soldiers and border police are stationed and readied to transform it into urban battle space, putting to use a vast arsenal of high-tech weaponry to target signs of Palestinian objection to colonial control. Those who supply the weapons and other security technologies inside the checkpoint compete for contracts in Israel and overseas, marketing their wares as "battle-tested" in the control of Palestinian land and population. Control, however, is of course not absolute: this part of Palestine remains steadfastly Palestinian as social and political life negotiates or counters Israeli rule. This book examines these multiple political geographies of Checkpoint 300 to tell the story of colonial space in Palestine.

A part of this story that must be foregrounded is that Checkpoint 300 is a border crossing that regulates the movement of Palestinians from one part of Palestine to another. To exit Bethlehem and emerge on the Jerusalem side is to remain on land owned by Bethlehemite families that has been sequestered by the Israeli state. It should also be remembered that the Green Line—the demarcation between territories that are internationally recognized as Israeli and Palestinian—is still approximately two kilometers to the north (see Map 1). As I will reiterate at various points, everything described in this book takes place on Palestinian land, and this applies to definitions based on both historic Palestine and United Nations (UN)-defined Palestinian territories.[1] This is not, then, a crossing *between* Palestine and Israel but a crossing *within* Palestine, a colonial imposition that funnels Palestinian movement through Israeli security architecture. Checkpoint 300's location at this point is highly strategic; it is built across the historic Hebron Road (Tariq al-Khalil and sometimes Road of the Patriarchs), which runs from the south through Hebron, Bethlehem, and Jerusalem and northward to Nablus and Nazareth. In the Bethlehem section close to the checkpoint is Rachel's Tomb (also known as Bilal bin Rabah Mosque), a site of religious importance in the three main Abrahamic faiths and one that has been entirely enclosed by the ten-meter-high wall that Israel has built. Rachel's Tomb and the intersection to its immediate south are historically considered the northern entrance to the city of Bethlehem (it is, in fact, not coincidentally, the site where British soldiers would check documents during the Mandate period [1920–48]) (see Figure 1). A veer left after the tomb follows Manger Street to the Church of Nativity, the birthplace of Jesus; continuing straight leads to Hebron, twenty-five kilometers away, the burial site of Abraham and the Patriarchs of Abrahamic religions. To the north, of course, is Jerusalem, the city of Palestinian cultural and political importance that Israel seeks to control through a regime of segregation and elimination. Access to Jerusalem for West Bank Palestinians[2] is restricted by a bureaucratic permit system that is materially enforced by Checkpoint 300 and other checkpoints that dot the eastern perimeter of the city (e.g., Qalandia Checkpoint, between Ramallah and northern Jerusalem).

These restrictions are relatively recent, especially when set against

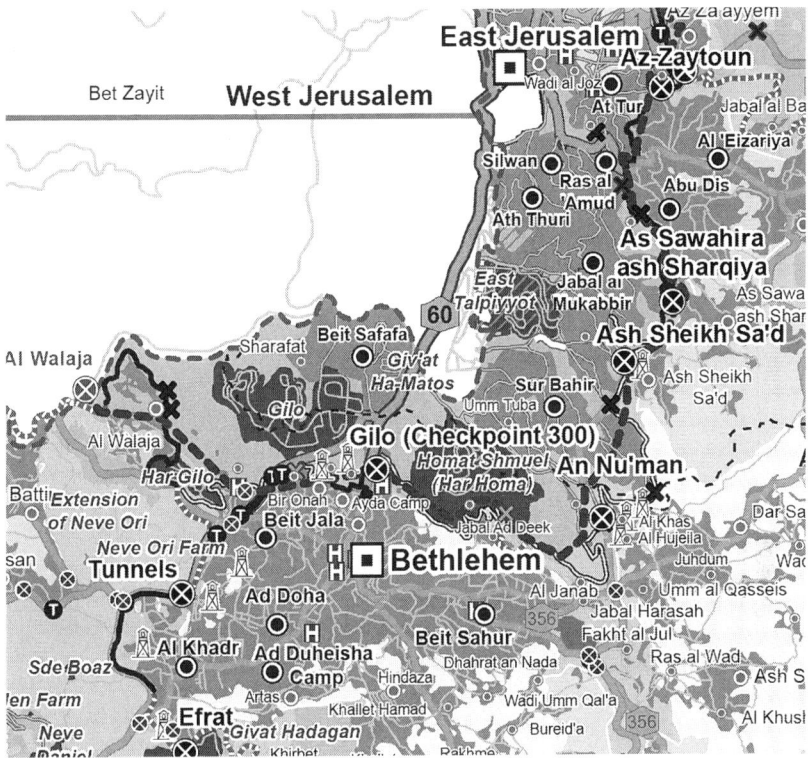

MAP 1. Contemporary colonial restrictions: a map of the many barriers and checkpoints between Bethlehem and Jerusalem. Detail of West Bank Access Restrictions Map (May 2023) published by the UN Office for the Coordination of Humanitarian Affairs (OCHA).

the biblical history that (only partially) defines the area. People in Bethlehem recount stories from up to the 1990s of more or less free passage across historic Palestine, of daytrips to the coast and longer trips to Damascus, Beirut, and Cairo.[3] An afternoon watching the sun go down from the beaches and ports of Jaffa or Haifa was an appreciated but entirely routine pleasure for Bethlehemites and all Palestinians. Israel's occupation of Palestinian land has made these mobilities not only impossible but almost unimaginable, especially to the generations that have grown up with the restrictions that tightened during the First Intifada (1987–93) and again in the period immediately post-Oslo (the accords signed between Palestine and Israel in 1993 and 1995), before reaching toward current levels during and after the Second Intifada (2000–2005). To be clear, it is not that

FIGURE 1. Historical colonial restrictions: British soldiers search Palestinian farmers for arms outside Rachel's Tomb in 1936. From the Matson (G. Eric and Edith) Photograph Collection held in the Library of Congress, Prints and Photographs Division (LC-DIG-matpc-18200).

these events and Palestinian resistance are the cause of security restrictions—as the State of Israel claims; rather, they respond to Israel's continued presence and belligerence on Palestinian land. Before Checkpoint 300 was built, movement restrictions materialized in so-called flying checkpoints, impermanent and unannounced stop-and-search operations carried out by the Israeli army that would appear close to Rachel's Tomb through the 1980s and 1990s. In the mid-1990s, a facility was built approximately one hundred meters north of the current Checkpoint 300.

Bethlehemites referred to this as the "carob tree checkpoint." It comprised a roadblock and a walk-through check booth on the pavement—in the shade of a large carob tree (now cut down)[4]—with a temporary-looking watchtower above (Figures 2 and 3). To travel northward, Palestinians had to present a valid ID card (or birth certificate for under-sixteens) and pass variously light or heavy interrogation. There are many stories of denied passage, intimidation, and military violence at that checkpoint, and there were frequently periods of enclosure when the main route from Bethlehem to Jerusalem would be either entirely blocked or practically so because of go-slow ID checks and gridlocked traffic. This was a precursor to the more systematized regulation of Palestinian movement that began with the construction of the West Bank wall from the early 2000s and Checkpoint 300 in 2005. The new checkpoint was justified by the Israeli government as simultaneously a "defensive, temporary, passive and effective measure against terrorism" and a transfer of security to "civilian" authorities as a "humanitarian step" in managing the Palestinian population.[5] Checkpoint 300 and similarly styled "checkpoint terminals" (e.g., Huwara, south of Nablus and Qalandia) would, the Israeli narrative goes, increase speed and efficiency for law-abiding Palestinians wishing to travel around the West Bank and Jerusalem. Of course, this has never been the case; the new terminals have merely become efficient at disrupting the lives of greater numbers of people. No Palestinian in the West Bank can move without dealing with an Israeli checkpoint, of which there are many. At the time of writing, according to the UN, there were "565 obstacles to movement" in the West Bank and East Jerusalem (excluding Hebron, whose city center is divided by twenty-eight checkpoints),[6] including forty-nine permanently staffed (military or private) checkpoints, 139 "occasionally staffed" checkpoints, and 304 roadblocks and road gates.[7] Checkpoint 300 is thus but a prominent site in a vast security architecture that should shade all that is to follow in this book: the conditions in northern Bethlehem are replicated all over the occupied West Bank.

The 2005 construction of Checkpoint 300 and major renovations since (in 2010, 2014, and 2019) have produced a complex space made up of corridors and turnstiles, cameras and scanners, weapons and intimidation. Every morning, crowds of Palestinians gather to make the northbound crossing to reach their workplaces in Jerusalem or Israel. They do so only with permits that are granted by the part of the Israeli military that deals with civilian matters in the West Bank, COGAT (Coordinator of Government Activities in the Territories). Most permit holders are laborers who meet numerous other criteria that the Israeli state deems requisite for entry. Unmarried men are unlikely to gain a permit because they are considered an elevated terror threat; older men and women are not issued permits because they are less useful for low-wage sectors of the Israeli economy (e.g., construction,

FIGURE 2. Car barrier on the Hebron Road in the mid-1990s. Photograph by Jimmy Michael.

FIGURE 3. The "carob tree checkpoint" in 2002. Photograph by Joss Dray.

agriculture). Already, the segregating function of Checkpoint 300 comes to the fore; it is not only a mechanism that prevents Palestinians from entering Jerusalem but also one that sediments societal divisions as people are excluded from the checkpoint itself—and also from each other. Those who are sanctioned to enter must negotiate overcrowding, slow-moving queues, faulty equipment that delays, demeaning identity checks, and the looming possibility of military violence. Those who are not afforded entry may have to pick up extra domestic labor, cross the wall at weaker and even more dangerous points, or face lower wages and unemployment in the West Bank. With a permit, crossing Checkpoint 300 can take up to two hours, adding significant time and stress to the days of permit holders—and also, as is discussed in this book, to those of their families. At other times, crossings can be much quicker (one interviewee for this book considered forty minutes to be a smooth crossing); this seems to have become more often the case with the introduction of biometric "smart gates" in 2019. Still, the crushing crowds and violence persist, as do the more systematic issues of Israeli control over Palestinian mobilities, life, and land more generally. It is to this wider view that the book turns throughout, making connections between the details of Checkpoint 300 and Israel's wider colonial project in Palestine.

Viewed close up, Checkpoint 300 is revealed as both product and producer of manifold political geographies that span scales from the intimate to the global. As the mainly male laborers join the clamor of the early-morning crossing, subjecting their bodies to crushing and stress, their families are also reoriented to the long hours of absence and deficit in domestic labor. All around Checkpoint 300, businesses have closed or been forced to adapt to closure and military presence; many residents have moved away. Inside the checkpoint and around the wall, a vast armory of surveillance and targeting equipment has been assembled from a global network of weapons manufacturers. These and other political geographies come together through Checkpoint 300, shaping its spatial makeup as it resonates out to other spaces: the home, the neighborhood, and farther afield into research laboratories and international arms fairs. What might at first appear far-fetched is substantiated in the chapters that follow, in which a certain reciprocity emerges between otherwise disparate figures in colonial space. A Palestinian home and, for instance, an Arizona tech park or a Belfast research laboratory can thus be seen as partly co-constitutive spaces, each produced by the other. There are many extrapolations from this: a morning of crushing queues and exhausting delays is codependent on an expanded day of domestic labor in homes around Bethlehem and southward, on a technological breakthrough in crowd control techniques and capital investment, and on contracts and knowledge exchanges with government and private actors in a globalized military–industrial complex. The vision of Palestine that emerges from bringing these scales together is one of colonial space that inheres in yet also exceeds the colonizing state. This is not to dilute culpability but to recognize that Israeli colonialism in Palestine is also a collaborative project of international cooperation and complicity.

This has historical roots. The idea and establishment of Israel, it should be recalled, emerged as part of a European colonial movement and (latterly) the reach of American imperialism. Zionism was born of a specifically European context in the anti-Semitic desire to expel Jews alongside a colonial reflex to establish strategic outposts. Palestine was the paradigmatic space in which to deliver on those aims; under the British Mandate, there was a coinciding willingness to oppress an Arab population and to remove Jewish figures from domestic politics with a vision of satisfying a centuries-old obsession with capturing the "Holy Land."[8] The 1917 Balfour Declaration was a product of these political tensions and desires and is widely considered the precursor to the declaration of the State of Israel in 1948 and the subsequent Nakba (or "catastrophe") that saw Zionist militia kill or displace more than 750,000 Palestinians.[9] In the traumatic years that followed, those who were displaced became refugees in the southwestern part of Palestine, on the Egyptian border (Gaza); in the eastern part, on the western side of the Jordan River (the West Bank, including East Jerusalem); in neighboring states (Lebanon, Jordan, Syria); and farther afield (e.g., Chile, the United States). Even as the "international community" recognized Gaza and the West Bank as Palestinian territories in 1948 and declared the 1967 occupation of those territories illegal (UN Security Council Resolution 242), international, especially Western, and particularly U.S., support for Israel grew through the 1960s and 1970s.[10] This support has grown further, to present a somewhat accelerated history, in the spread of neoliberal governing structures (which gained purchase in Israel after the 1985 Economic Stabilization Plan), Palestine Liberation Organization support of the 1990 Iraqi invasion of

Kuwait, and the wider War on Terror and anti-Arab militarism after 9/11. This is not a book on international relations, but this history is an important context for better understanding the political geographies of Checkpoint 300 and the contemporary dynamics of Israeli colonialism in Palestine more generally. From an international relations perspective, overseas support for Israel can be distilled to three connected and consequential points: the U.S. government has repeatedly used its UN Security Council influence and veto resolutions that condemn the conduct of Israel in Palestine;[11] Israel is the recipient of the second-largest (after Egypt) overseas aid grant from the United States;[12] and Israel is positioned as a regional strategic ally of Western states and even as a contingent part of "the West."[13]

At no point in Israel's history have we seen these dynamics more viciously prominent than with the 2023–25 military attacks on Gaza (which, at the time of writing, may well restart). In response to Hamas's incursions and killing of twelve hundred Israelis and foreign nationals on October 7, 2023, Israel launched a massive offensive that has killed more than forty-five thousand people in Gaza, while many thousands more are missing (likely trapped or dead under rubble), and 1.8 million people (80 percent of the Gazan population) have been forcibly displaced. Hundreds of international law experts, including experts in conflict, genocide, and the Holocaust, have warned of potential genocide,[14] as did the UN International Court of Justice (ICJ) in its January 2024 ruling.[15] Despite this overwhelming weight of evidence, the Israeli military appears beyond sanction, and the lives of all Gazans remain in grave danger. Israel's impunity and military capacities are owed, as most readers will be aware, to an international community that is, despite some dissenting voices (notably in the postcolonial Global South, e.g., Brazil and South Africa), steadfast in support of Israeli military crimes in Gaza. Weapons exports continue, diplomatic discourses coalesce around an unqualified slogan that "Israel has the right to defend itself," and large-scale public protest in solidarity with Palestinians is either ignored or (often violently) suppressed. The political mainstream on the left and right in Europe and North America long refused to apply any sort of meaningful pressure to effect a ceasefire, let alone to make Israel answerable for the violence it distributes. When a ceasefire motion was passed by the UN Security Council (after *five* vetoed attempts), the U.S. ambassador took the unprecedented step of claiming the resolution as "nonbinding."[16] The ceasefire eventually agreed upon at the end of the Biden administration in early January 2025 (at the time of writing) holds—just. While we are still in a first-response stage to the crisis in Gaza, we can be sure in our initial analyses that the dead Palestinians and bombed-out hospitals and schools are Israel's crimes, facilitated and legitimized by international support.

The horror of Gaza is compounded by Israel's control of border crossings. The Rafah Checkpoint in the south is controlled in coordination with the Egyptian Border Guard, who manage day-to-day operations. Before October 7, 2023, this amounted to allowing very limited movements of prescreened people and subjecting them to arduous security checks.[17] Currently the Rafah crossing is beset not only by ground and air attacks by the Israeli military in the city to the immediate north but also by go-slow bureaucratic mechanisms that severely impede the entry of much-needed humanitarian aid. *Thousands* of trucks have at times remained gridlocked on the Egyptian side, while Palestinians inside Gaza—just a short drive away—suffer severe food and medicine shortages. The U.S. military's ill-conceived $320 million floating pier built on the southern shoreline of Gaza City was designed to circumvent this blockage (though, it must also be said, the pier was primarily a cynical exercise in promoting American humanitarian benevolence) but failed to deliver more than a single day's worth of land aid in two months of weather-affected operation. The other obvious option—aside from *not* razing Gaza—is Beit Hanoun (Erez) Checkpoint in the north, only seventy-six kilometers from Ben Gurion Airport, Israel's main aviation and cargo hub. It is indicative of the impunity afforded to Israel at this time of genocidal war that instead of building a pier, instead of photoshoot-oriented aid airdrops, and instead of blaming ever-complicit Egyptian security forces at Rafah, no journalist or diplomat has asked the simple question why Beit Hanoun has not been open to a constant flow of aid that would provide succor to the people of Gaza. The war on Gaza is of a different order to what this book addresses, but there are shared patterns in the control of Palestinian space via borders and checkpoints against a backdrop of international complicity and indifference.

This is not to disperse criticism of Israel across a global geography but to recognize the production of colonial space—and, by extension, colonial war—as an internationally dispersed process. To bring us back to Checkpoint 300, the dynamics to which we are witness in Gaza are similarly present (by quality, not to the same urgent degree) in the supply of arms and diplomatic support touched on in this Introduction and expanded on in this book. Yet multiple aspects of Checkpoint 300 (and Gaza) are particular to the form of settler colonialism that has taken shape in Palestine since the early part of the twentieth century. The checkpoint is a part of the two-tiered transport system in the West Bank whereby Israeli settlers move seamlessly on modern highways between Tel Aviv, Jerusalem, and settlements, while most Palestinians are forced to skirt around Jerusalem and negotiate a combination of the 565 "obstacles to movement" noted earlier.[18] This is a telling contrast that should be central to our political and ethical positions on Checkpoint 300: while colonizers move freely and comfortably on unceded Indigenous land, the Indigenous themselves are subject to a discriminatory and often violent border mechanism. That mechanism is formed also of a punitive bureaucratic system of permits that restricts not only Palestinians' rights to movement but also residency, development, and education.[19] To build on land designated "Area C" (approximately 62 percent of the West Bank), an Israeli construction permit is necessary;[20] to export goods from the West Bank requires an Israeli exportation license;[21] to reside with family born outside the West Bank is subject to an Israeli visa or residency document.[22] And to refer back to Gaza, Checkpoint 300 is situated surely within Israel's embrace of collective punishment for all Palestinians, where bombardment there leads to increased closure in Bethlehem and across the West Bank (as well as increased arrests and police violence for Palestinians in Israel). Sustained bombing campaigns against Gaza (in 2008–9, 2012, 2014, and 2022)[23] and any times of (often spurious) "heightened alert" lead to the closure of Checkpoint 300, including during the 2023–25 bombardment, when opening times were limited—and there were signs that many of the spatial effects documented in this book were greatly pronounced.

As I hope is clear, Checkpoint 300 is not simply an interesting colonial space in and of itself; it is also instructive of the wider spatial dynamics of colonialism beyond its corridors and turnstiles. It is, as I hope to convey in the chapters that follow, a codependent of Palestinian household intimacies *as well as* a coconstitutive site of the (big G) geopolitics that operate at all scales between those poles.[24] It connects material, bureaucratic, and discursive forms of colonial power as an imposing edifice that regulates via physical violence and documentation underpinned by the instrumentalizing logics of a terroristic Other. Checkpoint 300 is, as I show in this book, an entryway into understanding how colonial space is formed through security infrastructure that is both the product and producer of wider geographies of oppression, complicity, and counter.

The research for this book was conducted over many visits to Bethlehem over a nine-year period. I first crossed Checkpoint 300 in 2015 and was immediately struck by the scale and the complexity of the building, as well as by the investments of time and capital it takes to produce such a space. At first take, especially during the daytime, Checkpoint 300 is a quite unassuming addition to the West Bank wall, a protrusion of three corridors covered in corrugated steel surrounded by a clutch of street vendors and taxi drivers (Figure 4). Inside, the concrete and steel grayness is both palette and mood, an affective background to the hardware of surveillance and control: cameras, turnstiles, and scanners. Even now, many years later, I am still taken by an initial reaction of horror and incredulity at the coming together

FIGURE 4. Checkpoint 300 during the daytime. Photograph by Nadir Mauge.

FIGURE 5. Checkpoint 300 turnstile. Photograph by Nadir Mauge.

of architects, engineers, politicians, capitalists, and military who have (directly or indirectly) dedicated a part of their working lives to producing such a facility. The most striking aspect of Checkpoint 300, however, comes close to the end of the crossing process, where the racial politics of security checks come to the fore. I am white and British and have crossed through perhaps thirty times over the last nine years, and each time, I have been waved through, barely ever having to produce any form of ID. All the while, and as will become clear, Palestinians are subject to the most discriminatory and invasive forms of checks and validation.

Since that first visit, my research on Checkpoint 300 has been conducted during regular field trips and collaborations with different people in Bethlehem. In the first years (2015–17), I conducted observations mostly in the early mornings (four to seven o'clock) and walk-throughs at less busy periods, occasionally with the intention of interviewing permit-holding laborers but never fully pursuing the idea. I decided against interviews because the main part of the existing knowledge of checkpoints is focused solely on overcrowding and the (almost always male) laborers who cross at busy times (this is a key rationale for writing this book) and because the fact of my positionality (white, non-Arab) does not lend itself to entering a highly racialized security space where the stakes for potential interviewees are dangerously high. I was also not prepared to ask permit holders to spend precious free time recollecting their stressful workdays. Instead, from 2018, I began working with the activist-researchers Baha Hilo and Ala' Hilo and a political scientist (also based at Newcastle University), Jemima Repo, in a collaborative project with the Women's Group in al-Walaja, a village cut in half by the wall two kilometers to the west of Bethlehem.[25] The Women's Group is a collective that promotes members' participation in cultural, economic, and political life, for instance, by producing and selling furniture from a workshop in the village and amplifying women's political voices on the local council.[26] Lamees (a pseudonym), a prominent member of the group, joined the project as a (paid) researcher who conducted a series of interviews and focus groups with twelve women from al-Walaja whose husbands used the checkpoint daily as permit-holding laborers. The candidness of the accounts presented in chapters 2 and 3 is owed entirely to Lamees's skill as an interviewer and the trust she built with interviewees. Research for chapters 4, 5, and 6 began in 2020 with Baha and the Bethlehem-based filmmaker Nadir Mauge, for a documentary film project titled *My Tomb, Your Tomb, Rachel's Tomb* (2025) that was funded through Newcastle University. Nadir conducted hours of in-depth interviews with people who live and work in the vicinity of Checkpoint 300, taking hundreds of photos in the process. Nadir is a friend and an inspiration—as well as a meticulous researcher—and our collaboration opened my eyes to many details presented in the latter chapters of the book. The majority of the quotes and photographs used in chapters 4, 5, and 6 are from that collaboration. Chapter 5 also benefits from research I commissioned from Daniela Freund, a researcher for Who Profits (an excellent independent research center with expertise in tracing movements of capital in the Israeli security industry), whose diligent work in investigating companies involved in operating Checkpoint 300 adds vital detail to the analysis and connections to international exchanges in objects and ideas.

Throughout, the many people with whom I have spoken in Bethlehem about Checkpoint 300 have been welcoming and open to sharing their experiences. This will become clear in the book, but one thing I want to deposit here is the curious question of the checkpoint's distinctive name. To most, the site is referred to simply as *hajez* (،حاجز)—"the checkpoint"—and questions around its numerical suffix are generally answered with an unbothered shrug. For the record, Israelis refer to Checkpoint 300 colloquially as "Gilo Checkpoint" because it is close to the settlement of Gilo, while its official government name is "Rachel Border Crossing." As for the "300," there are no sure answers: some people speculate that it derives from an address and that the checkpoint sits at 300 Hebron Road; others have told me that it appears as the three hundredth on an Israeli list of military facilities. The answer I have heard most, though, is that the "300" refers to the number of meters between the checkpoint and Rachel's Tomb, telling us, if anything, of the close relationship between the holy and military sites. As telling is that no Palestinian refers to it as a "border" because it sits entirely on Palestinian land; where I refer to a border in the text, it is in the form of "border crossing" or "borderland," in recognition of the imposition of a border mechanism that is, like all borders, arbitrary and violently reproduced. As for what Israel calls the "separation barrier" or "security fence," I have gone with "West Bank wall" and "the wall," for simplicity and to reflect the ways in which Palestinians in Bethlehem refer to it. Finally, it goes without saying that throughout the book, I have made every effort to read colonial space from a Palestinian point of view and to set the testimonies included in proper context—I hope this is achieved in the chapters that follow.

The book opens with chapter 1, "The Punitive Commute," which attends to the Checkpoint 300 site itself and how Palestinians move through its corridors and turnstiles. I examine how the stratification of space and the discipline of bodies serve the settler colonial project via the incorporation of Palestinian laborers into the Israeli economy in a way that regulates the sexual division of labor among the Palestinian population. This is very much the book's "primary scene"—the most immediately striking aspect of Checkpoint 300, where Palestinians are corralled into an oppressive space for validation by charges of the Israeli state. Colonial space from this angle takes on a quite familiar form of colonizing authorities regulating the movements and rights to participate in economic and social life of a colonized population. I show how the affective space of Checkpoint 300 imposes disciplinary sequences on the daily movements of Palestinians that are related to Israel's biopolitical management of the occupied population *as a whole.* The checkpoint sifts for able-bodied, politically docile, male subjects to work in the Israeli economy while simultaneously shaping categories of excluded subject groups. This is a crucial argument for the entire book for the ways it directs us to the ways in which Palestinian lives are regulated *beyond the checkpoint* and into the multiple colonial spaces of Checkpoint 300.

Chapter 2, "Women at the Checkpoint," turns to women's pronouncedly gendered experiences of obtaining (and often of being denied) permits and travel through Checkpoint 300 as differently targeted and vulnerable subjects in a security setting. Women are less readily granted permits than men and cross mainly as caregivers (accompanying family members for medical appointments) or for purposes of prayer (e.g., at al-Aqsa during Ramadan). Crossing often involves gendered forms of harassment by checkpoint staff as well as the significant fact that checkpoints are especially unforgiving environments for children. The result is that many women seldom cross or avoid crossing altogether; Checkpoint 300 delimits women's participation in social, economic, and political activities in ways that exacerbate gendered divisions in both domestic labor and public life.

Chapter 3, "Beyond the Checkpoint," sustains the focus on gender by taking a closer look at domestic labor and the ways that family life is tethered to the temporalities of the checkpoint. If, in that "primary scene," those thousands of men have been awake since the early hours before a long day at work, the homes to which they eventually return are maintained by women: mothers, wives, and daughters who ensure that wages cover household costs and thus the reproduction of the labor force. The bureaucratic context here is important: to gain a work permit to cross Checkpoint 300, men must be married with at least one child. This condition radically changes the perception of the crowds in the mornings: every man enduring that punitive and protracted commute leaves a wife and child/ren at home, and each hour added to his day is an extra hour of absence from family life—an extra hour of tasks added to a woman's day. The checkpoint thus plays an integral role not only in keeping women in place but also in shaping daily routines, the distribution of labor, and the (sometimes partial) fulfillment of duties and, ultimately, in forming and maintaining intimate family relations as colonial space extends from Checkpoint 300 to the home.

Chapter 4, "An Urban Geography of Checkpoint 300 and the Hebron Road," picks up the notion of extended checkpoint spatialities in a survey and analysis of the surrounding Hebron Road area in northern Bethlehem, where a designation of "Area C" (nominally under Israeli control but within a Palestinian municipal area) has given rise to a particular gray zone of economic and planning activity that elevates the exposure of residents and businesses to bureaucratic and military violence. The narrative here comprises a walk-through of the area, telling the stories of buildings and businesses in the words of local residents and workers who share memories of a lively street that has been dampened in the last two decades. Palestinian life is thus depleted as the spatial effects of de-development and legal exception take hold and a once vibrant part of Bethlehem is made a borderland that is readily transformed into an urban battle space.

Chapter 5, "Producing Checkpoint Space," concentrates on the broader flows of *ideas, objects,* and *people* that come together to produce this borderland and that are thus crucial to Israel's capacity to effect control of Palestinian people and land. A global frame brings into view three important factors in making colonial space: (1) the international networks of security technologies whose innovations (smart surveillance systems, "nonlethal" crowd control weapons, biometric scanners) are produced both for and through the checkpoint; (2) the wider labor relations that govern mobilities like Israel's privatized domestic security market and its overseas "guest worker" programs that maintain levels of precarity in the Palestinian labor pool; and (3) the international movements of capital and people that have enclosed and fortified the Rachel's Tomb compound, around which so much security architecture is built. Seen through a global frame, Checkpoint 300 is revealed as a significant site in the international exchange of ideas, objects, and people where colonial space is produced through security commodities and rationalities, precaritized labor, and ideologized capital.

Chapter 6, "Re/making Colonial Space," finally, and not as an addendum but as an important corrective, attends to the ways in which Palestinians who live and work around Checkpoint 300 negotiate or resist Israeli control by re/making colonial space. We learn that even in the context of colonial spacio-cide, de-development, and legal exception, Palestinian life endures; commuters strategize, businesses adapt, and activism persists. This is in part owed to "ungovernability," or that quality of life that simultaneously calls forth and evades attempts to govern and therefore reveals the fissures and frailties of Israeli control over the future of the site—and the rest of Palestine.

A conclusion, "Geographies for a Decolonized and Free Palestine," draws out four key aspects of colonial space that warrant emphasis beyond this book—to do with borders, feminist approaches to geopolitics, less spectacular geographies, and the ethics of research at sites of pronounced political oppression—before then explicating the ways in which the critique offered here is angled toward an *actionable* knowledge of colonialism in terms of the broader material promise of decolonizing. As is most evident at this late stage of Israeli colonialism in Palestine, our political and ethical positions must—now as much as ever—be invested in keeping open and edging toward a decolonized Palestine, free of the colonial spatial control that violates Indigenous rights over land and life.

1

The Punitive Commute

DISCIPLINING PALESTINIAN LABOR

> The quintessential Palestinian experience, which illustrates
> some of the most basic issues raised by Palestinian identity,
> takes place at a border, an airport, a checkpoint: in short,
> at any one of those many modern barriers where identities
> are checked and verified. . . . For Palestinians, arrival at such
> barriers generates shared sources of profound anxiety.
>
> —Rashid Khalidi, *Palestinian Identity: The Construction
> of Modern National Consciousness*

> The fight for a piece of railing is the hardest of all. . . . Only the
> strong can climb the railing and hold tight to the barbwire fence
> for hours. Not everyone has the strength to keep hanging in
> the air all night, and only the strong survive. . . . The rest pray
> to God.
>
> —Ahmed Darajah, a quarry worker crossing Checkpoint 300

This opening chapter begins inside the Checkpoint 300 complex of
buildings to analyze the spaces and practices that effect control of Palestinian mobility. The main aim is not only to account for mobility but
to bring the question of movement into contact with the issue of subject making in the context of colonial power. How does power function
at the checkpoint? What kinds of subjectivity are produced through
checkpoint space? And, crucially, what is missing from a focus bound
by that space? Aside these questions, a complementing objective of
the chapter is also to convey—through both textual and photographic
imagery—something of the materiality of the checkpoint and as much
as possible of the experience of passing through its various spaces. To
these ends, I consider how various security technologies—turnstiles,
metal detectors, cameras, corridors, identity check booths—render

Checkpoint 300 a complex space where various affective and disciplinary techniques work toward the biopolitical management of the Palestinian population. As will become clear, the checkpoint's physical design—*its very materiality*—disciplines the flow and form of movement; the control of pace and direction; what people can move with (e.g., wheelchairs, strollers, walking aids) or carry (work tools); and, in turn therefore, *who* can move. Put succinctly, the checkpoint sifts for able-bodied, politically docile, male subjects to work in the Israeli economy, often as construction workers in illegal settlements in East Jerusalem. At the same time, the checkpoint and permit bureaucracies around it "leave behind" entire groups who do not fit a required profile—women, those who are differently abled, the blacklisted, ex-prisoners, unionists, and *even* (and significantly) childless and unmarried men—such that the checkpoint's effects extend far beyond the space of the checkpoint itself. It is this premise that prompts the chapters that follow this one. Here, though, as a key point of departure for the rest of the book, the move is to enter and examine the space of the checkpoint itself.

A key figure to bring to the fore in this task is that of a Palestinian laborer, one whose residence is registered in the West Bank but whose place of work is across the wall—in either Jerusalem or Israel—and who is thus required to hold an Israel-issued permit to commute through the checkpoint. In the mornings, Checkpoint 300 is packed with hundreds of such people, each attempting to make the crossing in time to complete a full workday—those who are late risk missing the transport connections that await on the other side. It should not be left without explication that during the busiest commuter times, most (perhaps *all*) people crossing this way are men who have obtained permits via their employers. Work permits, sometimes termed "eight-hour permits," allow for a single crossing in each direction for the purposes of work only and explicitly without permission to remain in Jerusalem or Israel overnight. Numbers fluctuate according to the needs of the Israeli economy, and "security threat levels" can result in closure (such as during bombardments of Gaza), but approximately eighty-seven thousand West Bank Palestinians with such permits together constitute a primary source of cheap labor for Israeli businesses.[1] An estimated thirty-six thousand of them work in Israeli settlements, mostly in construction—building the houses that are the first line of the occupation. In Andrew Ross's account of these workers, a common refrain in interviews was that "they demolish our houses while we build theirs."[2] The incentive for the men to take on this work and to endure the checkpoint each day is that they can earn up to five times more than they would in the West Bank, even despite settlement businesses often exploiting the legal ambiguity of settlements under Israeli law to employ Palestinians under worse conditions than they do Israelis.[3] Many receive no vacation or sick days and lack other social benefits, nor are they issued pay slips; the work is often "backbreaking," and health and safety regulations are lax. Only those willing or able to accept such conditions are "granted" permits to make the daily commute.

The Checkpoint 300 site is split between two main openings in the wall. A large gate about one hundred meters to the east of the Hebron Road regulates road traffic and is open only to Jerusalem- or Israel-registered vehicles carrying international visitors (mostly tourists visiting Bethlehem's holy sites) or Palestinian residents of Jerusalem or Israel. In the main, West Bank Palestinians are not allowed to pass through the road section and must commute through a separate area designated for pedestrian crossings—it is this section that forms the focus here. The pedestrian entrance has undergone extensive modification over the period of research conducted for this book (2015–24), with incremental modifications appearing every year, along with a larger-scale renovation in 2019. Though this project slightly reconfigured the points of entry (see chapter 5), for most of the last ten years, Checkpoint 300 has been crossed by foot through one of three lanes: one for the smaller number of Palestinians with 24-hour permits or Jerusalem residency;[4] a "humanitarian lane" intended for women, children, and the elderly; and another—the only one in use in the early mornings—for those with work permits. The bottom halves of the lanes are made of concrete, the top halves of galvanized bars with corrugated iron coverings, making for walkways closed in on one side by the gray slats that are characteristic of this section of the wall and on the other by a cage-like structure. The walkway slopes upward and curves for thirty meters before doubling back and opening into a small enclosure where two Israeli security personnel sit behind tinted glass monitoring CCTV screens and regulating the flow of people with a button that starts and stops an adjacent turnstile. Beyond this turnstile is an expanse of open concrete that leads to (what Israel considers) the Israeli side of the checkpoint. In this part is another caged corridor of approximately twenty meters that doubles back on itself and a shorter section flanked by tinted glass where soldiers observe and give instructions through a loudspeaker system. At this point, one must place all belongings on an X-ray conveyor belt and (if selected) enter a body scanner, afterward passing through a further turnstile and into a large, open space with automated "smart gates" behind which armed private security staff patrol. For a Palestinian to pass through this point, a valid ID card and permit must be presented and verified by fingerprint or facial recognition biometrics, along with a visual check from security staff behind the booth glass. There remains one more turnstile before the journey along the Hebron Road can continue toward Jerusalem.

This extensive infrastructure, according to a 2005 Israeli Civil Administration policy, is designed "to enable speedy and efficient security checks in a minimum of time."[5] There is nothing of substance to such a claim: crossings are marked by long delays and elevated levels of surveillance, humiliation, and stress—with an always-present threat of violence. These effects—and affects—are pronounced each morning between five and eight o'clock, when up to fifteen thousand men enter the middle lane at the beginning of the workday (Figure 6).[6] In fact, the men's days start much earlier; queues form from 3:00 A.M., and many have already traveled from south of Bethlehem (many from Hebron Governorate) to use Checkpoint 300, meaning some workers are awake from as early as 2:00 A.M. Just before the gates are opened at five o'clock, there is a jostling for position, and those at the front are continually squeezed as an effect of more and more men joining at the back. In 2009, a *Belfast Telegraph* reportage captured (in a way consistent with what I have since seen in visits between 2015 and 2024) a typical morning scene outside Checkpoint 300 thusly: "Before sunrise . . . there is scuffling when the tempers of the men, many of whom have been up since 3am, begin to fray as they compete to squeeze into the alley to queue for a lengthy series of Israeli security checks of their IDs, work permits, and biometric palm prints."[7] In these dawn hours, when the checkpoint is at its busiest, it takes ten to twenty minutes to progress through the bottleneck at the entrance and file into the first sloping corridor. It is too narrow for the volume of commuters such that tension and frustration seem inevitable; the architecture foments "scuffles" and "fraying tempers." Inside the entrance, where the walls and bars give form to the crowd, moods seem to calm as relative positions become a queue that advances in stop-start fashion. Men on the other side of the bars walk up and down selling bread, falafel, coffee, and cigarettes, while in the background *servis* (shared taxi) after *servis* delivers more men to join the back of the crowd outside the entrance. From 5:00 A.M., for the next three hours, the first corridors—which are visible from outside—are packed with men four to five abreast, slowly making their way to work. Thus begins the daily commute.

Halfway along the first corridor, something striking starts to happen. Where the bars do not quite meet the roof, a stream of younger men take advantage of the small gap, climbing through and forming a parallel and quicker-moving queue above the heads of the other men (Figure 7). It is an impressive sight: they nimbly pull themselves along the bars, moving quickly while trying not to kick the heads of the men below. To understandable remonstration, they inevitably do. When they have moved along as far as they can, they drop into the main group, saving themselves an amount of waiting time by adding it

FIGURE 6. The queue outside Checkpoint 300 in the early morning. Photograph by the author.

FIGURE 7. Men climb along the bars above the heads of others. Photograph by the author.

onto the wait of those now behind. For journalists and human rights organizations, this scramble has become something of a visual spectacle that illustrates the dysfunction of the checkpoint, as well as serving as a metaphor for the wider cruelty of Israeli military rule in Palestine.[8] A 2017 report in the *Washington Post* accompanies a set of powerful photographs with commentary that "the workers call them 'wall crawlers' and 'snakes,' the young who jump over and slither under the bars to cut the line. Those who did not cut in lines said the crawlers demeaned themselves—and that this was intentional, that the Israelis wanted this to happen. Why else would they let these conditions persist year after year, they asked."[9] Whether or not such strong terms are commonplace,[10] most relevant for the task to hand is to recognize that "wall crawling" is indicative of a space that produces a new ethics of relations between bodies, one that connects to Nasser Abourahme's observation that "at the checkpoint, social norms blur: gestures can be wildly misinterpreted, body movements can seem erratic and unpredictable, civility often hangs by a thread."[11] I emphasize here the fissures created *between* Palestinians—along axes of, for example, fitness, respect, arrogance, guile, courage, selfishness, or desperation—whereby the spaces of the checkpoint set workers in competition against each other in the race to cross. This refines the subject-making function from a broad category of permit holder to those with a capacity to endure, physically and mentally, this punitive commute.

By the turn of the first corridor, all the men on the bars have lowered themselves into the main queue. Twenty meters ahead of this point is a small control room where two security personnel work shifts monitoring and regulating the flow of people through the checkpoint. It is from this room, as Eyal Weizman has noted of checkpoints across the West Bank, that "soldiers regulate the pace of passage by using an electrical device that controls the turning of the gates. . . . Every few seconds soldiers stop the rotation of the turnstiles, so that several people remain caged between the gates."[12] From behind tinted glass at Checkpoint 300, security staff (who are not soldiers but employees of private contractors; see chapter 5) watch the crowd on two monitors that display images from cameras positioned at the turn of the first corridor. They press the button intermittently, orchestrating the pace of movement in the corridors and thus subordinating the men's bodies to the whims of the checkpoint guards and the technologies they command. This maintains a sense of unpredictability in this section of the checkpoint, where the satisfaction of each move forward is tempered by the halt that follows and another stretched-out moment of stillness. Though it is important to reiterate that I can never experience this type of crossing (i.e., at a busy time with a day of work ahead and as part of a targeted population), there are observable conditions whose effects cannot be ignored. From photographs and measurements of Checkpoint 300 and a method of crowd counting, at any given time between 5:00 and 8:00 A.M., 350–400 men squeeze into a space of 120 square meters, giving virtually no room—bodies are checked not only by the bars and walls but also by the physical intimacy with others—for meaningful agency in how, when, and (even) whether to move. In this setting, as the minutes tick by, the prospect of lateness looms larger. Delay—or rather, the *delaying* function built into the materiality of the checkpoint—is in this way not inconsequential; it sustains and intensifies the circulation of affects prevalent to such conditions: anger, boredom, despondency, resentment, humiliation, frustration, stress, fear, and so forth.

In this sense, even only the prospect of lateness can levy a high affective toll. This hinges on the transport connections imposed by the restrictions enforced by the checkpoint and wall. The checkpoint opens out onto olive groves on the southern tip of Jerusalem (or rather what Israel has defined as Jerusalem in its program to sequester more and more Palestinian land), and most of those crossing in the early mornings depend on a minibus link to their places of work. As the human rights organization B'Tselem reports, "drivers do not wait for late arrivals, meaning that delays at the checkpoints are not just exhausting and unnecessary, but may also end in the loss of a full day's work. Others have their pay docked for the hours they are late."[13] The pace-controlling corridors and turnstiles thus materially enact Israel's wider—and deliberate—"slow-motion" governing of the Palestinian population that targets and instrumentalizes the "precariousness of life as an instrument."[14] Precarity of employment is the chief instrument here: the potentially high cost of missing a transport link cannot but introduce a level of anxiety to the checkpoint crossing. In the first part of the queue (which is visible from the outside), it is the case that many of the men during the morning crossings check the time using watches and phones, crane their necks, and stand tip-toed to know something of what is happening ahead. These are movements of anxious bodies, evidence of waiting as it imposes an important political function of setting and intensifying one's place in the world. Waiting, as David Bissell has written, "heralds a heightened sensual attentiveness to the immediate spatiality . . . [and] to the physicality of the perception of the body itself."[15] There are important limits to what can be understood of another's embodied experience,[16] but there are sure grounds here to speculate that the body's immobility—the prolonged moments of stillness or crawling pace—imposed by the checkpoint elevates anxieties as the waiting men take in the immediate and bleak spatiality (the bars, turnstiles, concrete—the *overwhelming grayness* of security spaces) and contemplate the possibilities and consequences of lateness and lost work.

Aside this, the stillness, crowdedness, and staccato rhythm carry a further substantial threat. Incidents of physical harm in Checkpoint 300 have risen sharply in recent years with the increase in volumes of crossings outpacing upgrades to the checkpoint infrastructure.

Crush injuries, such as broken ribs and fainting, are troublingly regular, and there are documented incidences of worse. A 2019 *Al Jazeera* report on the issue claims that lengthened intervals between locking and unlocking the turnstiles inside have exacerbated both the physical effects of crushing and the psychological sense of urgency felt by people crossing.[17] Drawing from an interview with one of the checkpoint's long-serving coffee sellers, Abed Abu Sheira, the report includes the frankly shocking severity and frequency of crushing in the corridors: "Every morning, at least one or two workers [almost] suffocate and faint from the lack of airflow," and "legs [have been] broken after Palestinians fall off the steel bars where dozens of workers hang from. . . . Other times . . . workers get their ribs broken from the pressure of the crowd pushing forward each time the turnstile is unlocked."[18] On the morning of October 2, 2018, Yousef Jum'a Ghawanma, a resident of al-Arrub refugee camp close to Hebron, fell from the bars onto his head and died from the injuries he sustained.[19] Unsurprisingly, workers in the morning queues now frequently express fear of being crushed inside the checkpoint facility.

The always-present possibility of injury adds to the elevated risk of lateness to make for a notably affective dimension of power at the checkpoint, where colonized subjects are produced—at least partly—via the subordinating embodiments of stress, anxiety, and fear that are drawn from potential futures of lateness, harm, and lost wages. In the manipulation of time, the corporeality of waiting does not simply extend time but causes it to fold in on itself; time becomes dynamic, nonlinear, where the "imminence of the event-to-come" pulses through the moment of bodily stillness.[20] In these terms, the "event-to-come" carries the threat of missing work and thereby losing pay or future employment—threats that, of course, evoke manifold further potential consequences: on or under the surface, variously un/likely visions of financial straits loom. In his influential work, Brian Massumi terms this dynamic of threat an affective "virtuality" where an imagined—or "indeterminate"—"future/event" collapses time and obscures all other (more desirable) futures: "an eventuality that may or may not occur, indifferent to its actual occurrence. The event's consequences precede it."[21] More and more, we are seeing elements of colonial governing expressed in powerful future tenses where the very possibility of (or uncertainty around) nameable outcomes has become an effective mechanism of control.[22] In this temporal (re)ordering or

FIGURE 8. Corridors of Checkpoint 300. Photographs by Nadir Mauge (A, C) and the author (B, D).

A

B

C

D

(re)emphasis, "prospects shape both a range of everyday conducts and a deeper existential attunement to a foreboding loss of future, they show how Israel's governmental techniques instrumentalise the uncertainty and anticipation of threatening and ominous possibilities."[23] From this angle, the scuffles and heated exchanges, the clambering and jostling for position, the checking of watches and phones—each evidences something of the "virtuality" of lateness in the present: the prospect of lost wages plays out anticipatorily. Whether or not time is kept, lateness is an integral part of the power relations that form at the checkpoint crossing.

After twenty-five to forty minutes in the curved corridors, the men cross the open expanse to enter the "Israeli side" of Checkpoint 300, where the queue narrows to the tighter dimensions of the walls and ceiling of another double-back corridor. Another twenty-five to forty minutes pass before the men approach a metal detector where security staff seated behind the tinted glass shout orders over a loudspeaker. The low-quality public address system and bare concrete walls make for ear-splitting acoustics that add another layer of hostility to the brusque orders (mostly in Hebrew, sometimes in Arabic): "remove belt," "wait," "take off shoes," "step forward," "MOVE, MOVE, MOVE!" and so on. The detector's alarm sounds intermittently, and people hustle back and forth, each time depositing something more onto the conveyor belt for X-ray inspection. Once through the detector, the men shoulder for space at the other end of the conveyor to collect their belongings. The order of the queue at this point dissipates; the space is too small for so many people. There follows another short wait while each person passes through a turnstile—which every so often locks momentarily with people inside it—and then into an opening of space, a large atrium with signs on the wall: "WELCOME TO INSPECTION POINT: YOU ARE NOW ENTERING A MILITARY AREA. . . . PLEASE PREPARE YOUR DOCUMENTS. . . . PASS ONE BY ONE." In the years before the smart gates, there were six check booths of which rarely more than two or three were staffed, even at busier times. Those booths are still in place for Palestinians without the newer biometric ID cards and permits but are now flanked by smart gates, which provide a measure of regularity—without, of course, making for anything like a pleasant crossing; questions always remain around what information is held, how it is interpreted, and what levels of security checks are in place on a particular day.

It is in this checking area that one's individual identity must emerge from the crowd to be validated for passage toward Jerusalem. Emerging from the cramped conditions of the corridors, the opening of space provides a prompt to move, but in fact more stillness is required. One must remain at a certain distance from the gates and booths, behind an imagined line, before being gestured—by either a green light or a guard's reluctant nod—to approach. That the precise distance required between the booth and the front of the queue in checkpoints is not marked by a painted line is notable, as Hagar Kotef and Merav Amir have pointed out, for the way it maintains a level of arbitrariness and punishment: an "imaginary line is bound to be transgressed . . . [and] transgression carries penalties."[24] These penalties range from sending 'transgressors' to the back of the queue to detaining them for hours or denying passage; sometimes "whoever finds himself transgressing the non-existent demarcation is badly injured or even killed."[25] For the men, this is the final threat of checkpoint violence, one that demands a mode of self-discipline—remaining in one's subordinate place until beckoned by person or machine—to avoid being late for work—or risk not getting there at all.

The final stage of the crossing is the most important. For most, the check is brief; an ID card and fingerprints or face are scanned, and there is a click of the turnstile. For others, there is a gesture to move aside for bag inspection and questioning. Two crucial points must be emphasized here. First, the prospect of bag inspection carries a sense of vulnerability for the fact that so many of the men crossing in the mornings "are carrying table saws and joint knives" for their work in construction.[26] The very tools that make work possible become an invitation for punitive measures. It is a cruel irony that these tools are carried—and this entire commute is endured—by so many Palestinian men so that they can work on construction sites, providing cheap labor in the building of illegal Israeli settlements on Palestinian land. Second, as is widely discussed, those employed or contracted by the Israeli state to impose security measures vary markedly in their approach to the task, introducing a pronounced level of unpredictability or arbitrariness to decisions made in settings like checkpoints. As Helga Tawil-Souri writes of Qalandia Checkpoint, "perhaps the soldier [or security guard] frowned on one's perfume, disapproved of the amount of shopping bags in hand, perhaps he finds one's face of clothing suspicious, perhaps he's just having a bad day."[27] After everything—the bureaucracy of gaining a permit; the early morning; the crush in the corridors; the amplified threats of lateness, denial, and lost pay—at this end point, it comes down to the pettiest of sovereigns: a disinterested, low-paid, poorly trained, (often) young Israeli whose decision divines untold consequences.

Once through, it is easy to miss the final sections of the checkpoint in the rush to proceed along the Hebron Road. They are nonetheless noteworthy: "Welcome to Israel" signs are accompanied by "Visit Eilat" and "Visit the Dead Sea" tourism promotion images. They are hard to comprehend in any other terms than as a form of taunting arriving West Bank Palestinians who cannot visit Eilat or the Dead Sea, nor will they recognize Jerusalem as part of Israel. It is a particularly undignified display of colonial arrogance that adds provocation to mechanisms of control wherever possible. That said, I would guess that most Palestinians pay little mind to these images as they emerge from the checkpoint and turn right back onto the Hebron Road. From there they board transports to take them on to workplaces where, four, five, or six hours after waking up, they begin a full day of hard labor. Such is the routine, six days a week, with profound effects for those who cross, their families, and the broader issue of Palestinian liberation.

To the questions of power and subject making at Checkpoint 300, a crucial first point in response is to emphasize that checkpoints (and borders more generally) profoundly affect the lives of millions of Palestinians—practically *all* Palestinians. In fact, they are commonly positioned as somewhat central to an idea of Palestinian-ness: Rashid Khalidi considers checkpoints "the quintessential Palestinian experience";[28] Helga Tawil-Souri labels them "the new Palestinian icon,"[29] while Nasser Abourahme claims that "crossing barriers is perhaps the single most definitive experience in contemporary Palestinian life."[30] Yet, despite this acknowledged prominence of checkpoints in the lives of Palestinians, most commentary—nongovernmental organization reports, journalism, and academic writing—begins and ends in the time-space described so far in this chapter: the early mornings in which male laborers are funneled through facilities like Checkpoint 300. As such, there is a certain parallel between the ways in which the checkpoint and permit bureaucracies "leave behind" certain groups (women, those who are differently abled, the blacklisted, ex-prisoners, unionists, and *even* childless and unmarried men) and the tendency among researchers to leave out such groups from discussions of checkpoints. Put simply, that people are absent from checkpoints does not mean that they are unaffected by a broader checkpoint spatiality. This base observation serves as the rationale for attempting a dual focus that would enable an analysis of workers as they cross in dialogue with those who are excluded from crossing, all the while retaining the checkpoint as a crucial, yet not deterministic, node in spatial expressions of colonial power. The remainder of the chapter begins this process, considering the role of Checkpoint 300 in the making of plural subjects (i.e., not only male ones) that demands, as the chapters that follow address, an analytic of border spatiality that extends far beyond the confines of the checkpoint itself.

This process, perhaps counterintuitively, begins with close attention to the very materiality of Checkpoint 300 itself and the ways in which its spaces align modes of subjectivity with Israel's broader project of control in Palestine. A key part of this is detectable at the entrance to the entire complex, where the so-called humanitarian lane to the right of the lane for laborers is most often closed (I have never once seen it open), forcing members of vulnerable groups either to join the 'disorderly' main lane described earlier—"where pushing, fighting and yelling is commonplace"[31]—or to avoid travel altogether. Because of this potential for disorder, men whose bodies are aging or injured begin to be pushed to the margins of mobility, and thus the margins of the labor market, as an older man about to join the queue once told me: "I can't do this for [much] longer, standing here for hours this early is too much." As Ahmed Darajah—the quarry worker quoted in this chapter's epigraph—explicates, "only the strong . . . survive."[32] The closure of the humanitarian lane and resulting crowding also have important gendered effects to do with physical proximity, as Irus Braverman notes: "The physical design of the new crossings already excludes many Palestinians, especially traditional Muslim women, who must refrain from physical contact with male strangers."[33] The journalist Wajdi al-Jaafari reported in 2017 that "Israeli soldiers forced [two women] to remove their face veils in front of hundreds of other men and women—an act that can be degrading and embarrassing to devout Muslim women—despite the existence of special rooms in the checkpoint facility for Israeli soldiers that could have been used in order to provide privacy for the women."[34] Even where cultural expectations around gendered modesty are less pronounced—plenty of women do not fit a "devout Muslim" characterization—many (especially) younger women "dress for the checkpoint," purposely wearing baggier clothes and scarves to avoid the sexualized attention of checkpoint staff and the prospect of public inspection.[35] At Checkpoint 300, private inspection rooms do exist but are routinely out of service, as are the toilets and baby-changing facilities that were built in preparation for the 2014 visit of Pope Francis and have been locked ever since.[36] Additionally, the narrowness and frequency of the turnstiles make them obstacles for strollers, any kind of walking aid, and, especially, passing through with young children. To be clear, these points are made not in the interests of making the checkpoint more women-friendly—it should not exist at all—but to outline reasons why women, where possible, tend to stay away not simply, or primarily, for reasons of family or cultural norms but also because of the unforgiving design of checkpoint technologies.

When brought back into contact with the question of power, these preliminary observations on who can and who cannot cross open an important theoretical path. Significantly, we are led away from a predominant approach in academic work of the past two decades that discusses checkpoints as geographically discrete sites whose spatial effects are confined to—or at least *emanate from*—the space of the checkpoint itself. One important and illustrative analytic within this approach is to conceive checkpoints as "exceptions," a spatial designation (one that is discussed in more detail in chapter 6) that Giorgio Agamben developed to refer to "a space that is neither outside nor inside" the state,[37] where "[sovereign] power confronts nothing but pure life, without any mediation."[38] In legal terms, checkpoints—as well as other "threshold" spaces in Palestine and Israel, such as seam zones, closed military zones, and security buffers—are paradigmatic of exception; they are not subject to Israeli civil law yet are sequestered as sites by the Israeli state, mostly as military zones where a notion of martial law presides yet does not, in any meaningful way, protect Palestinians within that space. On entering the checkpoint, Palestinians are thus positioned wholly within Israeli space, with little or no recourse to protection from the sovereign that designates that space. In this thanatopolitical (the politics of death) making of space, Israeli border practices dehumanize Palestinians, rendering them "bare life" via simultaneous exclusion from juridical order and inclusion within sovereign territorialization. Set in dialogue with influential existing work that uses a thanatopolitical frame, everything presented so far in this chapter (and indeed everything researched for this book) valorizes *yet exceeds* a politics of death.[39] In Checkpoint 300, the elevated threat of state-sanctioned violence, the impunity of security personnel, and the abattoir-like conditions are each real and pronounced factors in the dehumanization of Palestinians—yet they remain only partial visions of a wider dispersal of power. The details of permit conditions and exclusions dictate that the question of subject making must be addressed beyond a notion of checkpoint–as–sovereign space alongside a recognition of a productive (i.e., not only subtractive) function of power. This is a significant theoretical turn: it broadens the field of observation outward from a legally indistinct site (i.e., the state-controlled checkpoint that is by some degree territorially external to the state) marked by pronounced state violence to bring these undoubtedly crucial factors into contact with persistent (and therefore unignorable) practices of familial, social, and political life. In base terms, the shift is from a spectacle- and male-centric mode of analyzing checkpoints that asks, simply, what wider power relations are detectable? These relations might be subtle (or not), they could be highly localized or global in nature, or they could be unspectacular (e.g., bureaucratic) yet pervasive in their effects.

Circling around to bring these theoretical issues back into contact with the empirical context, the concomitant imperative is to examine Checkpoint 300 as a regulatory site whose distribution of bodies and affects is productive in the divisions of labor that are materially bound up with the Israeli colonial economy. This angle is strongly informed by feminist readings of both thanato- and biopolitics that critique a tendency to adopt the "viewpoint of a universal, abstract, asexual subject" that diminishes the ways in which body politics, especially the regulation of a racial and sexual division of labor, are integral to the reproduction of capitalism and colonialism.[40] The light of these important interventions reveals a need to attend to bodies in both symbolic and biological terms, the organization of labor and intimate social relations, and their complex formations with/in expressions of colonial power—all of which is clearly central to the function of Checkpoint 300, but none of which can be brought into sharp focus through a thanatopolitical frame. Foucauldian feminist scholarship provides a crucial complementing direction toward the workings of power outside the confines of the state or law, urging a focus on how the organization of bodies, families, labor, and care is at the core of attempts to normalize and regulate populations. The disciplinary modality of power in this respect is not so much a matter of "deduction as of synthesis"[41] so that disciplinary sites, such as checkpoints, bring together various knowledges that effect the "controlled insertion of subjects and objects to the capitalist machine of production."[42] The practices involved in these insertions and control are always situated in "a certain 'political economy' of the body," where "the body is directly involved in the political field";[43] an array of political technologies, including security architectures, are thus deployed to target bodies; to know, control, and train them; to render them docile, submissive, and useful. This requires a focus on the *microphysics of power*, in other words, the forms of power that work "by reordering material space in exact dimensions and acquiring a continuous bodily hold upon its subjects" through techniques of discipline and persuasion that are both corporeal and affective.[44]

According to Michel Foucault, biopolitics, or the "political ordering of life,"[45] is organized around two axes: an anatomopolitics of the human body and a biopolitics of the population. The former is centered on "the body as a machine": its disciplining and optimization to maximize its usefulness and docility and its "integration into systems of efficient and economic controls."[46] If this pole is characterized by various disciplines, the other is shaped by interventions and regulatory controls targeted at the level of the population as a totality for its administration and calculated management. These two modalities of power are not opposed but complementary, functioning on different scales of the "controlled insertion" of subjects into economic and social life. The prison, school, barracks, and factory feature in Foucault's work as disciplinary institutions that distribute bodies through individuating practices that render them more productive through isolation and the enforcement of organized movement. Such practices are individualizing in the ways that they mobilize detailed knowledges of the human body to align the time of a person's life with the "temporal system of the cycle of production."[47] This is not only observable on a broad scale in the calculated direction of groups of bodies and the prevention of "imprecise distributions" (e.g., vagabonding[48]) that ties a labor force to certain localities and habits but it is also perceptible on a microscale, in the imposition of particular gestures and behaviors that make bodies more efficient.[49] Power on this microscale operates—to use one of Foucault's more visceral images—on the "soft fibres of the brain" that constitute the "synaptic contact of bodies-power."[50] Such an "anatomopolitics"[51] approaches "the individual as an affective being who can 'control' unruly passions through physical action"[52] to integrate conduct into efficient spaces of control. Individuating techniques, therefore, must be understood as corporeal, as generative forces that intervene in the body's capacities as constitutive elements of a totality of bodies or population, the combined coordination and regulation of which is at stake.

The push is therefore to draw out the affective impositions on the individual body that are tied to managing the population as a totality. Persuading the body to submit to power in this sense takes place in what Diana Coole terms "the 'somatic dimension' . . . where power is etched onto the body and communication takes place through a mute yet eloquent corporeal syntax."[53] The "synaptic contact" (to use Foucault's imagery) between bodies and power is made, Coole continues, in "material and affective worlds, where . . . violence assaults the flesh with raw immediacy."[54] Crucial to the analysis here is the recognition of an affective political pedagogy of disciplinary spaces where such "assaults" on the flesh—or affective experience—create shared places where "people learn political fundamentals through their experiences."[55] This disciplinary function rests on the notion that affective experience is significantly constitutive and is a central tenet for prominent writers on affect: as William Connolly writes, each sensory experience leaves a "deposit" in "'affectively imbued memory banks' [that] might later yet encourage a disciplined train of thought."[56] From this perspective, if we take seriously the Palestinian experience of checkpoint spaces as "sources of profound anxiety,"[57] and we recognize checkpoints as "geographic manifestations of Israeli control over Palestinian life,"[58] then it follows that thorough examination of embodied experience in such spaces of colonial control can bring insight into the broader subjectivizing processes that lie at the heart of Israel's biopolitical management of Palestinian life.

Through this theoretical framework, we can begin to analyze the ways in which the affective space of checkpoint terminals imposes disciplinary sequences on the daily movements of Palestinians that are related to Israel's biopolitical management of the occupied population *as a whole*. This theoretical position highlights how Checkpoint 300 disciplines the affecting body toward the biopolitical end of producing a submissive and useful population. More specifically, it directs us toward the ways in which Palestinian lives are regulated *beyond the checkpoint* via a distribution of bodies and affects and in terms of families, care, and community. The base argument I wish to build in the final part of this chapter is that Checkpoint 300 sifts for able-bodied, politically docile, male subjects to work in the Israeli economy while simultaneously shaping categories of excluded subject groups—ones that are brought more fully into view in the chapters that follow.

The first part of the chapter presented a largely descriptive account of conditions within Checkpoint 300 that are marked by prolonged delays and pronounced levels of stress and threats of violence. The second part built from that account a broader mode of analysis capable of a focus on checkpoint effects outside the space of the checkpoint itself. This enables, I argue here and throughout the book, a fuller appreciation of the deeper function of power detectable via careful attention to Checkpoint 300—and likely similar such security infrastructures. It is not only that the checkpoint is a place of visually evident colonial violence; it is also a node of less spectacular techniques of control that may be subtle in register but no less pervasive in effect. A crucial element of this is perceptible by zooming out from the site of the checkpoint to expand further on the strict permit system that precedes entrance into that space as a bureaucratic mechanism for identifying and regulating an admissible Palestinian mobile working population. Once again, the story begins with men, posing the challenge of tracking further vectors of power for the project to hand. Men are denied or made ineligible for labor permits for many reasons: having been detained by Israeli police or miliary (easily a majority of the male population);[59] being involved in union activity; having been dismissed from an Israeli company; or being either under the age of thirty, older than fifty, unmarried, and/or without at least one child.[60] The denied laborers—many with "black marks" on their West Bank ID cards—comprise an estimated thirty-five- to fifty-thousand-strong labor force whose exclusion from checkpoints forces them to find weaker points in the wall to cross "illegally" (without a permit) to their places of work, often at great risk to personal safety.[61] For the men in Checkpoint 300—negotiating the corridors, turnstiles, and delays—this is the alternative; those crossing without documentation are (even more) expendable and therefore (even more) exploitable. In this way, the checkpoint simultaneously produces and capitalizes on a population with few alternatives and thus takes on a subject-making function of producing a compliant labor force comprising—exclusively—only those men with bodies fit enough to withstand the physically demanding and psychologically demeaning commute. These bodily capacities, it follows, are harnessed into a "machinery of production"[62] that turns on backbreaking days of expendable and tractable labor.

A picture thus begins to emerge of how the disciplinary and affective register of Checkpoint 300, in Foucault's words, "increases the forces of the body (in economic terms of utility) and diminishes these same forces (on political terms of obedience)."[63] The delaying and anxiety-inducing microprocesses of the checkpoint space work to discipline and render docile the laboring bodies that flow through it. The enforced stillness, restricted movement, agitation, threat, fear, and so forth corporealize the coconstitutive hierarchical relations between colonizer and colonized. The embodied experience serves as an intense daily reminder to Palestinian commuters of their inferior status. As an "assault" on the flesh, as Diana Coole terms it, the concomitant and unquestionably negative political orientations embodied at the checkpoint might be likened to what Lauren Berlant referred to as "political depression," marked by "hopelessness, helplessness, dread, anxiety, stress, worry, lack of interest."[64] The stretched-out time— sometimes *hours*—spent on the checkpoint crossing are characterized by such depressive affects; the corridors and turnstiles come together to produce an apathetic body whereby subjects are too tired to think, much less to organize, calling to mind Helga Tawil-Souri's reflection that "the moment of the checkpoint makes it nigh impossible to contemplate more important—political—thoughts."[65] In this sense, the checkpoint works to wear down the political agency and community of Palestinians, diminishing possibilities of organizing and resisting. This grounds the first part of my argument in this chapter: that the disciplinary and affective functions of the checkpoint work to produce a specific kind of male Palestinian subject, one whose able-bodiedness and political docility serve Israel's wider colonial-capitalist project.

To expand briefly in closing on a specific part of this argument, it is important to recognize that a depoliticizing effect of the checkpoint is not ahistorical. The elaborate technologies of Checkpoint 300— and, indeed, the wall, *all* checkpoints, the overblown capacities of the Israel Defense Forces (IDF), and so forth—are sustained by the construction of the Palestinian (often male) Other, a figure whose strategic prominence reproduces the justifying logics on which such security infrastructures depend. The Israeli Ministry of Foreign Affairs claims that the "anti-terrorist fence" (West Bank wall) and "check terminals" (checkpoints) are built as a "defensive, temporary, passive and effective measure against terrorism."[66] Such is consistent with a by now familiar figuring of Palestinians in Israeli political discourses as "the world's premier 'terrorists.'"[67] It is a base point, however, that any purported "disorderliness" or "ungovernability" of the Palestinian population is born not of a vacuum but rather of lives lived in the context of often brutal oppression and dispossession.[68] Checkpoint 300 is one other site where this plays out as the distributive segments and practices of the checkpoint both perpetuate the sense of disorder that needs management and continually reestablishes the disciplinary effect of order. The checkpoint—as described herein—produces the unruliness it is tasked to order; to revisit one particularly illustrative scene, in the desperate conditions created by the Israeli state, some Palestinian men are prepared to climb over the heads of members of the same community. The spaces of the checkpoint therefore seem designed not simply to discipline uncivility but also to produce it in the first place in a way that—I would argue—is not contained within the checkpoint itself but tells us something of the broader logics of colonial power. As Timothy Mitchell wrote of the British colonial project in Egypt, the "question of achieving the continuous appearance of structure or order" runs parallel to the "problem of 'disorder.'"[69]

Of the second part of my argument—that checkpoints and permit bureaucracies around them "leave behind" entire groups such that the checkpoint's effects extend far beyond the space of the checkpoint itself—I have only begun to scratch the surface, but there is sure ground to suppose that the checkpoint's disciplinary and affective impositions work to disrupt manifold aspects of Palestinian life. In particular, all indications are that the checkpoint plays an important role in reproducing a heteronormative sexual division of labor in Palestinian society, a fact that is discernible even through a narrow focus on the men. Given the long hours that Palestinian men must give up for the commute, as husbands and fathers, they are left with little time to spend with their wives and children or to see friends and neighbors. As one Palestinian man traveling through Checkpoint 300 recounted, "it's cold and dark when I wake up, and the rest of my family is asleep. . . . I do this every morning . . . so I can cross through to work in Israel and make some money to feed my eight children. . . . When I get back, I have an hour or two before I have to sleep, so I can repeat the whole day again."[70] Prompted by feminist interventions on biopolitics, testimonies such as this open up a broad range of issues to do with the extensive *spatiality* of the checkpoint and, specifically, how it extends beyond the space of the checkpoint itself. With regard to the crucial question of what is missing in a strict focus on the checkpoint itself, therefore, the story presented in the first part of this chapter must be read as partial. The harsh conditions of Checkpoint 300 are only the epicenter of a wider dispersal of Israeli colonial power through Palestinian society. The hundreds of men deprived of sleep and time with their spouses and children are a clear pointer to a bigger story: of the checkpoint affecting women and families, of a security infrastructure that penetrates not only political life (i.e., in terms of docility) but also domestic life—the very target of biopolitical modes of governing.

At this early point in this examination of colonial space through Checkpoint 300, a key point of departure—put in the strongest terms—is that, just as a physically fit and compliant body is required to make the daily crossing through Checkpoint 300, so, too, are fitness and acquiescence requisite for "insertion" into the Israeli machinery of production. To the central questions on Checkpoint 300 I posed at the beginning of the chapter—How does power function? What kinds of subjectivity are produced? What is missing from a focus on the checkpoint itself?—I hope to have provided clear answers that indicate the lines of inquiry that are to follow. Power (while always a multiple and contested force and concept) operates in different registers toward producing a particular type of Palestinian subject. Most readily perceptible is the compliant laborer whose potential "disorderliness" or "uncivility" is simultaneously an ever-present liability in need of control and the underlying justifying logic of control. Less obvious—but by now brought to the fore—is the otherwise absent figure of a laborer's family or the groups excluded from Israel's permit system. This is what I see as missing from an analysis that focuses sharply on the checkpoint itself and what is given center stage over the next two chapters.

For workers, Checkpoint 300 imposes a disciplinary and affective space on daily life. They are caught within a swirl of subjugating affects—anger, boredom, despondency, resentment, humiliation, frustration, stress, fear—that set them within a clearly hierarchical colonizer–colonized relation. Waiting, or being made to wait, at the whim of colonial technologies and security staff makes this most clearly visible: men are positioned in a space marked by the dual threats of bodily violence and lost labor. The only answer is to make oneself comply with security restrictions, to try one's best to cross without incident and to therefore insert oneself into the colonial economy. This disciplinary function—one delivered in a heavily affective register—scales up to a biopolitical one, where a population of depoliticized (i.e., docile) male subjects are either too exhausted to politically organize or else simply (and understandably) reticent to risk losing a permit. Zooming out further, there is a deeper biopolitical function in which domestic lives are drawn into the commute. If a permit depends on marriage and fatherhood, it also depends on social reproduction, on the everyday labors of women and others. If checkpoints are, then, considered the "quintessential Palestinian experience," then we should recognize that women are not currently part of that essence. This brings us to a point of asking, simply, how is checkpoint space gendered? And more specifically, what are women's experiences of checkpoints? I answer this crucial question in two steps. In chapter 3, I investigate women's lives beyond the checkpoint by examining the effects of the checkpoint's impositions on daily life. First, though, in chapter 2, I remain within the checkpoint, documenting women's experiences of crossing the checkpoint themselves.

2

Women at the Checkpoint

THE COLONIAL PRODUCTION OF GENDER

> When it was my turn to pass, he asked, pointing at my belly,
> "What is there?!" I answered, "It's a baby, there is a baby." He
> said, "No, there is a bomb," to which I replied, "No, it is not
> a bomb, it is a baby." Then he told me to turn around, which
> I did, and then they were whistling again, making fun of me.
> The idea is that one has to do exactly as they say without
> making a big deal, as they might shoot us without caring
> even one bit. This is one of the miseries of Checkpoint 300.
> —Dina, al-Walaja

The work of this chapter is to remain focused on the space of the
checkpoint buildings with the objective of bringing women's crossings and dealings with permits to the center of discussion. As I have
pointed out, most of our knowledge of Checkpoint 300 (and checkpoints in Palestine in general) is concentrated on the experiences of
men crossing during the busy morning commute. The first chapter
began with that important context, while making sure gestures toward
the broader effects of control that are detectable only at various removes from that widely documented scene. What is brought into view
here is not so visually striking as, say, men scrambling across cage bars,
but there is no less colonial control effected by the materialities of the
checkpoint and the convoluted permit system that restrict the mobilities of women in Palestine. To pick up the theme of subject making,
women's roles and lives are consequently tethered to the checkpoint,
as it curtails women's social and political activities while splitting off
parenting and homemaking duties—amplifying the roles constitutive
of uneven gender relations. There are multiple factors in the formation of these relations, from the pronounced practices of humiliation
and intimidation by checkpoint staff to the deterrent function of the

permit system, each of which contributes—sometimes conspicu-
ously, most often subtly—to the instrumentalizing of uncertainty and
the making of women's lives through the masculinized logics of security.[1] Following and learning from important precedents that counter
the "politics of invisibility" of Palestinian women in military and security infrastructure settings,[2] the chapter forwards an understanding
of Checkpoint 300 as a markedly gendered—and *gendering*—space
through which wider patriarchal relations are formed and reinforced.

I base the arguments presented here and in the next chapter on
a series of interviews and focus groups with twelve women in the
village of al-Walaja, on the northwestern edge of Bethlehem. The research was facilitated by al-Walaja Women's Group and particularly
the research of Lamees, a member of the group who, as I outline in the
book's introduction, devised questions and conducted interviews for
the project. This approach set out to enable a feminist examination of
security infrastructure that "studies up"—from micro to macro—by
taking a personal and embodied approach to knowledge that makes
visible practices, experiences, and effects that might otherwise remain
obscured.[3] From the interviews emerges an account that makes two
contributions to the book's overall understanding of Checkpoint 300
as a colonial infrastructure of control. First, it shows how the movement of Palestinian women through the checkpoint brings the politics of gender and occupation to the fore, in particular the way that
colonial security mechanisms situate women within colonial patriarchies. As Palestinian women themselves articulate, their presence at
the checkpoint can be alternatively challenged or facilitated by Palestinian men, while the treatment they receive from Israeli security
staff is frequently intended to intimidate and humiliate. With (I hope)
appropriate qualifications to the limits of analysis possible from my
particular positionality, I relate these experiences to the broader social
and cultural positioning of Palestinian women within colonized space.
A second contribution is to connect Checkpoint 300 to the politics of
care and domestic life in the context of colonial control. As the previous chapter shows clearly, the checkpoint effects border crossings of
male wage laborers, thus positioning men as household breadwinners.
But what if, instead of foregrounding this function of the checkpoint,
we take women's experiences as a starting point? How do we then understand the making of subject categories at Checkpoint 300?

I address these questions by foregrounding and learning from the testimonies of women living close to the checkpoint. The discussion moves through different stages of mobility, beginning at dealings with permit bureaucracies before moving to the checkpoint itself to attend to women's experiences of attempting to cross. This includes sustained focus on crossing with children, a key aspect of women's experience of the crowds and security staff at the checkpoint. The chapter closes with an attempt to synthesize the various expressions and registers of power that work through the checkpoint and their effects on women's lives.

While those thousands of working-age, permit-holding Palestinian men cross the checkpoint every day, the exigencies of the Israeli labor market result in women using the checkpoint for different purposes. It is important to articulate something of the multiplicity of these purposes, for instance, a relatively small number of women hold permits to work in Israeli settlements, either in agriculture or as domestic labor; some students gain sponsored permits from institutions of higher education in Jerusalem; and Bethlehem's large Christian population has relatively easier (though by no means *easy*) access to permits through church relationships. For such groups, however, travel through the complex tends to be undertaken via the vehicle gate one hundred meters east of the pedestrian entrance. The majority of women crossing by foot do so after gaining one-off permits to attend medical or bureaucratic appointments in East Jerusalem or for social and religious purposes, such as prayer at al-Aqsa Mosque and iftar during Ramadan. Women's journeys through the checkpoint—like those of men—actually begin at the district coordination office (DCO), where applications are processed by the Israeli Civil Administration, a part of COGAT, the part of Israel's Defense Ministry that governs in the West Bank.[4] It is common that applications are submitted via representative organizations, such as village council groups, or, as in the cases discussed here, a civil society collective, such as the al-Walaja Women's Group. The processing of permit applications is notoriously opaque and subject to unpredictable delays and arbitrary refusals. An important part of women's relations to the checkpoint is formed through dealings with the permit system, and the knock-on effects on im/mobility shape women's participation in political, economic, and cultural life.

A recurrent story of checkpoints for women in al-Walaja, as well as around Bethlehem and all over the West Bank, is of not crossing due to a refused permit and of successful applications being both arbitrary and relatively rare. In addition, the process of applying is known for being particularly arduous, as it often involves an in-person meeting at the DCO. To understand anything of bureaucratic processes in the West Bank, it is crucial to emphasize the aspect that goes beyond form fill-ing and slow processing: the dreaded in-person encounter at the DCO, where Palestinian permit applicants are treated with open contempt. One activist from the group Checkpoint Watch records "trying physical conditions: endless waiting periods, lack of adequate shelter, toilets and refreshment facilities," where Palestinians have "no redress, no agency and very little hope.... Waiting seems longer because of the uncertainty as to when it will end and what its results will be. The very request for a permit is regarded as suspect, as insolence."[5] During the interviews in al-Walaja, Amani, who is prominent as the head of the Women's Group, spoke about her appointment at the DCO in the Israeli military base in the Gush Etzion complex of settlements: "It was very crowded.... I was waiting from eight in the morning until two in the afternoon.... When I got my turn, [without any explanation] they paused the process, and I had to wait another two hours until I got the permit. I finally left at four o'clock." The Etzion DCO is notorious among Bethlehemites for both openly intimidating personnel (including police, military, and privately contracted) and markedly inhospitable conditions, such as extreme heat or cold in the waiting areas and overflowing or locked bathrooms.[6] For any Palestinian—or indeed anyone researching Palestine—the experi-ence Amani recounts is a familiar one; a full eight hours of uncertain waiting in such a hostile environment takes a toll: "It was a very harsh day, and a cold day, and by the end of it, I was totally exhausted." The long waiting time is typical of Israel's invasive, segregating, and "slow-motion" bureaucracy that never operates to more than a bare-minimum standard in a contradictory performance of both recognizing and stall-ing Palestinians' human rights.[7]

For Amani on this occasion, the trying day at Etzion DCO did at least yield a permit. Many other applications are rejected, or a permit is granted only on very specific grounds. In the instances when permits are not issued, the Civil Administration offers little explanation, save for vague references to "security concerns." In this way, the bureau-cratic process functions as a wall before the wall—or what Julie Peteet has termed a "paper wall of bureaucracy"—that excludes women not only from Jerusalem but also from the checkpoint itself.[8] This is significant for the fact that most of what we know about checkpoints centers on the site of the border crossing itself, thus overlooking the regulation of mobility via dispersed mechanisms of bureaucratic control. The mechanisms set in place by the Civil Administration provide for two main grounds on which women's checkpoint permit applications are more readily accepted: for medical appointments and for prayer. Immediately clear is both a quantitative and a qualitative difference in the ways that the Israeli permit system contributes to the respective roles of Palestinian women and men. Karima, another active member of the al-Walaja Women's Group, explicated this in an interview: "Many more men have permits than women, so they can pass and go to work. For women, you have to have some kind of medical document, because even for family visits, you don't get a permit—so men have more chances because of their labor, but we only get a permit when it's Ramadan or hospital—or we don't get it at all." As a survey of the checkpoint permit system, Karima presents a keen sense of gendered discrimination: large numbers of men can cross for work; significantly smaller numbers of women may cross, most usually for prayer or medical treatment. Though no official figures are published, it is sure that of the eighty-seven thousand and more work permits for West Bank Palestinians to cross into Jerusalem, only a tiny percentage is held by women. For context, OCHA reported 320,000 people passing checkpoints into Jerusalem for Friday prayers during Ramadan in 2019, when the gender balance was pronouncedly reversed: temporary regulations allowed "women of all ages, and men under 16 and above the age of 40 to cross without permits [while] men between 17 and 39 years of age needed to apply for permits."[9]

For medical appointments, women cross the checkpoint either for their own clinical care or to accompany children or husbands to appointments at hospitals in Jerusalem. Significantly, none of the women interviewed had been accompanied on her own appointment; women act only as *carers* and not as the *cared-for*. Also notable is the denial of checkpoint permits to further the cultural and economic activities of the Women's Group; applications are repeatedly ("two to three times a year") denied. The permit system thus foregrounds and backgrounds different aspects of women's lives, women who, in addition to being wives and mothers, are variously engaged in part-time work, the village council, and the carpentry practiced at the group's workshop. This is not to negate deeply gendered divisions of labor that exist in

the West Bank (and everywhere) but to highlight a way that Israel regulates Palestinian women's visibility in Jerusalem and beyond along
normative figures of a religious and caring wife or mother. It bears
pointing out that crossing is not possible as, for instance, a furniture
trader, local councilor, or civil society organizer—not to mention a
more politicized role as a campaigner for women's rights. Nor is it possible to gain a permit for cultural or leisure activities, and many of the
women regret not being able to spend free days at parks or beaches or
"anything that would make us feel less trapped," as one woman put it.
The toll of immobility on women's well-being is palpable, and the very
narrow conditions of mobility—to do with the "traditional" subject
position of pious caregiver—do not leave room for women to pursue
their varied interests.

But even the roles that are more permissible do not guarantee a
smooth crossing through the checkpoint. In fact, from an important
perspective, given that checkpoint staff arbitrarily deny passage, all a
granted permit does is displace the possibility of denial from the bureaucratic mechanism to the checkpoint itself. As such, a "successful"
negotiation of the permit system also marks the beginning of a period
of anxious waiting: "Once I got [the permit] I was very happy—but
it came with fear, because you get the permit and then you remember you have to go to the checkpoint—and you feel like you're going
to a prison" (Randa). Such nervous anticipation is consistent with a
broader proliferation of anxiety-inducing security strategies of maintaining uncertainty in Palestine and beyond and, on many occasions,
is well founded. One woman recounted,

> Once during Ramadan, when they [the Israeli Civil Administra-
> tion] announced that all women could pass through any day, I
> went to the checkpoint based on that assumption. When I arrived,
> the soldier[10] said I was forbidden from passing. When I asked
> why, he said that I was not fifty years old! I told him, "At Ramadan
> women below fifty can pass!" He started yelling at me, "Go back,
> go back!" On this occasion I responded that I do not want to
> become fifty—I was forty-five at the time—and I did not want
> to pass. It's unjust—I was angry and returned home. (Tala)

Such arbitrary application of a temporary (and thus malleable) rule is
commonplace, as checkpoint staff either do not know or do not care

about regulations, which can change from checkpoint to checkpoint, shift to shift, and mood to mood. There is apparently limited incentive for them to learn and apply rules because they act with almost total impunity, given the little recourse for Palestinians to appeal a decision (and little point, because an appointment is already missed anyway). These "petty sovereigns"—who are often young, disengaged, and poorly trained (see chapter 6)—make unilateral decisions, enforcing the borders of the state on a whim with sometimes serious consequences, such as missed medical appointments.[11]

While Tala did not regret speaking her mind on that particular occasion, it is frequently the case that checkpoint encounters enforce silence whereby any sign of dissent compromises the chance of entry, even with a valid permit. This puts a strategic choice on women when checkpoint staff threaten to deny entry: "I want to know why, [and] if I argue, they might change their mind, but if they're stubborn and decide to deny me entry, especially when I have kids, I won't make a scene because I might be arrested or taken away" (Karima). In other instances, women speak of having to endure the demeaning tactics of checkpoint staff without protest when the rotation of the turnstiles is delayed in a way that increases bodily proximity—"we are not allowed to object or speak, so women stay silent, but men get irritated [and shout]" (Dina)—or when invasive security checks are enforced: "For a woman, it's difficult, because they body scan and humiliate you while you have to keep your mouth shut" (Randa). Significant in each of these scenarios is the imposition of a further condition on women's mobility: "keeping [one's] mouth shut." We can thus add detail to the claim that women's use of the checkpoint rests on a particular subject position to do with piety and caregiving: passage can additionally be dependent on maintaining the familiar silence of the submissive or subaltern colonized woman.[12]

Yet, even as women adopt such subject positions, there remains no guarantee of safe passage through the checkpoint. One can obtain a permit and behave as required but still be refused passage at the security check stage. The women involved in the research in al-Walaja were each able to recount multiple cases of being turned back, most of the time without explanation from checkpoint staff:

I often can't go to Friday prayer during Ramadan because I can't take the kids along because it would be exhausting for them and you can't leave them alone at home, because I might get stuck on the way, or not being sure about what time I would come back. . . . This year I gave up my only opportunity to go there. . . . Sacrifices are always there, like visits, traveling. The mother gives all her life and time to her kids at home to make sure her kids don't feel left out because we can't always cross. Therefore, often the mother stays with the kids at home. (Karima)

Karima's words here bring together in very clear terms some of the themes discussed so far in this chapter. It is not only the case that women are prevented from engaging with Jerusalem's cultural, economic, and political life (as evidenced in the Women's Group's repeated denial of permits), or even that they are denied entry on religious or medical grounds—there is something deeper to the power of the checkpoint to do with uncertainty, anticipation, and self-governing. For Karima, and for others who fear, through experience and precedent, that they "might get stuck," the checkpoint has become a prospect they are unable or unwilling to face, a deterrent. Importantly, this extends through the initial bureaucratic process—"I wanted to apply for a permit . . . but it's an awful hassle so I didn't apply" (Amani)—to the final stage of security checks: "I wished to go, but [because of] the fear of soldiers . . . I stopped applying for a permit" (Hanan). The permit system and checkpoint in this way come together as deterring elements that discourage even attempted mobility. As importantly, the decision to remain im/mobile in this way is not limited to the relatively small al-Walaja Women's Group but extends via friends and family to the wider Bethlehem area: "According to what people have said lately [around the area] about crossing the checkpoint, it's a struggle. Some women went through with their children and said it was very difficult and exhausting and they would never do it again. It's very crowded, and there isn't a line for women. . . . They said it was very difficult and they would never try to pass again" (Amani). In the continual reformulation and reiteration of such difficulty is a pervasive discourse, one with a material effect of deterring women even from entering the checkpoint, let alone Jerusalem.

To this point, the story of women's dealings with the checkpoint centers on bureaucratic processes of subject making that foreground specific roles (piety, carer, motherhood) that contrast starkly with those of permit-holding men (low-wage laborers) and a keen sense that crossings are made more difficult—or "exhausting," to use a recurrent framing—by a lack of provision for women's specific (and, in part, *forced*) needs, such as traveling with children. This culminates in a powerful discourse of the checkpoint as an inhospitable space to be avoided wherever possible, which is a decision many women understandably make in al-Walaja and beyond. This part of the chapter moves back into the space of the checkpoint itself to examine the roots of that discourse in the ways that Palestinian women are treated, specifically in terms of how Israeli security practices target female bodies and the parameters and possibilities of embodied subjectivity. A key point made here is that women's movement through the checkpoint involves intrusion, intimidation, and violence that are not imposed on an already-established body but are rather "part and parcel of the production of the various bodies that are subjected to violence."[13] The affective, embodied dimensions of the checkpoint thus come to the fore as instrumental in the processes of gendering Palestinian bodies and thereby realizing difference between men and women.

An important contextual backdrop to developing this claim is the account presented in the previous chapter, where the packed corridors, security technologies, and policing practices inside the checkpoint make it a challenging—and often dangerous—route of crossing for *any* Palestinian. This broad point holds even if the most part of critical attention (from academics, human rights workers, or journalists) is focused on men crossing, and mostly in the early mornings. Little is said or asked about the ways that, for instance, turnstiles, proximity, and body searches affect women specifically or the ways that pregnancy, mothering, and caring roles heighten the vulnerability of women at the checkpoint. These are obvious gaps in our knowledge that women during the research in al-Walaja were keen to speak to through thoughtful, sometimes contrasting, but always complex experiences and opinions on competing, gendered dynamics at the checkpoint. For instance, some women report occasions when Palestinian men showed a great deal of empathy or care for women as they made their way through the corridors and turnstiles: "We Palestinians make it easier for each other. . . . When [men] see a woman approaching and wanting to pass, the men open the way for her to go right through" (Ameera). At other times, no such grace is offered, and women come up against an embodied disadvantage in the queue:

"[Instead of waiting,] if I were a man, I would jump like them over the fence and skip the queue." It is not only that "wall crawling" is not (as) physically possible as it is for some of the younger male bodies; it is also that imposing and exposing the body in that way is significantly less socially acceptable for women. In other cases, men are not empathetic but explicitly hostile: "Some men shame women. . . . They don't understand that we are passing for medical purposes, they start questioning why we are at the checkpoint and so on. . . . This is from the side of the unskilled workers" (Tala).

There are some notable consistencies within these contrasting examples that map closely onto women's perceived positions in Palestinian society. In a field of possibilities where one could alternatively be afforded eased passage or subjected to shaming behaviors (blocking, comments), there are two fixed constants: either option is, first, subordinate to the whims and wills of men and, second, tied to the materiality of the reproductive or "modest" body. Put this way, there are obvious connections to the figuring of women in Palestinian society under Israeli occupation. In addition to the considerable discriminatory practices of the Israeli state, many Palestinian women—though prominent in anticolonial struggles[14]—face substantial pressures (like women of all nations) to uphold the integrity of family life and maintain religious norms of femininity.[15] In this light, being allowed to pass, being shamed, or feeling it unsuitable to climb the bars can be rooted in a longer history of women's societal and colonized positionality. As two discernible possibilities that are brought to the surface and intensified in the colonial setting of the checkpoint, *welcomed-and-eased* or *blocked-and-shamed* neatly encompass the simultaneous and contradictory struggles of many women in Palestine and add to the analysis by illustrating the ways that women's encounters at the checkpoint reveal the dual movement—both exogenous and endogenous—of colonial patriarchies.[16]

There is far less ambiguity in the ways that women are treated by Israeli security staff, however. As mentioned in the previous chapter, despite the presence of a "humanitarian lane" (ostensibly for women, children, the differently abled, and the elderly), it is most often closed, forcing all groups to join the general lane. The result for women can be quite distressing, especially during crowded times, when safety is most compromised; being pushed to the side and against the bars is commonplace, as are resulting bruises and even cracked ribs. Women also report a heightened sense of discomfort in physical proximity to so many men, as well as an elevated vulnerability that comes from accompanying family members. "It's difficult alone, but if you have children with you, you can't even imagine how bad it is" (Dina) was a reflection that resonated with many. Also apparent is that "*they* do not care," referring to the security staff, who seemingly make little effort to ease conditions at the checkpoint. Ameera recalled a time when a crush prompted a panicked attempt to escape the crowd: "I broke down in tears and started climbing the cement walls to get out of the crowd. I am tall compared to other women—shorter women with children had a tougher time. They squeezed us in the crowd so that no one could go forward or backward, it was rough. . . . From that day, I decided never to go again. . . . There was no mercy [from checkpoint staff]."

The threat and stresses of the corridors are only the beginning, however. Once the crowds are negotiated, women's exposure to harm turns psychological as checkpoint staff practice specifically gendered modes of intimidation and humiliation, including comments on physical appearance, such as body shape (typically comments on being "overweight") and a general provocation of self-consciousness among women. One interviewee, Suad, described in general terms the experience of the security check area inside the checkpoint:

> It's so crowded and there are men and women, so usually we
> are forced to be pushed against each other even though we try
> to prevent it. And when you pass the first gate, you go through
> a metal door to the metal detector. Sometimes you have to take
> everything off, including a hair tie. . . . Sometimes she's taken
> aside to be searched by a female soldier, and sometimes it's a small
> thing that makes the machine go off, like a piece of metal in your
> shoe that you can't see. . . . It feels submissive. . . . They humiliate
> us as much as possible.

It is, by all accounts, "very common" for women to have such problems passing through metal detectors, and this exposes women to sometimes extreme levels of distress. Suad recounted one specific occasion when

> there was a woman in front of me who kept making the metal
> detector go off. Again and again she was sent back by the soldier

[through a loudspeaker] to take something off and try again, it happened so many times. She took off so many things that she got scared and started crying. I told her not to be scared and asked the men to go back so we could lift her cover dress. . . . It was terrible—it's a struggle and a humiliation, especially for a woman.

There is an obvious and pointed threat to corporeal sovereignty in this case that rests on specific cultural and religious bodily norms that are purposefully ignored or exploited by checkpoint staff. The woman's distress builds to a breaking point with little sign of any "humanitarian" provision that might preserve dignity. In all senses, such treatment seems needlessly cruel. Checkpoint staff habitually degrade women during security checks in this way. They exercise total control of the women's right to present themselves as they wish, and this is routinely expressed via insults or the order to remove items of clothing in view of others. Understandably, many women feel a profound unease at undressing in security spaces, and this contributes further to the sense of trepidation and considerations of whether to attempt travel.

One more key dimension of the gendered dynamics of power at the checkpoint warrants sustained attention. As discussed, a main reason that women apply for permits is for access to essential medical care in Jerusalem for themselves or as named accompaniers of older relatives or children. It is not an exaggeration to claim that this latter purpose of crossing—one that is, it must be reiterated, formalized in the Israeli permit system—amplifies everything described so far. The materiality of the checkpoint takes on new significance once children are present: the tight corridors, turnstiles, and metal detectors are unforgiving for anyone traveling with strollers or wheelchairs (see Figures 9 and 10). And although it might go unnoticed to the early-morning laborers that facilities like toilets and baby-changing rooms are permanently out of service (or have been for the last nine or so years), when women join the queue with babies and toddlers, that lack in provision can add further stress to the crossing. The treatment by checkpoint staff takes on a new tone once children are present too, whereby the threat of violence emerges at a more immediate and visceral register. It is apparent that "Israeli soldiers don't consider your situation, whether you're pregnant, or with kids, or older" (Karima) or, worse, that they *do* consider these factors and yet use them to further target women. Each of

FIGURE 9. Passing through Checkpoint 300 with children. Photograph by the author.

FIGURE 10. Passing through Checkpoint 300 with children. Photograph by the author.

these three factors—the materiality or architecture of the space, the lack of provision for children, and the consistent targeting of women *as mothers* by staff—amplifies the gendered power dynamics at the checkpoint.

Unsurprisingly, the crowded and chaotic space of the checkpoint makes it difficult to ensure the safety of children. This is the case even as children bring forth a communal sense of care among other people crossing, who show levels of courtesy and assistance, especially for younger children, opening the way and generally trying to keep mothers with their children to avoid distress. Nonetheless, keeping track of children at the busiest times is difficult and worrying:

> One time . . . the kids were in front of us and there were lots of people, nobody knew how to move forward. People were pushing and my children had trouble breathing because of the number of people who were stuck. . . . I passed through the narrow lane and got stopped at the gate [while they were ahead]. . . . I didn't know where my kids were. (Lamees)

On occasions like this, the checkpoint is a dangerous place for children, where a lack of air and the possibility of getting lost or trampled demand extra exertions from women. And this is an importantly affective exertion, as women's stress, anxiety, fear, worry, anger, exasperation, and so on—the embodiments that the checkpoint provokes—are greatly intensified for the fact of traveling through with the heightened vulnerability of children. This is starkly illustrated, along with a sense of pragmatism, in the example of Randa's quite routine description of what she does with her children when the crowd is tight: "When there is traffic, the kids can't breathe, so I hold them up in the air so they can breathe." It would be difficult to conjure a more shocking image of—both oppressive *and* negotiated—gendered colonial power at the checkpoint.

Aside from the issue of separation in the crowd, a prominent consideration on the issue of taking children through the checkpoint is separation at the security check stage. It is commonplace that security staff, often without discernible reason, are given to splitting family groups by either delaying or denying the passage of different members. Making this worse is the fact that the staff insist on processing children's checks individually, and they apparently do so with an intimidating demeanor entirely unsuited to communicating with younger people. The predictable result is that children become scared. They cry and protest, especially when they pass through the final security check and have to then wait to see if their mothers will be admitted. That wait can vary from minutes to much longer:

> Once I had my seven-year-old son with me, and he was allowed to pass. It was very difficult; my son was holding my hand, and I was not allowed to go through. He would not let go of me [because] he wanted to be with me. Eventually he had to go on with his family [aunties], so I gave him some pocket money and told him to go ahead with the family members that passed. But he was in tears the whole time while with them in Jerusalem, and he did not have fun at all because his mother was denied spending the day with him. I had to go back home and stay on my own. (Randa)

Arbitrary (and, it must be said, *cruel*) decisions at the checkpoint in this way disrupt family plans and relationships. Randa reflected on this and other similar instances of separation at the checkpoint as "the most difficult situation in my life. . . . When I am denied access with my children, then I am not there for them. I am not allowed to pass with my husband, so I am not there for him. . . . If they pass and I don't, then I have no role to play in their lives that day." Suad and Karima shared similar experiences: "When you want to cross with your children, and they let most pass but only one is denied access, you have to go back with them. Especially because they're young, and can't get back alone, it makes you feel very bitter" (Suad); "I took the kids and went toward the checkpoint. It was overcrowded as always[, and] that day we got separated. Two of the children passed, and I and one of them was stuck in the checkpoint. I had to search the crowds! It was really horrible" (Karima).

What is perhaps not conveyed in these printed words is the affective register in which these stories are told. In person, these checkpoint scenes are gestured, embodied accounts of frustration and anger, permeated by shared moments of silence that cannot but provoke reflection—and some disbelief that it has come to this, where travel even to Jerusalem, only a few kilometers away and so culturally important to Palestinians, is made so difficult in precisely this way; where rights of mobility and protection are not extended *even to children* and the right to family life is threatened for all; and where women are targeted *as mothers* by security infrastructure. In the longer, final quote of this chapter, these elements come together in a most appalling way:

> My mother-in-law was in front of me, and the soldier told her to raise her hands up. She is an old woman wearing a dress [*thoab*] covered with a *V*-shaped *shal,* which the soldier told her to remove and turn around, and when she turned, another soldier started whistling, they were bullying and making fun of us. . . . When it was my turn to pass, he asked, pointing at my belly, "What is there?!" I answered, "It's a baby, there is a baby." He said, "No, there is a bomb," to which I replied, "No, it is not a bomb, it is a baby." Then he told me to turn around, which I did, and then they were whistling again, making fun of me. The idea is that one has to do exactly as they say without making a big deal, as they might shoot us without caring even one bit. This is one of the miseries of Checkpoint 300. (Dina)

If, at this point of the discussion, the taunting of an elderly woman reinforces the sense of inhumanity afforded to Palestinians at the checkpoint, then the threatening actions toward a pregnant woman push this to even more sinister levels. The reproductive body is instrumentalized to the ends of extremely demeaning colonial subordination, all of which must be endured "without making a big deal." "It makes you so sad you want to cry," summarized another woman, Hanan, in response to this account. "The soldiers torment us, then they search us. . . . My girls are scared. . . . We'll never do it again."

The key themes discussed in this chapter converge in this final reflection. The checkpoint clearly invokes fear and, in doing so, takes on an effective deterrent function that is significantly gendered. Generally, if children stay home, so do their mothers. From this angle "the wider sociopolitical functions of barriers" come into view—what checkpoints do "beyond blockading."[17] We get a clear sense of the ways in which women's interactions with and within the checkpoint facility are profoundly shaped by their role as caregiver and, in turn, how this role is challenged and delegitimized by crowdedness and security checks. At base, the challenges women face are amplified to the extent that claims that crossing is an anxious experience "for *all* Palestinians" must be understood from a specific perspective of motherhood: facing the inhumane and subordinating process of crossing the checkpoint is rendered all the more anxiety inducing when undertaken in the role of mother or of protector of children from the harmful environment of the checkpoint.

In this final part of the chapter, I return to the question of power and how we can understand its function through the checkpoint when we take women's experiences as a starting point for analysis. In many ways, there is nothing remarkable about the women's experiences at the checkpoint, except to add women's voices to the idea discussed in the first chapter that crossing checkpoints is something of a "quintessential Palestinian experience." What is remarkable, however, is how the women experience the checkpoint in a markedly different way, *as women*—and women, albeit with important exceptions (prominently in the work of Rema Hammami and Nadera Shalhoub-Kevorkian[18]), are not routinely thought of as part of this "quintessential" experience. When women are brought to the center of a consideration of the checkpoint and power, a picture builds of how a permit system and security space gender through im/mobility, embodiment, and relations of care. To close the chapter, I make some points on power and women's checkpoint experiences to do with the political substance (or "governmentalizing") of uncertainty, the prevalent effect among women of self-governing, and the obfuscating function of deterrence.

Aside from its obstructive materiality, the checkpoint functions as a symbolic wall that effects enclosure from afar: women are deterred by a convoluted and arbitrary permit process and by the prospect of an exhausting, unpredictable crossing with no guarantee of entry into Jerusalem. At each stage, from permit application to security check booth, women are faced with opaque processes, arbitrary decisions, and an accompanying sense of deep uncertainty. Focusing closely on this uncertainty provides a way of uncovering some of the more subtle yet pervasive machinations of power that function through Checkpoint 300. In the first instance, where the encounter with the checkpoint is bureaucratic, a permit application can have two outcomes: an (arbitrary) refusal that is met with understandable disappointment or an issued document that is received with a foreboding sense of a grueling crossing to come—"you feel like you're going to a prison" (Randa). The entire process is thus shot through with uncertainty, even to the point where the colonial state's own issued documents are subordinated to the whims of uncaring, unthinking, or simply cruel checkpoint staff, who can refuse entry right until the last moment, as we have seen. An issued permit is no more than a "fluid" or "unstable" document that produces, as Yael Berda has demonstrated in her study of Israel's permit system, "consistent anxiety and uncertainty for all Palestinians in the West Bank."[19] To take this unstable document into the space of the checkpoint is to enter a wider field of uncertainty, on which Rema Hammami writes so lucidly: "The logic of power materialised through the checkpoint regime aims to create a constant state of uncertainty (is it open or closed? Does this permit work or not? What's the mood of the soldiers?). Rather than an effect of it, this constant state of uncertainty is the very logic of Israeli sovereign violence that checkpoints instantiate."[20] Hammami documents this elsewhere as partly a "checkpoint of the mind" that fuses uncertainty and anxiety and thus captures something of an internalized border whose effects extend spatialities and temporalities.[21] Uncertainty in this way is not a by-product of inefficient techniques of governing; it is instead central to an effect of control.

There is little doubt that this dynamic is deeply prevalent for the women interviewed for this research—and for countless more around Bethlehem and the wider West Bank. Again and again, set in the comfort of the al-Walaja Women's Group workshop, it was obvious that the checkpoint forms a source of considerable uncertainty and anxiety for women, with significant effects on their lives: "When I last went to the checkpoint I was nervous because of *unexpected* issues. . . . *Anything* can be done by the soldiers in the checkpoint that would put me in trouble" (Hayam). The political substance of this pronounced uncertainty is realized in the decisions of many women to avoid travel through Checkpoint 300, and therefore to Jerusalem. Immediately clear is that the permit system and checkpoint take on a different function than that of simple closure or blocking; a deterrent forms through anxiety-inducing qualities that prompt a decision to self-govern. The question of Checkpoint 300, im/mobility, and subject making is thus opened out into different domains of life as reduced mobilities for women affect the arrangement of domestic and waged labor, as well as the pursuit of political and social activities. We should thus see the unreliability of permits and the intimidation of the checkpoint for the way they function as mechanisms of control: less a failure or absence of governing than an effective mode of governmentalizing or, in Michel Foucault's words, "arranging things so that this or that end may be achieved through a certain number of means."[22] This influential analytic of governing—or governing-as-arranging[23]—attends to those forms and techniques that act indirectly and the ways that power "operates on the field of possibilities in which the behaviours of active subjects is able to inscribe itself."[24] What this offers to the case at hand is a useful parsing of the checkpoint's various registers of power, which range from a sovereign enforcement of closure (i.e., visible, direct, readily traceable) to a governmentalizing effect (i.e., subtle, indirect, less perceptible) of curating the "possible field of action."[25] When situated within an arranged field, for instance, one that comprises arbitrary, intimidating, and/or humiliating practices in both the permit system and the checkpoint itself, *the endurance of which does not guarantee safe passage,* subjects conduct themselves in an anticipatory manner—and in ways that choices are made in relation to perceived threats and possibilities.[26]

In this way, control and action merge into a process of "governmentality" whereby those targeted by state power negotiate a delimited set of possibilities; it is from this position that the "decision" not to cross Checkpoint 300 is importantly agential, while also entirely subordinate to a narrow range of choices. "Torment," "fear," "humiliation"—all powerful and recurrent themes documented here—are hence significant as affective prompts toward certain decisions, or acts of self-governing that keep women in place.[27] And this brings us to a deeply consequential effect revealed through the accounts presented in this chapter. Taking women's experiences as a starting point for analysis, the checkpoint is not only a crowded, violent space of control, or a space where those effects are amplified for women; it is also a space to be avoided. Checkpoint 300 thus becomes a spatializing deterrent that contributes to the distinction between the active and mobile male worker who participates in the (extremely exploitative) labor market and the passive and immobile female homemaker who is tethered to domestic life. While a part of this distinction is undoubtedly endogenous to Palestinian society (as it is the world over), it is also bound up with colonial security infrastructure and bureaucratic impositions on colonized women. As Nadera Shalhoub-Kevorkian also found in her study of school-age girls and checkpoints, "in some cases parents decided to prevent girls from pursuing their education, fearing the effect of military checkpoints on their safety and security. In other cases, young girls were unable to cope with the daily humiliations and hardships, and decided to quit schools; in yet others girls agreed to an early marriage to escape the daily oppression."[28] It would appear from this, then, that focusing on the *avoidance* of the checkpoint is key to understanding its gendered effects of restricted mobility and the ways in which women—from school-age girls to al-Walaja's Women's Group—thus come to inhabit a "small world" of "physically and socially shrinking space" whose delimited confines coincide with delimiting gender norms and boundaries.[29]

In the broad project of understanding the manifold effects of the checkpoint, it is important to think through such avoidance in conceptual and methodological terms. Where the intimidations and humiliations of the permit bureaucracy and checkpoint space are enough for women to decide *preemptively* to remain in place, there are clear issues to do with detecting both the experience and scale of the issue. That is, if women report that crossings are so difficult that "they would never try to pass again" (Amani), then there is a gesture toward uncountable numbers of women deciding never even to enter the space of the checkpoint or to endure the bureaucratic procedure of applying for a permit. Inquiry thus runs up against a methodologically elusive research object for the simple fact that *deterrent* denotes a disengagement from a sight of focus, leaving nothing to apprehend.[30] But this cannot prevent an attempt to gain some purchase on the (absent) effects of deterrence, and it might rather signal a need to take seriously a notion that certain formations of power function precisely *to make nothing happen.*[31] From one angle, for instance, the early-morning crowd, there is a somewhat unremarkable absence of women: who would wish to enter such a space? Men endure the poor conditions of the checkpoint in exchange for wages; what incentive is there for women to do so? But these important questions set clear bounds on any potential response, almost completely foreclosing the possibility not only that women are denied permits but also that the *very possibility of denial* deters an application in the first place. And the real, evidence-based fear of intimidation inside the checkpoint facility reinforces a decision to stay away. This would mean that there is no document or recordable account of an unsuccessful attempt to cross the checkpoint, but it would, nonetheless, denote an effect of the checkpoint of restricting mobility. That women self-govern, therefore, is a prevalent if somewhat unquantifiable dimension of the power of the checkpoint to affect people's lives in Palestine.

In closing, then, what are the relations between permits, the checkpoint, and gender? And more specifically, what is the role of Checkpoint 300 in shaping women's lives? The answers provided here are clear (yet partial, as chapter 3 explicates). At base, beginning from the experience of women renders a quite different version of the checkpoint from that of the first chapter. Yes, the checkpoint still presents a crowded, anxiety-inducing space that constantly holds a potential for violence, but how that is both textured and experienced differs significantly between women and men. While men are permitted to cross as politically docile, low-waged laborers, women must cross as caring or religious subjects, ones that surely do not contradict some aspects of their everyday lives but that do foreclose manifold other social, political, and economic pursuits. The women interviewed here are variously involved in local government and women's rights movements, and a main al-Walaja Women's Group initiative (funded by the German government) is to grow a furniture-making business from a workshop in the village. Involvement in these activities denotes a plurality to women's lives in this part of Palestine that is denied as a condition for travel to Jerusalem. It is significant that Israel does not allow women to pursue such activities with any mobility, both on a legal plane of human rights and as a pronouncedly gendered form of discrimination that exacerbates difference. Relations of care and the domestic division of labor are thus (further) skewed; women have little choice but to remain in place, taking on more homemaking duties than their husbands, whose days are consumed by the punitive commute described in the previous chapter.

This is the question I take up in the next chapter, where the focus moves from the checkpoint itself to developing an understanding of the checkpoint "beyond the checkpoint," or the ways in which the border permeates the intimate spaces of the family home and women's lives.

3

Beyond the Checkpoint

DOMESTIC LIFE IN PALESTINE

> Knowing it was too early for the dawn prayers, I wondered
> how many of the village mothers, wives and sisters had got up
> at this odd hour of the night in order to prepare the coffee and
> breakfast for the bread winner(s) of their families.
>
> —Suad Amiry, *Nothing to Lose but Your Life:*
> *An 18-Hour Journey with Murad*

> It takes my husband three and a half hours to reach his
> work. . . . There is so much lost time, he leaves when his
> children are sleeping, and he comes back when they are
> sleeping again.
>
> —Randa, al-Walaja

> I feel a lot of pressure and stress because of the extra
> responsibilities. I have to deal with all of it on my own because
> my husband is absent at work all day . . . then when he comes
> home late, he's stressed, and I've had a long day [too] and I'm
> also stressed. . . . There's no time for you to spend together, to
> talk about problems—so you postpone talking and problems
> pile up.
>
> —Amani, al-Walaja

In that primary scene, the one that spurs and sustains most interest in
the checkpoint, thousands of men queue from the very early hours in
the morning. Many of them have been awake since 2:00 or 3:00 A.M.
and face an arduous day's work before returning home in the evening.
Most usually, the homes to which they return—very much a *secondary
scene* in our current imaginaries of checkpoints—are maintained by
women: mothers, wives, and daughters who ensure that wages cover

household costs and thus the reproduction of the labor force. The bureaucratic context to the making of these two scenes is notable for the way it sifts Palestinian society for wage-earning capacities, setting aside those of lesser (wage) labor value, such as women. The temporal and spatial makeup of people's lives in this way is closely tied to checkpoint permits, and this, in turn, is inseparable from the making of gender. But the story is not simply that male laborers gain permits more easily than women and that that difference can thus be attributed to the exigencies of the Israeli economy. This is partly the case, of course, but the permit system has a deeper influence on the sorting of women and men and the entrenching of respective roles. Crucially—and this cannot be overemphasized—in addition to depoliticizing permit conditions (e.g., a permit holder cannot have been involved in union activity or have spent time in an Israeli prison), the Israeli Civil Administration stipulates that permit-holding men be married with at least one child. This regulation should radically alter our perception of the crowds in the mornings: every man enduring that punitive and protracted commute leaves a wife and at least one child at home, and each hour added to his day is an extra hour of absence from family life—an extra hour of tasks added to (most usually) a woman's day. The checkpoint thus plays an integral role not only in keeping women in place but also in the shaping of daily routines, the distribution of labor, the (sometimes partial) fulfillment of duties, and, ultimately, the formation and maintenance of intimate family relations.

The checkpoint must therefore be seen as central to the ordering of family time. It also—and this is an important claim made in this chapter—modulates affective and emotional exchanges within that temporal order. That is to say, checkpoint delays both orchestrate daily rhythms and dictate their tones. This might appear an obvious point, but it bears repeating for its significance in understanding the extensive spatial reach of Checkpoint 300: its delaying function sustains and intensifies the circulation of affects constitutive of colonial control. Anger, boredom, despondency, resentment, humiliation, frustration, stress, fear, and so on thus mark the days of those who pass through the checkpoint (as we have seen in chapter 1) and—*crucially*—of many who do not. This argument emerges from further work with the al-Walaja Women's Group and a research focus on the effects on the homes of laboring men who travel through Checkpoint 300 to reach their places of work. As the women themselves make clear, in addition to the checkpoint's role in shaping domestic divisions of labor and daily routines, in affective terms, the checkpoint enters the home. Husbands return exhausted from a day's labor and commute and are often anxious in anticipation of the following day. They are regularly frustrated or angry at having to endure that punitive crossing and also regretful or bitter that family time is so greatly reduced. This cannot but alter familial relations in the home. Partnering and parenting are strained, and women pick up surplus domestic physical and emotional labor. They fill the gaps—cooking more, caring more, and worrying more—as a traceable result of the family's reliance on checkpoint permit–enabled wage labor.

In this way, for all the threat and violence of security staff, crowds, corridors, and turnstiles, the first two chapters merely scratch the surface of the deeper effects of checkpoints in Palestine. And if a discriminatory permit system and hostile checkpoint space deter women from travel, this is only a partial story of gender and Checkpoint 300, whose very capacity to control depends on the domestic labor of women. All that we witness *inside* the checkpoint is dependent on women's reproduction of home life *outside* it—that which ensures that those men return each morning. A key difference, of course, is that the effects on men's lives are more visible and more widely documented, while women's lives are affected in the less visible spaces beyond the checkpoint. The task of this chapter, therefore, is to document life in that space and the ways in which many Palestinian women—even as they do not regularly cross Checkpoint 300—are drawn into the wider geographies of Israel's infrastructure of control. This is pivotal to the overall project of examining the wider colonial spaces of Checkpoint 300 for the ways in which temporalities and spatialities of borders open out beyond territorial demarcations. By this I mean that the extension into the home of Israel's manipulation of Palestinians' temporal rhythms prompts a key methodological move to "separate the border from the wall."[1] We are thus brought to a spatially and temporally broadened view of the processes of bordering that are otherwise distant from a territorial frontier. From this important angle, the relations between Checkpoint 300 and colonial space multiply with each step taken away from the building itself. This chapter takes that first step to demonstrate how Checkpoint 300—via its subjugating affective and disciplinary technologies—shapes the activities (eating rituals, sleeping patterns, marriage, parenting) that are constitutive of "home." Less a secondary scene, the home in this way should be held as a primary site of the checkpoint's effects of control in Palestine.

First, some details on methods that I expand as the chapter proceeds. All of what follows draws from work with the al-Walaja Women's Group introduced in the previous chapter. The difference here is that the information that founds the analysis comes from a series of one-to-one interviews conducted by Lamees, one of the central organizers of the Women's Group. Whereas the previous chapter includes interview and focus group accounts where I was present, the themes here required a different level of comfort and positionality. Lamees wrote a series of more personal interview questions and was engaged as a paid researcher for the project; none of what follows would be known if it were not for her diligent work and ability to ask questions and leave space for deep reflection. The candidness of the accounts is owed entirely to Lamees's skill as an interviewer and the trust the women have in her.

An underpinning point that women made to Lamees on the theme of the checkpoint's effects on their lives was, quite unsurprisingly, that long queues and delays prolong the absence of men from the home from the early mornings into the evenings. Men's crossings can take anywhere from forty-five minutes to two (or more) hours, and most leave the house in the very early hours (three to four o'clock) and return late (seven to eight o'clock), leaving little time for activities other than eating and sleeping. Hayam broke down a typical daily routine as follows:

> My husband wakes up at 2:00 A.M. and leaves home for the checkpoint at 3:00 A.M. He gets there around 3:15 or 3:30, when, of course, the checkpoint is already horrible. People are on top of each other, the workers push each other—it's really overcrowded. And, of course, the checkpoint is sometimes closed by the soldiers and won't be opened to make things easier for people. The soldiers check all details, and many workers are delayed and get to work late, all the time they are held in a packed place. . . . So it takes until 6:00 A.M. for him to be able to pass through, he gets to work at 7:00 A.M. and works until 4:00 P.M. and gets back home by 7:00 P.M. He comes home and barely has time to eat and go to sleep, he has no time to spend at home or do anything other than

going to work and coming back; most of his time is wasted on trying to get to work and trying to come home.

For Hayam's husband, this makes for a four-hour commute in the morning and a two-hour return—an addition of six hours to an already physically demanding day of labor as a welder on a construction site. Other women reported their husbands making two- or three-hour journeys in each direction and a cutoff of around 6:00 A.M., when it becomes too late to get to the checkpoint to make it to work on time. As a result, mornings are generally hurried and stressed; breakfasts are eaten on the move as workers seek to secure an advanced place in the checkpoint queue. Word spreads quickly through the crowds of conditions on any specific day, which can range markedly depending on combinations of equally predictable or unpredictable events: national or religious holidays, (rarely specified) security threat levels, raised tensions and national strikes, checkpoint staff shortages, fewer functioning check booths or smart gates, and even the whims and moods of commanders and soldiers. It is pointed out more than once in conversations on these issues that living around Bethlehem is an advantage because thousands of workers must travel to Checkpoint 300 from the southern West Bank—such as from Hebron—and thus need to go through these processes even earlier in the morning.

But it is not so much men's routines as the temporal effects on the entire household that tell us most about the power of checkpoints to shape family life in Palestine. It is the way that time is orchestrated for all in the household, determining the hours of waking, cooking, and eating, as well as levels of availability, energy, and stress, that provides a fuller understanding of colonial control. And it is through a careful analysis of Checkpoint 300 as "a woman's *eib* [burden]" that we come to grasp something of the gendered effects of security infrastructure beyond a notion that women simply "stay home." At a fundamental level, therefore, it is important to note that women's daily routines, just like those of men, are shaped by the rhythms of the checkpoint:

My husband wakes up at 4:00 A.M., and I wake up with him to prepare for his departure to work. When he goes to work, I start working in the house, like cleaning, getting my children ready for school, preparing food before they come back, and also prepare dinner for my husband when he comes home late. My children want to eat at a certain time, and he comes home late, so I prepare the meals twice. We don't usually have our meals together because my husband comes home late. (Amani)

To explicate the way that gendered divisions of labor are exacerbated, because of the male-selective permit system and the 4:00 A.M. start and late return, Amani wakes earlier, looks after the children longer, cooks more often, and dedicates more time to caring for her husband's needs (or, in broader terms, the needs of the Israeli labor market). A second account—that of Suad—reveals more of the daily routine:

On a Friday at least, we can sleep until 8:00 or 9:00 A.M., but on a weekday, my husband goes to work very early in the morning, sometimes before dawn prayer [4:00 to 4:30 A.M.]. An hour or two after he leaves, I wake my children to get ready to go to school. I make them breakfast and I take them to school and I take my daughter to university. I work around the house all day and tend to the garden. If I have work to do at the Women's Group or the village council, I go to do that for a couple of hours. Then I come home to prepare food for my children before they come back. They used to wait for their father to eat together, but these days he comes home later because of the checkpoint. While we wait for him, I or my [elder] daughter help the children with homework, and I prepare his food for when he gets back around 7:00 P.M. or sometimes 8:00. He eats, sits with us for half an hour, then goes to sleep to go to work again the next morning. I make sure there's some breakfast ready. This is our daily life.

The detail here uncovers a deeper connection between a man's absence and the reproduction of gender, whereby Suad's daughter is also called on to make up an amount of the deficit in domestic labor. This is contrasted with Fridays, a day of no checkpoint or work for him and therefore no (or less) work for Suad and their daughter. For both Amani and Suad—and many other women—their routines are tethered to checkpoint times that allocate and order household activities in such a way that historical gender roles are amplified: women have little choice but to dedicate (even) more time and energy to cooking, cleaning, parenting, and other domestic tasks.

This is not for one moment to reduce women to a secondary role in this particular geography of the checkpoint. Rather, the matter here is that women's responsibility for social reproduction is substantially expanded as chores and tasks that might be shared more evenly are added to a woman's duties: "I clean our house, I go shopping, cook, pay electricity bills . . . *everything* that involves the house, I'm responsible for; *there's no other way*" (Hanan); "I have to deal with family duties alone, *we can't share responsibilities*[, so] I have to organize all family issues, house requirements, deal with the children" (Hayam); "I take on extra . . . responsibilities for the children like helping them study, taking them for medical visits, I even look after his in-laws—all these responsibilities are now on me" (Randa). These women are thus required to step into different roles—"I cover for the husband and the wife at the same time!" more than one interviewee exclaimed—with a strong assertion that this is a specifically *adaptive* mode to externally imposed conditions. It is because of the checkpoint and labor regime that "there is no other way," a statement that speaks on a practical level while communicating something wholly different in ideal terms: *it would be different were it not for stolen time.* To be clear, the point here is not that were there no permits or checkpoints, domestic labor would be shared equally. This would be to deny gendered norms in Palestine and everywhere to do with women's roles in the home. But it is also clear that men's forced absence and tired presence exacerbate the gendered division of labor. It thus serves to remember that Palestinian women, in common with other colonized women, face layers of patriarchy, where underlying "endogenous" processes of gendering are exploited and exacerbated by a colonizing force.[2] It is beyond the scope of the discussion here but entirely relevant that all discussions of Israel's supposedly progressive policies on women and gender should begin from its abuse of Indigenous women's rights, such as those we witness in al-Walaja and all over Palestine.[3]

For Palestinian women in al-Walaja and beyond, Israel's infrastructure of control is thus central to a gendered ordering of routine whereby women's less visible labor articulates with the more publicized crowds and delays of checkpoints. For the women included in this research, this routine entails rising at dawn and staggered mealtimes, often involving preparing two breakfasts and two dinners. The hours in between are filled with the responsibilities that *both* wife and husband would carry out if both were able to be more present. Women are thus keenly situated within the temporalities of the checkpoint, even as they cross it much less frequently than men. On a conceptual level, we can begin to include women more surely in considerations of the ways in which Israel's colonial (i.e., spatial) project functions on a temporal plane. This is a useful approach to apprehending mechanisms of Israeli colonial power that control either by accelerating processes like land confiscation or house demolition[4] or by slowing others, such as bureaucratic procedures and mobilities.[5] Julie Peteet's sustained attention to these issues clearly illustrates the way in which Israeli power functions in large part by restricting Palestinians to hierarchical "spatiotemporal zones," where the colonial state "steals" time from the colonized population.[6] As we have already seen in chapters 1 and 2, nowhere is this more readily visible than in the space of the checkpoint itself, where the manipulation of time—via forced overcrowdedness, delays, and immobility—is an integral mechanism of discipline. In every way, Checkpoint 300 steals masses of time from those who enter its corridors. But, as we have witnessed so far in this chapter, there are similarly profound effects beyond the checkpoint, in the family and home. We are thus partway toward including women in the power dynamics at work between control, the checkpoint, and temporality.

A significant further step to this end is to think through an effect of stealing of time that is common to the otherwise discrete spaces of checkpoint and home: waiting. The women in al-Walaja, even as they work and carry out their duties, are given to waiting—for news of a safe crossing in the morning, for updates on the workday on the other side of the wall, and for the sound of an opening door in the evening that marks the start of brief and precious family time. This is not described as an all-consuming experience of worry but rather as a persistent source of background stress that adds to the already-increased workload. "It is *very* exhausting waiting for him every day to come home until as late as 9:00 P.M.," emphasized Amani, while Tala put it this way: "For me and the kids we remain uncertain about his day, don't know if he passed, how his day went, so it's emotionally difficult *for us too.*" Without extrapolating too much, the three final words— "for us too"—remind us that not only does checkpoint time apply to the home but also something of the quality of that time is similarly extended. In other words, it is not that women simply go about extra tasks in the home but that these tasks are comparable—*perhaps* by degree, but *definitely* by quality—because they, too, come with significant levels of *exhaustion* and *uncertainty*. There is a clear attunement here with the embodied experiences of men who enter the checkpoint, and as is evident in chapter 1, waiting is not an inert imposition but one whose dynamics are expressions and indications of wider power relations. To expand further here, waiting and making wait are inherently political positions, as a range of theorists have expounded. Ghassan Hage's well-known work, for example, centers on the issue of "who waits for whom" by asking the simple but incisive question "who has the power to make their time appear more valuable than somebody else's time?";[7] the answer to this question, for Pierre Bourdieu, directs us to the sovereign and the extent of its reach: "The all-powerful is he who does not wait but who makes others wait."[8] Waiting in this sense is a signifier of power relations, and thus attending to the dynamics of waiting is a critical task.

On specifically waiting in Palestine—where there is no doubt around the question of the "all-powerful sovereign"—existing work emphasizes that waiting is somewhat constitutive of the (or *a*) Palestinian condition. Helga Tawil-Souri's discussion, focused on checkpoints in Palestine, makes the wider existential point that the "disjunctive temporality" of waiting "produces deep ontological insecurity: there is no continuity, stability, or routine. There is no ability to plan ahead, no ordered sequence, no continuous narrative, no cause and effect.... Existence here does not plot itself on a chronological timeline but collapses in on itself";[9] Laila el-Haddad eloquently gets to something of the deeply painful yet irreducibly hopeful practice of waiting under Israeli colonialism:

> [We are] always waiting. For this is what the Palestinian does:
> we wait. For an answer to be given, for a question to be asked;
> for a marriage proposal to be made, for a divorce to be finalized;
> for a border to open, for a permit to be issued; for a war to end;
> for a war to begin; for a child to be born; for one to die a martyr;
> for retirement or a new job; for exile to a better place and for
> return to the only place that knows us; for our prisoners to come
> home; for our homes to no longer be prisons; for our children to
> be free; for freedom from a time when we no longer have to wait.[10]

These words guide us toward less public sites of waiting, from the stasis of the visible and documented checkpoint queues to the more private, bated anticipation of a return home. From here what we currently know about checkpoints—for example, from a focus such as that of chapter 1—takes on a pronounced duality. Turning back to Tawil-Souri's evocative writing on "checkpoint time" provides a critical incision to open up this duality.[11] Writing on Qalandia Checkpoint, where Palestinians from Ramallah and the northern West Bank pass into Jerusalem, Tawil-Souri describes the "crowd of male labourers between 3 and 5am" as a "haunting scene": "[The workers] arrive early because there is no knowing how long—or if—one will get through the checkpoint. They have no control over their time: they do not know if they will get to work on time (if at all) and must wait for their return to come through the turnstile, into the corridor, and through the next turnstiles."[12] Particularly "haunting" here is the uncertainty of not knowing, of not being in control of one's own movements through time, of an inability to fulfill one's daily labor duties for the family—and this constitutes a powerful mode of colonial subordination. A very similar dynamic plays out in an articulating "haunting scene" where women must also wake early—to prepare breakfasts, attend to children, look after the home, run errands, and then prepare evening meals—while somehow also waiting for their husbands' safe return. Tawil-Souri further argues that at the checkpoint, Palestinians learn "to accept that their fate and time is not under their control . . . [that] power is not simply exerted in forcing people to wait; it is also in having them stay put" as they are stuck between the turnstiles and corridors inside checkpoints.[13] The women of al-Walaja, too, "stay put" and await a safe passage, but the passage is not theirs, and their waiting is done while carrying a significant burden of social reproduction. It must therefore be recalled that the power dynamics of waiting—alternatively, the power to make wait and the powerlessness of being made to wait—is replicated in the home among family. Occupation-time-as-waiting occurs, too, in this more private domain that is, as the experiences recounted by Amani, Suad, Tala, and others show, no less potent—and all the more burdensome given the additional weight of uneven divisions of gendered labor.

But there is something more than simply a connection between the women's lives discussed here and the temporality—or *duration*—of the checkpoint opening times and delays, something more closely to do with the qualitative nature of temporality or the *endurance* of crossing. As time is stretched, people's nerves are strained; the delayed pace of the checkpoint does not merely "steal" or order time but also imposes a quality to the way time is passed. Laboring men return from a checkpoint-extended day (even more) exhausted, angry, stressed, frustrated, despondent, anxious, and so forth; this cannot but impress on the household's affective balance. A common experience for the women interviewed during the research is that checkpoint conditions noticeably affect men's moods. Suad, for example, presented a sharp contrast in her husband "before and after getting a permit. . . . Lately my husband has become an angry person. He wasn't an angry man [before,] but with all the pressure and the exhaustion between work and the checkpoint, he has become angrier and more short-tempered. . . . Before, he was a calm and patient person, but nowadays, with the checkpoint and work, he is angry around the house." This is just one example of women speaking candidly on this sensitive subject and the detrimental effects the men's protracted time in the checkpoint has on the emotional exchanges in their households. Before continuing, it is important to address an ethical and methodological approach taken to this aspect of the research. On the specific themes of moods and frustrations, Lamees reflected that it was the "most difficult part" of the interviews and that women had a "hard time answering and talking about [the husband's] relationship in the family when he comes back home from work. . . . Most of the women felt shy talking about this." Cognizant of this, I discuss the ways in which the oppressive conditions of the checkpoint enter the home in a manner that I hope conveys sensitivity and respect.

Suad's candid comment on the checkpoint shortening her husband's temper is one that many echo, and it is a common incidence for workers to return home in a markedly agitated state. Tala shared,

> It is exhausting for him to wake up so early. He is a worker, he will work all day, but before [working] he has to pass the checkpoint. It's always overcrowded and it affects him physically, once he came home with a broken rib because of the pushing and squeezing. Of course, he will get angry, it is not easy for him, he wakes up early and goes into the overcrowded place with gates and inspections. This affects him at work and affects him when he comes home, because

he will be angry at home too. . . . He is tired emotionally, and for us we remain *uncertain* about his day, don't know if he passed, how his day went, so it's *emotionally difficult* for us too. (Tala)

And Hanan (quite starkly) conveyed, "My husband never comes back happy—*ever*. He always stresses about the checkpoint . . . delays, inspections, crowds—or, in the worst cases, 'this guy suffocated and died' or 'got hit and died.'" Hanan explicates: "The checkpoint has become a *nightmare*." Both Tala and Hanan here make reference to a pronounced physical threat inside the checkpoint (discussed in chapter 1) that has grown in recent years, whereby suffocating crowds, fainting, and broken ribs are not uncommon. These are shocking—or "nightmarish"—conditions in themselves that are then amplified from the perspective of the women: "If it's crowded, he comes home angry. . . . If it is particularly bad, he is irritated . . . and projects his frustration at everyone in the house" (Nariman). This is an explicit figuring of the checkpoint as a regulator of men's moods, whereby, put simply, when it's "bad" in the corridors, anger, irritation, and so forth are heightened also in the home.

Women spoke at length of how the crowdedness and delays at the checkpoint have a direct bearing on their own emotional lives. Karima presented a particularly clear example of this when she explained that part of her and her husband's morning routine includes "calls from other workers [already] at the checkpoint who warn him about how crowded it is," and when it is crowded, "we both have to get up an hour earlier than usual so he will not be late for work." "Because of this," Karima makes clear, "often I don't get enough sleep, it makes me feel exhausted for the rest of the day—I don't have time for a nap." It is not only, then, that the checkpoint dictates the times at which Karima wakes, cleans, and cooks; it is also a key referent for her own daily state of mind. In this way, and in important ways, there is a strong contingence between the workers' fatigue and her own. Karima expanded:

For him, he's physically exhausted, because he wakes up early and goes to work for long hours. . . . It makes me also feel nervous and worried about him. Because of lack of sleep, I get tired and short-tempered more than usual. I would like to rest and sleep but there is no time for it, because you have to keep up with housework responsibilities.

The significance of this is that such checkpoint-connected nervous-ness, worry, tiredness, and short-temperedness ordinarily go unno-ticed. Women like Karima are not included in the extensive work that oriented around the "profound anxiety" of checkpoint queues, turn-stiles, and security staff, yet her testimony emphasizes that she is—in an obviously profound way—affectively drawn into the conditions of the checkpoint itself.

The women talked further about how these effects extend to their children. Hayam, for example, expressed concern that her four chil-dren do not receive the attention they would "in a more normal situa-tion [because] my husband always feels nervous and angry because he has no time to rest," and this "affects the family life in a negative way; so even if I have trouble with one of the kids, I can't discuss it with him, because he will have a nervous or angry reaction." In a similar dy-namic, Lamees related that her husband "really tries" to remain awake after work despite being overtired: "He stays up with the kids to make them feel here's here, but he [can] get angry, even for small things, you'll find him screaming and angry." Lamees expanded further: "It depends on the day; when he's feeling good, it's the perfect family. But when he comes back home angry, the kids avoid even talking to him and are scared of doing anything that might piss him off. . . . When he has holiday and no work, he is mentally comfortable. He is the one who's excited to go out and take the kids and see people or go on a hike. But on a working and checkpoint day, if anybody speaks to him and he's angry, it's a tough situation." Lamees said she understood why this happened and, like many of the women, expressed a sympa-thetic position. This was echoed in Karima's words, which serve as an important corrective to emphasize that the men do not come home consumed by any one emotion (such as anger) but are entangled in a swirl of feelings that, as Karima movingly put it, includes a deep sad-ness: "When he comes home late, he's not only exhausted because of the long hours he's been away from the family but he's also upset that he didn't see his children before leaving for work nor after coming home. Because he comes home after the kids' sleeping hour, he's tired and sad. It's true that he's angry because of our living conditions [and] because of work, but [he's] also really sad. He keeps trying to make it easier, but life doesn't work this way."

As might be expected, the limits set around parenting grow con-cerns around children's upbringings. Typically, men's absences are so prolonged that time with children is restricted and often quite tense. The following is just one example of a response to a question about the impact of the checkpoint on children:

> It has a big impact on them. The children don't know their father, they don't understand what he wants, and he doesn't understand what they need. For example, if he's angry, the children don't understand why. There is no time for them to ask why he's angry, and there is no time for him to ask his children about their day, their problems, about their school and what they did today. There is no time for that because he only wants to eat, shower, and go to bed. He is already stressed about the next day. (Amani)

The claim here that the father–children relationship has broken down is particularly perplexing. It suggests that the stress of the checkpoint continues through the evening, disrupting bonds between family members. It also suggests that the production of anxious subjects through security infrastructure extends not only through space into the home but also in time and into future generations.

Additionally, and finally, it needs to be emphasized that the passage of stress into the domestic setting is not only centered on the men. Regarding their own relationships with their children, the women openly reflected on parallel dynamics whereby "pressure and stress," as Karima puts it in the following quote, penetrate also mother–children relationships in the home:

> I feel more responsible because I have to care for the kids, who should not feel like there is anything wrong. I feel pressure, I'm always under stress. I should not get angry, but internally, I'm angry and stressed out. But I should not show that to my children and relatives. I have to act calm and try my best not to raise my voice at home and not to project my stress on my kids. . . . It's just more pressure than any mother should have to deal with when on her own.

Karima's account here is disconcerting for the palpable sense that she is suffering for having to continually "act calm" even as her considerable responsibilities threaten to overwhelm. This internal conflict was referenced, too, by Hayam: "He's always nervous and angry[, and] this affects our life in a negative way; if I have a trouble with one of the kids, I can't discuss it with him because he will always have a nervous reaction." The sense here is that Hayam must also "act calm" and not add family problems to security anxieties for fear of "nervous reactions." There is a sense, too, that marital relations might become strained, as Amani reflected on this sensitive topic:

> I feel a lot of pressure and stress because of the extra responsibilities. I have to deal with all of it on my own because my husband is absent at work all day . . . then when he comes home late, he's stressed, and I've had a long day [too] and I'm also stressed, this creates problems between us, and we don't know how to deal with them. . . . There's no time for you to spend together, to talk about problems—so you postpone talking and problems pile up.

Like in Karima's and Hayam's, there is a foreboding tone to Amani's words, a feeling that pressure is building with no readily perceptible release. This evidences a contingency between the embodied impositions of the checkpoints—spoken of mostly in terms of exhaustion, anger, frustration, and so on—and emotional exchanges in the intimate spaces of the home. Caught within these exchanges, the women's relations with their children, husbands, and even themselves (in the imperative to "act calm") are therefore also shaped by the overcrowded and oppressive conditions of the checkpoint itself. It is in this way that the checkpoint enters and is importantly constitutive of domestic space.

The first objective of this chapter was to follow the trajectory set in the previous chapter by considering further the relationships between women, gender, and Checkpoint 300. This is driven also by an obvious but frequently overlooked point that although checkpoints and other Israeli infrastructures of control are considered central to the Palestinian condition, women are so often backgrounded, if not set outside the frame altogether. This chapter built on the previous one to arrive at a fuller account of women's experiences both at the checkpoint and *in the context of* the checkpoint. There is much to learn from this approach. We are brought to an understanding of geopolitics as importantly embodied, intimate, and quotidian, rather than as a constellation of power relations that play out at the level of the state in terms of international strategy or territorial claims.[14] This comes through a feminist approach to security and geopolitics—one that I have attempted here—that "studies up," beginning with otherwise marginalized voices rather than with the state and so-called high politics,[15] with an objective of "traversing scales from the macrosecurity of states to the microsecurity of people and their homes; from the disembodied space of neorealist geopolitics to a field of live human subjects with names, families, and hometowns."[16] So while the checkpoint is produced through Israel's territorial claims and readiness to visit military violence on a colonized population, this violence is only narrowly conceived if it is witnessed either from the viewpoint of the state or from within the checkpoint itself. The work with Lamees and the Women's Group of al-Walaja has enabled a move between the scales of a state-imposed security infrastructure and the intimate relations of family life in the home, shedding further light on the ways in which "'the Palestinian family' is enmeshed in patriarchal, state and colonial forms of power and violence."[17] Within this, as Chris Harker has long asserted, there are differentiating exposures to precarity and its associated stress, anxiety, and so forth that (re)produce gender.[18] It is not a coincidence in this sense that there are broad patterns of anger, frustration, and withdrawal among men and of worry, stress, and increased emotional labor among women. This is a distribution of affects born not of a predisposed body but of the conditions in which it is set, or in other words, the colonial making and maintaining of gender. The most significant factor in Palestinian women staying at home and taking on high loads of domestic and emotional labor is the presence and nature of Israel's colonial security mechanisms. Surely there are other factors for women in al-Walaja, but none as prominent as Checkpoint 300.

Because gender is not the central focus of this book, I am wary of making too grand a claim around this point, but it is important to recognize the role Israel plays in shaping gender roles in the land it occupies. It is a base tenet of (especially Second Wave) feminism that "sexual asymmetries in the social organisation of gender" rest on making a woman's "primary location . . . the domestic sphere" and that asymmetry emerges from the hierarchical ordering of spheres: "Culturally and politically, the public sphere dominates the domestic, and hence men dominate women."[19] The al-Walaja Women's Group is in many respects a response to this social order; its premise is to bring women's voices into political and economic spheres through the furniture workshop and engagement with the local council. The need for the group, however, stems precisely from the designation of women to specific roles and the devaluation of those roles. That Israel's infrastructure of control plays a part in this invites contrast with the prominence of Palestinian women in political life and resistance, from the Balfour Declaration and Mandate period[20] to the Nakba,[21] First Intifada,[22] Oslo Accords,[23] and the contemporary period of increased militarization.[24] This is not to dismiss the presence of Palestinian patriarchy but rather to highlight that women are diversely positioned in Palestinian political struggle and social life more broadly. Their struggles are thus connected not only to an immediate, Indigenous patriarchy but also to the patriarchy of occupier; there is a long colonial history of exploiting, violating, and exacerbating gender relations in Palestine,[25] and Checkpoint 300 should be seen as fully part of that aspect of colonial power.

Julie Peteet excavates some of this colonial history, revealing a shift in the organization of women's days from a pre-1948 Palestine where "women's time had been organised around agricultural labor and the production of consumable foodstuffs and household management and childrearing" to the introduction of mass education, which meant that "women's daily routines were now heavily shaped by schooling."[26] Peteet argues that "mass education's temporal rhythms reaffirmed and reproduced gendered inequality. Mothers drew upon elder daughters' labor to meet the needs of the younger children for an education."[27] Precisely this dynamic is evident earlier—explicitly, for instance, when Suad's elder daughter is required to help with the care of her younger siblings—except with the important addition that it is not only the temporal demands of schooling that order familial roles; it is also the demand on time placed by the checkpoint and permit system that orders the women's daily rhythms. This perspective further nuances a fuller integration of women into the notion of "occupation time"; it recognizes checkpoints as *one more* facet of women's struggles against patriarchal formations that emerge from and are intensified by Israel's occupation. In every sense, therefore, the home is a site of political struggle, of the "big P" politics[28] that give important insight into the spatial workings of colonial power.

This has further significant *spatial* implications. If it is true, as I hope to have convinced the reader of by this point, that women's daily routines, even as they do not regularly cross checkpoints, are intimately tied to checkpoint opening times, in terms of delays and crowdedness, and the conditions of crossing, in terms of exhaustion, anger, and frustration, then what other spaces are un/made by the checkpoint? If the home is partly constituted by an otherwise geographically distant checkpoint, then what other aspects of social and political life are affected, and where? This brings us to a key conceptualization not only of the chapter but of the book as a whole. Explicitly, this takes us to the border/checkpoint as remote from the border mechanism itself. The clear connections between the lives of women in al-Walaja and Checkpoint 300, 3.4 kilometers away, disclose a ubiquitous quality of the border—in terms of profiling, curtailed mobilities, induced fear, and so forth—that stretches into the village in ways that suggest (though perhaps with some qualification) that "the border is effectively everywhere."[29] If not true in toto, it certainly feels that way in those moments when it seems that every minute and emotion is inseparable from the checkpoint.

This spatial expansion sets the trajectory of the two following chapters. First (in chapter 4), I consider the effects of Checkpoint 300 on the wider Hebron Road area, on the northern edge of Bethlehem, and second (in chapter 5), I track the global geographies of technological and labor capitalism that contribute to making checkpoint space.

4

An Urban Geography of Checkpoint 300 and the Hebron Road

Hebron Road? You're talking about life, vibrancy . . .
everything that came into Bethlehem over the past four
thousand years came on that road. *Everything.* Joseph and
Mary came on that road! All the trade between Jerusalem
and the city of Hebron, a sixty-five-hundred-year-old town,
happened on that road through Bethlehem. . . . What do
I know of the Hebron Road? What I know is that for the
first time in its history, the road is completely destroyed
and blocked.

—Baha Hilo, political activist from Beit Sahour

In the past, tourists and workers all came here. I swear I was
the king of Bethlehem! . . . Now I'm just a poor beggar. . . .
How does one forget the work of a lifetime? How do I forget?
I have toiled here for 40 years.

This was the Beverly Hills of Palestine! Now look at it.

—shop owners on the Hebron Road

The Hebron Road (Tariq al-Khalil)—or sometimes the Road of
the Patriarchs—is the route on which stands Checkpoint 300.
It runs from Jaffa Gate (Bab al-Khalil) on the south side of Jerusalem's old city to Hebron (Khalil), the largest city in the Palestinian
Authority–administered West Bank. This is a route of great historical and religious significance; Bethlehem is the birthplace of King
David and Jesus, and Hebron is the burial site of Abraham and the
patriarchs of the Abrahamic religions. The one matriarch not buried
in Hebron—in the complex known to Muslims as Ibrahimi Mosque

(al-Haram al-Ibrahimi) and to Jews as the Cave of the Patriarchs—is Rachel, the second wife of Jacob and mother of Joseph and Benjamin. Rachel is buried 25.5 kilometers north of Hebron, in Bethlehem, 6.7 kilometers south of Jaffa Gate, where the weave of walls is built around Checkpoint 300.[1] The pedestrian part of the checkpoint is set at the northernmost part of the Hebron Road accessible to West Bank Palestinians, whereas the vehicle gate now sits on the parallel Caritas Road, one hundred meters to the east. From the checkpoint looking south, the road continues for approximately two hundred meters, and the wall skirts the backs of the buildings on the right. It then cuts back on itself and loops around the well-known Anastas family residence, enclosing it on three sides before again doubling back and turning south for another three hundred meters or so, where it meets the confluence of Manger Street and the Hebron Road at the old Sansur Building (also commonly referred to as the old cigarette factory). This busy point is perhaps, religious sites excepted, the most photographed in Palestine (Figure 11). It is where a military watchtower protrudes most pronouncedly into urban Bethlehem and where countless confrontations play out between the youths of the adjacent Aida and the close-by Azza refugee camps (armed with stones) and the IDF (armed with everything). The area can be particularly volatile on Friday afternoons and evenings, when shouting, tear gas, and gunshots fill the air.

Aside the watchtower is one of three "Gates of the Patriarchs," imposing five-meter-high, reinforced steel gates that are opened twice a year for the visit of the Catholic and Orthodox patriarchs from Jerusalem to Bethlehem at Christmastime. In front of the gate are concrete blocks of the type the Israeli military uses as a shield when firing into the crowds that gather during protests. The blocks also mark a quite unique subcategory of Area C. Whereas elsewhere in the West Bank, Area C refers to nonurban land that is under Israeli administrative and military control (this designation applies to 62 percent of the West Bank), the approximately five-hundred-meter stretch of the Hebron Road from the blocks to the checkpoint is very definitely Palestinian urban space, without clear jurisdiction of either side. The particular Area C produced between the blocks and the checkpoint is thus marked by unregulated economic activities (and opportunities), unprotected households and businesses, and unfulfilled municipal services. This is a legally undetermined area, one that Israeli personnel avoid, save for military attacks on protesters and nonprotesters, and

FIGURE 11. The watchtower and Gate of the Patriarchs at the intersection of the Hebron Road and Manger Street. Photograph by Nadir Mauge.

that Palestinian police cannot enter without Israeli permission, and only then unarmed and out of uniform. A parking free-for-all, antisocial behavior, and general disorder thus exasperate local residents and visitors—as well as the Bethlehem municipal government. To walk along this section of the Hebron Road is to move through manifold political geographies; it is a borderland produced by colonial encounter whose intricacies I seek to convey here, both descriptively and theoretically.

The chapter works through two main sections. In the first, I attempt to relay something of the current character of the area via a walk along the Hebron Road from the checkpoint to the point where Areas C and A meet. This is based on many hours spent alone and with friends and other researchers on the now-circuitous route. The second section turns its focus to Rachel's Tomb, the site that must be seen as generative of this entire spatial division. The tomb was subject to a last-minute exchange in the early-1990s Oslo negotiations between Yasser Arafat and Yikzhak Rabin, which resulted in an amendment that premises all that is discussed here. Rachel's Tomb is now enclosed within one of the most striking urban security architectures in the world. The tomb and the surrounding wall, including the watch-towers and military personnel that loom over the Hebron Road, is each considered in detail here, descriptively and critically. Through-out the chapter, I draw on ethnographic materials I gathered while assisting, as part of this research project, with filming the documen-tary *My Tomb, Your Tomb, Rachel's Tomb,* directed by Bethlehem-based filmmaker and photographer Nadir Mauge. The in-depth interviews collected during the making of the documentary provide firsthand accounts of the ways in which the checkpoint and wall are built to carry geographically dispersed effects to the entire area and beyond. In conclusion, I expand further on consequent understandings of space and the colonial borderland—through prisms of colonial spacio-cide, urban battle space, and exception—thus developing the themes that hold this book together. The Hebron Road, I argue, is a paradigmatic case of colonial land sequestration and spatial apartheid that is in-structive of Israel's wider colonial project in Palestine.

At any time of day, there is a clamor of taxis and vendors around the entrance to Checkpoint 300. The wall has created a choke point where flows of mobility and capital stop or pause. In some cases, they re-form on the other side, for instance, as permit-holding laborers traveling on foot; in others, they remain within the colonial boundary. Fruit and coffee sellers do business with those leaving and arriving, and taxi drivers and parking lot operators have adapted to curtailed mobilities. Because West Bank Palestinians can only cross by foot with a permit, they travel only this far by car. This "checkpoint economy"—which Helga Tawil-Souri wrote of as an ad hoc adaptation in the first years of the West Bank wall[2]—has matured: orchards have been paved over to accommodate cars, new supermarkets thrive in a gray zone for tax, and buildings have sprung where planning regulations are newly lax. The area immediately outside the checkpoint, at the northernmost point of the Hebron Road before the wall, takes multiple forms. In the mornings there is the bustle and crowdedness described in chapter 1, whereby thousands of workers arrive by foot or car and jostle for a space in the queue. Peddlers offer coffee and *ka'ek* (Jerusalem bread) through the bars of the first corridor to workers, many of whom have served this economy for more than a decade now. During late morn-ings and early afternoons, a trickle of people passes both ways: students and other (nonlaborer) permit holders and the occasional tourist who strays this far from the artworks on the section of the wall farther down the road. Taxi drivers smoke and drink coffee, awaiting the rush of returning laborers through the checkpoint gates, which starts at around four in the afternoon. At this point, the area is alive again with taxis filling up and parking lots emptying out as everyone seeks to leave the area as quickly as possible. Then there are the holidays— Christian, Jewish, and Muslim—that regularly disrupt these rhythms. For some Jewish holidays (Passover, Yom Kippur), the checkpoint is often closed completely, and at Christmas, the three Gates of the Patriarchs are opened along the street so clergy and functionaries can travel from Jerusalem to the Church of the Nativity in Bethlehem.[3] During Ramadan, and at Eid al-Fitr especially, the area is transformed completely: the Israel Border Police have taken to erecting temporary check booths and closed-in walkways where ordinarily the taxis wait. On these days, checkpoint users are not laborers but the Palestinian Muslims whom Israel allows to pass without a permit for prayer at al-Aqsa Mosque in Jerusalem: women, children, and the elderly—those deemed less of a security threat to the colonial state. Such are the mutable, lively, tense spaces on this side of Checkpoint 300.

On the other side, there is a complement economy of mobility where Israeli-owned transport awaits workers in the mornings to take permit holders to their places of work. Many are provided by

FIGURE 12. An aerial view of Checkpoint 300 and the Hebron Road area. Encircled left to right are Jacir Palace, the Sansur and Harb Buildings, the Bnei Rachel complex, Rachel's Tomb, the Anastas house, and Checkpoint 300. Photograph by Ala' Hilu.

employers, who deduct a small fee from wages for this convenience, plus there is the 163 Superbus service that runs from "Gilo Terminal" (that is, Checkpoint 300) along the Hebron Road (or Talpiot Road) to Jerusalem Central Bus Station, west of the old city, on Jaffa Street. The Superbus is used mainly by Israeli visitors to Rachel's Tomb; most Palestinians who wish to take a bus join the 234 South Buses service that leaves from the Jerusalem side of the checkpoint. There is also the 231 service from farther south down the Hebron Road, but that is not accessible to West Bank ID holders and is used mainly by foreigners and Jerusalem ID holders. In these mundane details of transportation services lie the logics of segregation: separate systems for separated groups in one land.

Across from the 234 bus stop, in the unkempt olive groves on the west side of the road—which belong historically to Bethlehem families who can no longer access them—are many makeshift shelters (see Figure 13) where workers, apparently, rest before the day's work. That is, after waking at two, three, or four o'clock in the morning, if a relatively quick crossing of the checkpoint allows time, workers use this to gain precious extra moments of sleep. The shelters are a stark illustration of the punishing nature of this mode of cross-border labor; if all sleeping routines are somehow subordinate to wage-earning capacities, here they are subordinated in the most extreme form. On the journey north from this point, the road is made of smooth asphalt and widens through a series of neat-looking intersections. The cars and public transportation are newer, of course. The six kilometers into the center of Jerusalem begin inside the Green Line[4] and run between the Gilo settlement to the west (behind the olive groves and shelters) and the Har Homa settlement to the east, two of the eight so-called ring settlements that Israel has built in East Jerusalem to limit the growth of Palestinian neighborhoods and fragment Palestinian space. Gilo was established in 1973 on land confiscated from Beit Safafa, Bethlehem, Beit Jala, and al-Walaja and now houses approximately thirty thousand settlers; Har Homa was built on land taken from Umm Tuba and Beit Sahour and is home to approximately twenty-five thousand settlers. The Hebron Road (at this point signposted "Talpiot Road") crosses the Green Line on the eastern edge of Beit Safafa, historically closely identified with Bethlehem but now part of the Jerusalem Municipality. The Zion Towers are the first landmark, on the right-hand side of the southern boundaries of the Arnona and Talpiot neighborhoods;

FIGURE 13. Resting places in the field after Checkpoint 300. Photograph by the author.

FIGURE 14. The wall cuts across the Hebron Road. Photograph by the author.

apartments in the towers sell for millions of dollars, prices that have been boosted by plans for more high-rise residences, the recently established U.S. Embassy in the area (on land that straddles the Green Line), and a planned extension of the Jerusalem Light Rail along the Hebron Road. It is important to keep in mind that the main part of these projects—the front line of Israel's "civilian occupation"[5]—was built with the labor of those Palestinian men who cross the checkpoint in the early mornings.[6]

Back on the Bethlehem side of Checkpoint 300, the Hebron Road running south is not marked by expanding construction projects. It is instead an evolving colonial space of a different type, one that has changed rapidly in the years since the checkpoint and wall were first built in 2005. In general, Bethlehemites[7] who are old enough to remember the area before 2005 recall this northern part of the city with some affection. "It was the Beverly Hills of Palestine!" recounted one person, "a place where you could eat pizza, drink a beer, smoke narghile—you could see families eating out, enjoying their time." A shopkeeper spoke of the economic vibrancy of the area: "There was the busiest and most modern supermarket in Bethlehem, you could buy everything. . . . There were Palestinians and Israelis passing through, it wasn't perfect but there was a real mix of people spending money here." At first glance of the desolate shop fronts closest to the checkpoint, there is little evidence of this; while the taxis and parking lots are buzzing with activity, a furniture store is shuttered, a plant nursery does slow business, and the numerous souvenir shops are either closed or struggling to sell often dusty trinkets and icons. Before the wall, these businesses had thrived. Lucy's furniture store—whose sign is still visible—sold bamboo and wicker chairs to both middle-class Palestinian families and residents of the nearby Israeli settlements, such as Gilo and Har Gilo (Figure 15). An Israeli who grew up in Gilo told me that she distinctly remembers her childhood bedroom being furnished with Lucy's products. The plant nursery, in fact, still displays Hebrew signs to cater to a long-disappeared clientele, and in the souvenir shops can be found, with a bit of searching, menorahs and Stars of David, objects that denote a different arrangement of space. The Jewish holidays were, I am told, "also a holiday for us. . . . In the 1980s and 1990s, you wouldn't believe how many Palestinians there were on this street selling Jewish foods to settlers—it was also a Palestinian feast [financially]!" I do not make any idyllic claims of peaceful

FIGURE 15. Lucy's furniture store. Photograph by the author.

FIGURE 16. The Balloons pizzeria, circa 1996. Image courtesy of Hanan Isachar/Alamy Stock Photo.

coexistence—this earlier period was of course a time of accelerating settler colonialism that has brought us to this current moment. But these memories serve to set in contrast the character of the Hebron Road in contemporary form. Where once businesses flourished and capital circulated there is now a markedly spacio-cidal effect of the enclosing function of the checkpoint and wall. "In the past tourists and workers all came here. I swear I was the king of Bethlehem! . . . Now I'm just a poor beggar. . . . How does one forget the work of a lifetime? How do I forget? I have toiled here for 40 years," as one former shop owner commented.

A place referenced frequently in stories of past glories is Balloons Pizza, which opened in the mid-1990s in the building across the street from Lucy's and the nursery (Figure 16). As one of the first restaurants in Bethlehem to serve pizza, Balloons quickly became "the best spot in the city," as its former owner recounted, with twenty-five waiters, seven chefs, and space for two hundred diners. In the basement was a bar called Memories, which became popular for its arcade games and a gambling machine. A little farther down the road is Christmas Restaurant, which used to cater to "high-class Bethlehem families," serving a mix of international and Lebanese cuisine, and which was known as a place to be seen, especially among Christian families on Sunday afternoons after church. A taxi driver once told me that on Sundays in the late 1990s, he and his brothers would walk from Beit Safafa through the olive groves of Mar Elias monastery to meet people, eat pizza, and drink Coca-Cola: "it was so busy on that road, so full of life!" he recalled with visible delight. Now that walk is possible only via the checkpoint and with a Jerusalem (blue) and not a West Bank (green) ID, though no one would now pass through Checkpoint 300 for something so trivial as a restaurant meal. Besides, Christmas Restaurant now serves only fast food for workers going to the checkpoint, and Balloons and Memories are long gone, closing, the former owner recalls, "between day and night." "The army started some 'sudden checkpoints' in the late 1990s, sometimes for twenty minutes, sometimes for two hours. We had a nice outside area with marble tables and umbrellas, and the Israeli soldiers started to sit there in 2000; from that point, no one wanted to come." The building is now residential but uninhabited, and its sizable (approximately five dunams) former gardens and orchard have been paved over to make parking space. A white booth stands at the entrance, from which an attendant charges fifteen shekels for a day's parking. Spaciocide and ecocide go hand in hand in this particular case.

Walking farther down the road away from the checkpoint, one finds the Awwad supermarket—the one remembered as "the busiest and most modern supermarket in Bethlehem" in the late 1990s and early 2000s—whose owner highlights the zoning problem of this part of the Hebron Road and its effects on his business. In other parts of Area C, usually in the West Bank outside of built-up Palestinian areas, Israel retains civil and military control. This part of the Hebron Road is unusual because it is Palestinian urban space that is thus—*in any sensical way*—the responsibility of Bethlehem Municipality, yet it is also nominally under the control of the Israeli military. One result of this is a patchy application of tax recovery in the area where older, more established businesses, such as the Awwad supermarket, are undercut by the newer and more informal vendors who are able to remain out of reach of municipal taxes.[8] In addition to tax matters, there is little clarity on who can be called on in matters of law and security, and the Awwad family is one of many business owners and residents to have joined efforts to lobby the Municipality for more services, including controls on unauthorized vendors and parking. Despite the Advisory Council of the Bethlehem Governorate taking up this cause—asking for greater law enforcement to tackle unauthorized parking—the Municipality has not responded, much because Bethlehem police have no jurisdiction in the area.[9] As might be imagined, this causes ongoing problems for residents and businesses; for the long-established businesses, it means that nonlicensed vendors undercut prices; for nearby hotels, it means that valuable parking space is frequently blocked off. Hotel owners readily emphasize how important coach access is to their businesses: "If the coach has to leave the tourists down the street and they have to walk they're not happy and we immediately have a bad start [to their stay]." There are also more pernicious effects: one hotelier recounted a time when a fight broke out among guests at a party. He called the Palestinian police, who told him to call the Israeli commander at the checkpoint. The soldiers refused to come, and as the confrontation got worse—a person's life was apparently threatened—another call to the Israeli commander yielded permission for the Palestinian police to attend, but only out of uniform and unarmed. The situation was eventually diffused, but the hotelier is still visibly affected by the violence and vulnerability: "We don't allow parties like that anymore."

On the side of the street opposite Awwad supermarket are some impressive buildings that speak of a grander past. The Nasser house (Figure 17) is a mid-twentieth-century design classic that was once a textile factory, and next to it are the curved, art deco balconies of the Awwad family residence (Figure 18), which was built in the 1930s. Both buildings stretch back quite a way from the road but are now only partially inhabited by contracting rather than expanding families. "No one wants to live around here, so close to the checkpoint." They are decaying and beautiful buildings whose former splendor haunts the new adaptive and functional checkpoint economy that struggles around them. A little farther down the road—with the checkpoint now two hundred meters behind—the wall comes back into the road, where a second Gate of the Patriarchs blocks daily passage. The wall at this point has run across (and split) the rear lands of the Nasser and Awwad properties and those of their neighbors before changing direction to cut eastward across the road before making four more sharp turns south, east, north, east. The effect is a carved-out plot around the by now famous Anastas family residence. The closing in of the house on three sides has made it a symbol of Israel's wall and its grabbing of Palestinian land; the house is the subject of countless profiles in international media.[10] Seen up close, the site is extraordinary: there are no more than three meters between the house's external doors and windows and the concrete gray of the wall, and even at three stories, the house appears miniature against its very particular backdrop. Its former gardens are covered in rubbish and the remnants of demolition and construction. The story in short is that either by a negotiated deal with the Israeli planning authorities or by fortune,[11] the house was spared demolition, while most of its lands were confiscated, resulting in the striking enclosure of the site today. On the ground floor of the property was a shop that sold kitchen utensils; it now sells Holy Land and "alternative" (wall-focused) souvenirs; on one of the upper floors, the family opened Banksy Guest House in 2007, capitalizing on the then recently appeared artworks in the area by the famous British artist. The family are on record saying that having tourists stay "defers once frequent night-time raids by Israeli soldiers" and that the business (which has a listing on Booking.com[12]) has helped them remain in the area. For this research, I did not interview the family for a feeling that

FIGURE 17. The Nasser house. Photograph by the author.

FIGURE 18. The Awwad family residence. Photograph by the author.

their experiences are amply recorded and widely published. A quote from Claire Anastas stands out among the large number of interviews she has been asked to conduct on living in the area: "We call it like hidden fighting. More than a direct fight to kill us. It's killing our soul. For me it's more hurt than other things. When you live injuring your heart slowly, that's another kind of death. It's more terrible actually."[13]

The Anastases' Banksy Guest House is now named Anastas Walled-In, as it now serves as an annex to one of Bethlehem's—and the West Bank's—best-known contemporary landmarks: the Walled Off Hotel, curated by the British artist Banksy in collaboration with the Palestinian businessperson Wisam Salsa. Another widely documented site, the Walled Off is situated two more right-angle turns of the wall southward from the Anastas house. Set in a former pottery shop between the Hebron and Caritas Roads (but on the route that now most closely follows the Hebron Road), the hotel has attracted masses of journalistic and academic commentary.[14] By turns an ironic, solidaristic, and (for some) opportunistic or shallow, tourism initiative, the Walled Off has become a must-see and must-discuss for almost all nonpilgrim visitors to the West Bank, many of whom search out Banksy's original works in the area, such as the dove in a bulletproof vest and girl frisking a soldier that are also ubiquitous in the city's souvenir shops. On the hotel itself, my own opinion does not matter, but all discussion might consider that the hotel's aesthetic is avowedly anti-British, anticolonialism, and antiapartheid, and it is now an "independent local business" that showcases artists from both the West Bank and Gaza with an "aim to break even and put any profits back into local projects."[15] The ground floor has two bars that are elaborately decorated in British colonial outpost style, complete with a self-playing piano, vandalized artworks, and clusters of CCTV cameras—all consistent with the aesthetics of Banksy's wider work. There is also an informative museum that begins at the Balfour Declaration—complete with a mechanized, life-size model of Arthur Balfour signing the document—and an audio loop with clipped British vowels that explains the colonial context of early Zionist settlement. The four rooms that follow take visitors through a familiar chronology of the 1948 Nakba, 1967 war, and 1995 Oslo Accords and with a particularly interesting section on the contemporary situation, including a critique of the international aid and arms trade that sustains Israel's occupation. A final room—an important corrective that is too often missing in Western views—is of Palestinian cultural and political life, making visible not only sites of resistance but the persistence of creativity and art for Palestinians in Palestine and the diaspora. The gallery upstairs continues this work with a display of works for sale across two rooms, one for West Bank artists and another for Gazans. The whole effect is clearly angled (knowingly) toward a Western audience, but this is a crucial audience that too often lacks knowledge and that otherwise might not be open toward such critiques of Israeli colonialism.

From the Walled Off, the street drops steeply past a souvenir shop and a coffee stand, then turns at a right angle to the left and continues for around one hundred meters past a number of buildings that now face the wall: the Waqf Ministry of Religious Affairs, the Kando gas station, and the Saca Cultural Heritage Center. The coffee stand is run by a man called Issa, who always offers coffee and a chair to passers-by; he also hands out Palestinian flags and points out some of the infographics that have been pasted on the wall by activists at the close-by Arab Educational Institute. One time, Issa led me through an abandoned building behind the Walled Off to his home, which is now surrounded by the rubble of semidemolished buildings—it is, at this point, an isolated and quite basic two-room structure with intermittent utilities. He says he owned the land it stands on and ten dunums that are now behind the wall. "I'll never leave," he insists. Aside Issa's small plot looking toward the wall is the Waqf—a ministry of the PA government—which operates in a surely unique setting: it is a government office standing on land that the state does not control. I have tried many times to speak with staff at the Waqf about working in the area, but to no avail. A curiosity across from the Waqf is that the slats of the wall are not uniform and have two vents built in at about three meters aboveground, from where, at quiet times, one can hear the activities of settlers on the other side. The vents sit directly opposite the site of Rachel's Tomb, on a platform that enables soldiers to file past to survey the area.[16] Next to the Waqf is a car garage and the Kando gas station, preferred by some because fuel tends to be cheaper, avoided by others because of rumors of low-quality or counterfeit gasoline. It cannot pass without mention, even as a mere curiosity, that Kando is a famous family name both locally and internationally as the finders of the Dead Sea Scrolls in the Qumran Caves (approximately forty kilometers to the east of Bethlehem) in 1946. Across the way from the gas station, veering off the Hebron Road toward Bethlehem city center, is

Banksy's famous *Armoured Dove* (and usually a knot of tourists) on a wall adjacent to the Cultural Heritage Center, which is run by the Saca family and has a quite wondrous collection of traditional Palestinian dress. The center opens out onto a tea garden, the final plot in Area C in the southeasterly direction of the city (see chapter 6).

Orienting again south toward Hebron, after the gas station, the wall makes another sharp turn where the Hebron Road intersects with Manger Street and runs westward, skirting around (and running through) the Muslim cemetery that is part of Rachel's Tomb from an era in which it was known more widely as Bilal bin Rabah Mosque. This intersection is, I believe, the most photographed nonreligious site in all of Palestine. It is where a Gate of the Patriarch is flanked by an imposing watchtower that marks the southernmost point of the wall in urban Bethlehem and sits between Aida and Azza refugee camps, both of which are targeted by nighttime IDF raids and both of whose communities are known for antioccupation resistance.[17] This watchtower and the next—known locally as "sniper towers"—differ from others in that they are covered not in street art but in pockmarks, scorch marks, and paint (a common tactic of Palestinian youths is to throw paint at military personnel carriers), and there is a constant presence of soldiers on lookout. The open space below and the widened part of the Hebron Road that stretches farther southward are readily transformed into an urban warzone when Palestinians, armed mostly with stones, are met with the full—often lethal—force of "nonlethal" methods of containment: tear gas, sound bombs, rubber bullets, skunk water.[18] It is one of the most teargassed places in the world, where residents deal with high levels of stress and the long-term psychological and physiological effects of living on Bethlehem's (or Aida Camp's) "death row."[19] Whether protesting or not, throwing stones or more (e.g., paint, burning tires, Molotov cocktails), advancing or retreating, Palestinians in the area—*in this built-up Palestinian urban zone*—face a constant threat of lethal military violence. In 2013, fifteen-year-old Saleh al-Amarin was shot in the head as he approached the wall with a catapult; in 2015, thirteen-year-old Abed al-Rahman Shadi Obeidallah was shot in the chest at a range of two to three hundred meters from the wall.[20] Both deaths are memorialized in murals close by the entrance to Aida. These killings are mourned, of course, but are not (to allow a generalization) thought of as exceptional; people (young men, especially) are routinely targeted by soldiers around the Hebron Road.

One man who was shot at the intersection in early 2023—a teenager from Azza Camp—gave important details of how this usually plays out: "We mostly use stones, paints, and burning tires and they open the gate [of the Patriarchs] and pull people in [for arrest] and shoot from the tower or from the concrete blocks when they advance. . . . If jeeps enter, they come through the gate from the base next to the tomb." The references here are to a small army unit just on the other side of the wall and to the set of concrete blocks on street sides in the area that serve a dual purpose of providing shielding to soldiers and marking the boundary between Areas A and C (Figure 19). "I think I

FIGURE 19. Concrete blocks on the Area A–Area C boundary outside Jacir Palace. Photograph by the author.

was shot from the tower. . . . It was a 'tutu' [also written 'two-two'] bullet, one that explodes on entry. The doctors said I didn't die because it was one centimeter away from a main artery—I was lucky!"

To visit by day, on a calm day, it is difficult to imagine such scenes of violence. Most of the time, the meeting of the Hebron Road and Manger Street is just another busy intersection in just another city where high volumes of traffic and pedestrians pass generally unbothered. Whereas, viewed from the north, the watchtower looms with a threat of military violence, the view south is composed of some of Bethlehem's most significant buildings. This was once the grand entrance to the city, where, in pre-occupation times, a banner hung by Jordanian authorities read (in English and Arabic) "Welcome to Bethlehem," with the elegant Sansur Building and Jacir Palace as backdrops and a roundabout fountain centerpiece in the road (which, apparently, was destroyed by Israeli soldiers soon after 1967).[21] For most of the twentieth century, this combination of buildings was the beginning of the city on arrival from Jerusalem and farther north; a veer left leads to Manger Square and the Church of the Nativity, whereas continuing straight leads to Hebron. Each building tells a particular and instructive history of colonialism in Palestine.

The Sansur Building was built between 1910 and 1914 and was for a long time the first building of the city for arrivals from Jerusalem. Its history is a history of the city itself: built on lands that stretched for eleven dunums as a residence for the middle-class Halabi family (the building is also referred to by some as the Halabi Building), it was hardly lived in and eventually rented in the 1920s to Shibli Sansur, who established a cigarette factory on the top floor. The building is still referred to colloquially as either the Sansur Building or the cigarette factory, and over the mid-century decades, the Sansur brand was ubiquitous in Jerusalem and the southern parts of the West Bank. The lower floors of the building have been home to different ventures—a notary's office, a newsstand, an antiques store—but what stays in people's memories is when a part of the lower floor was called "Stock," a bar that was established in the late 1960s and remained into the 1970s.[22] During that time, it is said, some rooms were given over to a brothel. As might be expected, details are hard to come by, but consistent among those who speak about it is that it was run by a Jewish man named David with two Jewish women whose clientele were Palestinian men. It is extraordinary to think of this arrangement now in a space only twenty meters from the watchtower. The building has been recently purchased by a Jerusalem-based businessman who is, at the time of writing, in the process of renovating with a view to establishing a center for Palestinian culture. Depending on whom one speaks to, this is a courageous, ambitious, provocative, foolish, collaborative, egotistical, colonial/anticolonial act. There are layers and layers to such a diversity of opinion on the project that have to do with religion, class, and Israel's ID regime. The new owner himself, however, is insistent that maintaining a Palestinian cultural presence in the face of the wall is crucial: "I wanted this place because it's Area C.... We want to show that we're human and to live in dignity and this is a perfect place." I focus on this important insistence in chapter 6, but for the moment, I want to recount the quite extraordinary circumstances of the building's renovation.

After years of lying derelict, the renovation process has been impeded by the planning gray zone; the building is the last but one in this part of Area C. Bethlehem Municipality planning authorities would not give the usual permission and assistance with installing toilets and a lift to the point that work stalled—"there were real problems; I called the Palestinian police, called the Israeli police, the army, I called the Red Cross, nobody would come." A turning point was when Bethlehem Municipality officials came to the site to stop work on a lift in a shared area with a neighboring building, and during the ensuing commotion, a soldier descended the watchtower and attended the scene. Eventually, the IDF commander appeared and said to the owner-developer, "I'll give you a permit, Abu-[redacted], you don't need a license from them [the Bethlehem Municipality].... I'll even give you the workers to complete the work if you need and a floodlight from the tower." It is difficult to overstate the significance of this—and the ripples it may cause among Bethlehemites reading this: a built-up Palestinian area granted planning permission by an Israeli soldier using a Palestinian name of endearment.[23] The plot thickens. In the next weeks, the building owner organized a bus to carry a delegation of police and army to visit the development for it to gain more favor among security personnel. The chief concern among the army and police was that the building had become something of a flashpoint during "clashes" and that Palestinian youth had used the roof to throw stones at the watchtower and the soldiers who would then emerge from the gate below. To rubber-stamp the deal, the commander asked for a guarantee that the roof would be secured and a promise that "nobody would enter the property or get on its roof without my knowledge." At this, the commander expressed satisfaction, saying, "We're happy to have you as our neighbor."

Across from the Sansur Building are three further buildings of note. First is the Wi'am (in English, "cordial relations") Building, a grassroots civil society organization focused on Palestinian conflict transformation that runs creative arts and education programs for women and children. Outside the complex, directly in the shadow of the wall, is one of Bethlehem's best-appointed children's playgrounds, maintained by Wi'am. The building and playground are frequently threatened with tear gas—and, occasionally, skunk water—which the military uses to disperse crowds. The next building is the Harb Building, a structure that was begun in the mid-1990s on the promise of the Oslo Accords as a hotel and commercial units. The Harb family lives on its ground floor, while the upper floors remain a structural shell and are littered with tear gas cannisters and rubber bullets (Figure 20). The owner tells us that the IDF maintains a right to commandeer access to the higher levels during times of heightened violence. After that, and after the blocks that denote a boundary between Areas C and A, is the magnificent Jacir Palace. Known to all as the grandest building in the city, the palace was built in 1909 as a home for the Jacir family, who fell into financial hardship in the 1920s and were forced to sell. The British then used it briefly as a prison in the 1940s before it became a school during the period of Jordanian rule (1950–67). It has also been used as a temporary base by the IDF (especially during the First Intifada) and most recently was developed as a high-end hotel that—by all accounts—always struggled to be profitable. A 2015 *Haaretz* report quotes a waiter in one of the hotel's restaurants joking that "the tear gas has become our perfume. . . . We wear it on Fridays but the lounge is mostly empty. We hope this will end soon."[24] It did: as the Intercontinental Hotel in 2021, Jacir Palace closed down at the beginning of the Covid-19 pandemic, and its two hundred rooms, its swimming pools, gymnasium, and grand dining rooms, remain locked. The complex is now also littered with the residues of urban warfare (Figure 21).

Going backward a few steps, a walk along the wall on the perpendicular to the Hebron Road—and then past another two right angles in a short stretch of fifty meters—moves along the Muslim cemetery

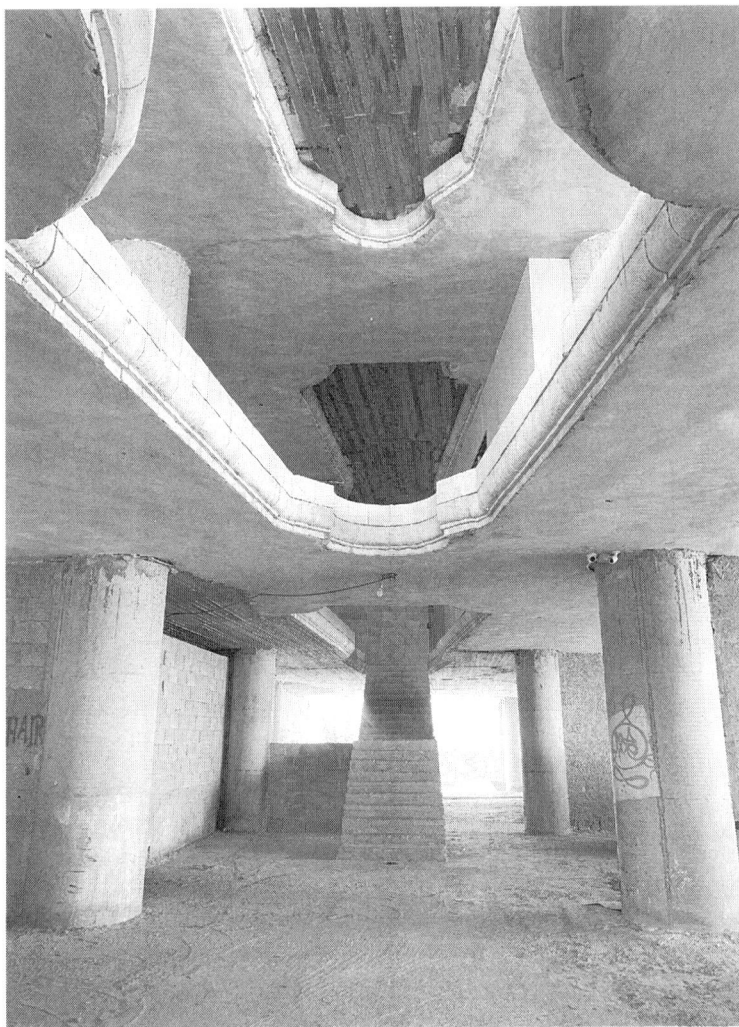

FIGURE 20. The Harb Building. Photograph by the author.

sometimes referred to as the Fawgreh Cemetery to arrive eventually at another gate from where Israeli troops enter to conduct nighttime raids on the Aida refugee camp (the camp's famous key monument is directly opposite the gate). On a quiet day, one can hear children shouting in Hebrew, the rhythms of Talmudic prayer, and the general din of another social and cultural world just meters away. This is the site most commonly known as Rachel's Tomb, the external walls of

FIGURE 21. Jacir Palace in 2023. Photograph by the author.

which reach into the Muslim cemetery. This is the edifice on which all of this convoluted security architecture and urban rearrangement depends. It is, in fact, a foundation for all that is discussed in this book.

Rachel's Tomb—or in Arabic Qabr Rāḥīl, in Hebrew Kever Rahel, and often also referred to as Bilal bin Rabah Mosque—is regarded (though this is contested)[25] as the burial site of the biblical matriarch

Rachel, one of Jacob's (a son of Isaac and thus a grandson of Abraham) two wives, who died during the birth of her son Benjamin. The tomb is a modest structure built in the eleventh century in the *maqam* (shrine) Islamic style typical of Palestine and Syria. Its significance has oscillated in the one thousand years since, and it has at various times fallen into disrepair or disregard. The structure has been used as a mosque and as a general site of worship for the three main Abrahamic faiths; nineteenth-century travel writers in English portray something of a "shared site" of more or less equal reverence for pilgrims of each of the three main Abrahamic faiths.[26] Undisputed is that there is a reason for the tomb's modesty: the first approximately seven hundred years of Rachel's Tomb are relatively unnotable, especially in relation to the greatly contested Jerusalem sites in those centuries. In the mid-nineteenth century, a Jewish British financier and proto-Zionist, Moses Montefiore, funded a renovation of the tomb, adding an arched entrance on the north side facing Jerusalem and—significantly, and most probably on the insistence of the Ottoman government at the time—a mihrab on the southern wall, pointing toward Mecca for Muslim worshippers. This configuration remains to the present day, except that the mihrab is currently covered by plaster. During the early period of Zionist settlement, two sets of keys were held—one by the Sephardic Oriental Jewish Community and the other by the Ashkenazi Western Jewish Community—and Muslim access became more restricted, even as British Mandate authorities included the site as part of a "Status Quo in the Holy Places" policy aimed (ostensibly) at harmonious interfaith relations. This policy is represented in a famous 1932 British postage stamp that features Rachel's Tomb and the word "Palestine" written in English, Arabic, and Hebrew. After 1948, Jordanian rule in the West Bank severely reduced Jewish presence at the tomb, and the site, once again, became known as Bilal bin Rabah Mosque to Muslims and as Qabr Rāhīl to Christians.

Up until the early 1950s, the area was semipastoral (Figure 22). An older resident recalls, "We had gardens at home, and we had apricots, olives, grapes, and everything. People used to make a living out of crops. They would pick apricots, then get on donkeys and take the harvest to Jerusalem to sell it there. . . . Once, a hyena chased them while they were going to Jerusalem! We had only disorganized agricultural land plots." As the Bethlehem economy grew in the mid-1950s, the Hebron Road became an important commercial center, and two buildings were constructed on the plot aside the tomb for commercial units, including a welding shop, mechanic workshops, and an automotive scrap dealer. Many of the buildings described earlier in the chapter were also built around this period, as were, of course, the refugee camps of Aida and Azza, transforming the Rachel's Tomb complex from a periphery of Bethlehem into a part of its urban fabric. During the Jordanian period of control, Jewish Israelis were not allowed to enter holy sites in the West Bank. After the Six Day War in 1967, which forced Jordan's withdrawal, Israeli prime minister Levi Eshkol ordered Rachel's Tomb to be annexed to the Jerusalem Municipality, but, owing to objections by defense minister Moshe Dayan, this was never implemented. Instead, control of the site was turned over to the chief rabbinate of Jerusalem, and Rachel's Tomb was formally recognized as a multifaith site. Older generations in Bethlehem recall the tomb as a generally shared place during the early years of occupation, where "you could meet Jews, Christians, Muslims, not really talking [to each other] but they were all there." One person recalls specifically that inside there was "a slab of stone where Muslims washed the dead before burial, and there was a cloth with gold thread where Jews came for prayer." Another, one whose workshop was on the plot adjacent to the tomb, recalls, "Back when there was no wall or anything . . . I would go inside the tomb [complex] and sleep there [in the afternoons]. . . . I would go to sleep there—it was a mosque and people would go there to pray."

The contemporary roots of the current arrangement of space around Rachel's Tomb have grown from, as is often the case in the West Bank, the Oslo Accords. In the draft agreement, the northern part of Bethlehem was originally assigned as Palestinian Area A, until—one story goes—a direct intervention in 1994 from Rabbi Menchem Porush, who, when told the news by Yikzhak Rabin, "started to cry, [pleading,] 'But Yikzhak are you going to leave our own mother outside our borders? How can we be without mama Rahel?' he cried. . . . Rabin's shirt was wet with his tears." On this show of emotion, apparently, "Rabin called Shimon Perez and told him to tell Arafat that Kever Rahel is not included in the agreement!"[27] In response, Arafat is reported to have exclaimed, "I cannot agree to this! Next to Rachel's Tomb there is a Muslim cemetery, and the holy place is located in Area A and I myself am a descendant of Rachel."[28] Whatever the truths and embellishments of these exchanges, the eventual text of the 1995 agreement confirms a change in course:

FIGURE 22. (A) Rachel's Tomb in the 1930s, from Wikimedia Commons. (B) The Hebron Road in the 1930s. Photograph from the Matson (G. Eric and Edith) Photograph Collection held in the U.S. Library of Congress, Prints & Photographs Division, LC-DIG-matpc-15858.

Oslo II Agreement, Annex I, Article V, Section 7

Rachel's Tomb

a. Without derogating from Palestinian security responsibility in the City of Bethlehem, the two sides hereby agree on the following security arrangements regarding Rachel's Tomb which will be considered a special case during the Interim Period:

   (1) While the Tomb, as well as the main road leading from Jerusalem to the Tomb, as indicated on map No. 1, will be under the security responsibility of Israel, the free movement of Palestinians on the main road will continue.

   (2) For the purpose of protecting the Tomb, three Israeli guard posts may be located in the Tomb, the roof of the Waqf building, and the parking lot.

b. The present situation and existing practices in the Tomb shall be preserved.[29]

In the years immediately after Oslo, these conditions generally applied. In fact, it was in this period that the Hebron Road area experienced something of an economic boom that saw the construction of hotels (e.g., the Harb Building), and eateries and bars—Balloons and Memories, for example—prospered. "People started to invest, they saw security and prosperity in the future, the Hebron Road would be busy again and a good place to do business." Such was the hope that grew during the mid-1990s, which fueled construction projects in the area focused on leisure and hospitality.

Hope waned as the promises of Oslo went unfulfilled and the Second Intifada (2000–2005) prefaced a new era of Israeli spatial control. From 2003 onward, various plans surfaced for a separation barrier that would sever one part of Bethlehem from the other. In the beginning, it was not clear precisely which parts of the city would be brought within Israel's direct control, and there was, in fact, disagreement within Israel's coalitional and regional powers. The Zionist National Religious Party and Haredi (largely non-Zionist) Shas Party, with the backing of Ehud Olmert, Jerusalem's mayor, lobbied to include Rachel's Tomb inside the Jerusalem "Security Envelope." At a Security

Cabinet meeting in September 2002, interior minister and Shas chairperson Eli Yishai "reminded the ministers in attendance that the Rosh Hashanah haftorah reading included a reference to Rachel weeping for her children—and the passage ends with the phrase that the 'children shall return.'"[30] Security Cabinet Decision 64/B was passed, rerouting the proposed wall five hundred meters south to annex Rachel's Tomb. The new structure would now reach farther into Palestinian space to grab the land around the tomb with all the effects discussed in this chapter so far. In the months that followed, eviction notices were issued and slats were lowered, gradually closing in buildings and closing out Palestinians. Tawfeek Natsheh, a welder whose workshop was subsumed, described his experience of this time:

> After they started building the wall, I spent two years going to my workshop around its construction. The soldier used to let me go but then more and more he would ask what I was doing there. I told him, "I work, I need some means of living." Then two or three weeks later, every time I tried to pass to my workshop, they would stop me for three or four hours. Eventually, my day would be gone, and there was no point in going to my shop. The last time I went, I was also asked where I was going. "To my workshop." At that point, they didn't allow me to go for two weeks. . . . I lost everything.

There are dozens other similar experiences among residents and workers in the area,[31] ones of watching their homes and livelihoods disappear behind ten-meter-high T-walls with little or no recourse to legal counsel or challenge. Tawfeek, at least, was able, in the end, to take his work to a new building and now runs his business from a unit down the hill from Jacir Palace.

The original welding shop was in a building of particular significance, known by Palestinians in Bethlehem as the Musallam Building.[32] One of the large, three-story, multiuse buildings of the 1950s, its north side flanks the Muslim cemetery at Rachel's Tomb. Until the 2000s, it was owned by three brothers from the Musallam family, who used the space for their various businesses, a pottery store and sandwich shop, and rented out units for other businesses, such as the welding workshop. The place is prominent among longer-term residents of the area talking about life on the Hebron Road before the wall because of its proximity to Rachel's Tomb and its eventual fate. One interviewee went so far as to say,

> If I want to describe the beautiful street to you, the street of the entrance to Bethlehem, I will tell you that, first, there was someone selling sandwiches called Hanna and Khalil Musallam. . . . I used to have lunch there every day. Every day, I ordered food and they delivered it to me. Imagine how comfortable life was! I had a Palestinian restaurant next to me that would bring me whatever food I wanted for me and my guests. It was very easy. Now, this same place has a wall that closes it entirely.

The enclosure of the building is documented in a set of photographs from 2006 that depict the gradual appearance of concrete slats that encroach and restrict (see Figure 23); they were initially an inconvenience that could be worked around, but, in the end, they are a formidable and unnegotiable barrier to Palestinian movement and livelihood. At first, the northernmost part of the Musallam Building was sealed off with a T-wall, before the West Bank wall consumed the entire plot and its adjacent outbuildings and lands.

These details are important because the Musallam Building now forms part of the Bnei Rachel (Sons of Rachel) complex, a yeshiva and accommodation quarters for Jewish Orthodox families. I discuss this transformation from Palestinian to settler use further in chapter 5; for our purposes here, it is important to note that for settlers, on an ideological level, the Musallam Building was seen as an opportunity to establish a Jewish presence in "Beit Lechem" (Bethlehem) "for the first time since King David" that has drawn funds from (mainly American) sources to gradually develop the main structure and area around it.[33] The Bnei Rachel organization, a Jerusalem-registered nonprofit, alongside a host of associated organizations, develops and fundraises for the site as an educational center (see chapter 5). A kollel was established in 2003 that, shortly after, became a yeshiva before two Jewish families moved into the building in October 2004 (on the Hebrew calendar, the eleventh of Heshvan, the anniversary of the death of Rachel). The years that followed were marked by military restrictions on the use of the building—a curfew was set at 5:00 P.M., then 7:00, and eventually 10:30—and overnight stay for students was prohibited on security grounds.[34] IDF commanders and rabbis eventually

FIGURE 23. Construction of the wall in 2006. Photograph by Anne Paq/Activestills.

FIGURE 24. Rachel's Tomb (encircled) and the visitor parking lot. Photograph by Nadir Mauge.

reached an agreement in 2014 for free use of the site, opening the way for a one-story extension of the main building and the establishment of a community that is now home to eleven families, seventy students, and fourteen permanently stationed IDF soldiers (Figures 25 and 26). Bnei Rachel's website advertises an "events hall [for] up to 80 people suitable for covenants, bat mitzvah, chalka, tefillin placement and more, as well as lectures and various events in the Rachel's Tomb complex." The tomb itself now receives five hundred thousand visitors per year.[35]

This now thoroughly Jewish Israeli settler space thrives not only on Palestinian land but in Palestinian buildings, ones that are fondly remembered and sorely missed. They are also totally inaccessible to all Palestinians, including those who own them. In the current division, children of the small settlement play on the plastic turf against the gray backdrop of the wall and under the protective eye of soldiers in the watchtower. A stream of religious tourists file through the strange, gray corridor that this protrusion into Bethlehem has created; they mourn and pray for Rachel, to them a specifically and uniquely Jewish matriarch. For those without access, Rachel remains the mother of Yaʿqūb/Jacob and Yūsuf/Joseph or also merely, but importantly, the name given to an almost-forgotten shrine that is now enclosed behind a vast security architecture that has reshaped the entire northern part of Bethlehem.[36] Viewed from above—for example, from the top floor of St. Michael's Hotel or via drone—the strange intimacy of two disparate worlds is mapped out. Tons of painted, graffitied, attacked concrete slats carve a circuitous path from Checkpoint 300 along the elegant buildings that were once restaurants and bars; around the Anastas house; past the famous Walled Off Hotel, Waqf, and Kando gas station; and down to the watchtower that looks over the Sansur, Harb, and Wi'am Buildings as well as Jacir Palace. From the other side, a pristine gray concrete runs both sides of the parallel path along a smooth asphalt serviced by Jerusalem public transportation and past a visitor parking lot (behind the Anastas house) and the open entrance to Rachel's Tomb (with its recently painted blue dome) before opening out again to the yeshiva (Musallam) building, playground, and storage buildings (Figures 25 and 26). This is a geography of colonial division like no other, a built-up area that has been transformed into an ethnoreligious, militarized security borderland that has slowly diminished Palestinian social, economic, and political life on the Hebron Road.

FIGURE 25. On the other side of the wall: Bnei Rachel Yeshiva (the Musallam Building). The entrance to Rachel's Tomb is under the shaded section toward the watchtower. Photograph by Nadir Mauge.

FIGURE 26. The other side of the watchtower: the storage areas and playground of the Bnei Rachel compound. Photograph by Nadir Mauge.

There are many and no ways to conceptualize power–space relations in all that is described here. Or, less obliquely, even as there are ready views through influential conceptual frameworks (which, no doubt, many readers will have already spotted), I do not think it possible to tie everything together in neat, theoretical abstractions. Nor do I think that that would be a desirable outcome, and I purposely set out here, first and foremost, to render the Hebron Road area in rich textual and visual description. That said, and without subordinating the illustrative work of this chapter to critical frames, there is much to learn from the Hebron Road on wider relations of power, space, and Israeli colonialism.

To untangle something of the ways that power functions in the area chronicled here, we might begin with a fairly uncontentious assertion that the checkpoint and the wall of which it is a part are only the beginnings of a broader borderland within Bethlehem. It is a borderland marked by pronouncedly *spacio-cidal* effects that are produced through de-development strategies, or the purposeful diminishing of Palestinian economic relations,[37] and a heightened exposure to the possibility of military violence that deters both visitors and residents, resulting in depopulation and economic degradation. We can thus add detail to our understandings of Checkpoint 300 by recognizing it as part of a wider security architecture in Bethlehem whose spatial effects reach beyond familiar processes of displacement, demolition, construction, enclosure, and the regulation of mobilities. Though the confiscation of land and im/mobility are clearly central to the significance of Checkpoint 300 in Israel's colonial project, control is also produced in the immediate locale, resonating outward through urban space, along the Hebron Road and surrounding areas. Also crucial to note is that this extends beyond what is documented here into the center of Bethlehem and across the southern West Bank, where all Palestinian social, economic, and political life is marked—to different degrees—by spacio-cidal effects that trace back to the choke point function of Checkpoint 300. Documenting these wider effects is part of another research project, but one simple fact of Checkpoint 300 would bear this out: at times of planned or unplanned closure, permit-holding workers are unable to earn their wages, a majority of hotel guests cannot arrive, and businesses cannot transport goods between north and south. To different degrees, then, the killed-off vibrancy of the Hebron Road is replicated in areas remote from the area considered here. In this order of control, *place* is the primary target of colonialism, where depopulation and curtailment of social and economic activities evidence the spacio-cidal effect of "transforming the Palestinian *topos* to *atopia,* turning *territory* into mere *land.*"[38] For many Bethlehemites and West Bank Palestinians, this once vibrant area of the city is now "a dead area only for workers and people stuck there." It is, in core geographical terms, *place* reduced to *space,* or the stripping away of the meaning-making activities that make *somewhere* knowable, nameable, experienceable. At a push (a claim that I complicate in chapter 6), it is the transformation of somewhere into *nowhere.* No communal Palestinian life—whether political, economic, familial, social, or religious—can freely flourish in the shadow of the wall that skirts the Hebron Road. It is subject to the dehumanizing processes of extreme urban degradation or, to use a term synonymous with spaciocide, a subject of *urbicide.*[39] Checkpoint 300 is, in this way, an epicenter from which resonate deadening effects that *unmake* Palestinian space.

But this view is only partial. Space might be unmade as whatever prompted the (albeit tongue-in-cheek) comparative "the Beverly Hills of Palestine" is systematically dismantled, but it is also *remade* in a very important sense. The entire area, as I have hinted throughout this chapter, can now be very quickly transformed into a theater of urban warfare where an always-mobilizable military force has planned and reserved positions to counter and attack. As we have seen, often on a Friday, often as a response to peaceful or else stone-throwing "provocation," the Hebron Road very swiftly turns into battle space: the concrete blocks that mark Area C become low turrets for either resistance or "neutralizing," high buildings (e.g., the Harb Building) are commandeerable as surveillance- or sniper-fit vantage points, and the always-ready watchtower and Israel Border Police/IDF units are on hand with an awesome arsenal of weaponry to put down those fighting for their political rights. One particularly illustrative example of this is at a residential property close to the Wi'am Building, where a family lives on the upper floor and the vacant lower floor has "south" and "west" spray-painted in Hebrew aside the unglazed window frames to orientate soldiers during operations (Figure 27). The family is ordered to retain the markings in permanent readiness for transforming the building from a home to a military shooting post. There is no realistic way of knowing for sure, but it is not difficult to imagine that the fourteen soldiers permanently stationed at Rachel's Tomb and the local border police and

IDF units—even as they are subject to turnover and rotation—retain something akin to muscle memory as they take up familiar positions that entirely repurpose, or remake, places in the image of their own belligerent ends. To a family, the ground floor is storage space; to the colonial military, it is decidedly battle space, the two uses greatly contrasting yet conveniently (for the colonizer) functionally coexisting. In this way, dual use is woven into the urban fabric of the area so that on the all-too-commonplace occasions when the area is swarmed by military personal and contaminated with tear gas and "skunk water,"[40] a military urbanism—that planning, architectural, and aesthetic turn identified by Stephen Graham[41]—is readily realized.

If these are the effects of either careful or ad hoc military urban planning, then the legal complement is undoubtedly the production of a space of exception. Though I do think that this is a somewhat overused category of analysis among (mainly Western) writers on Palestine,[42] there are strong indications here that this is a paradigmatic case. Take, for instance, the issue of policing on the section of the road just described, where there is a clear decision maker (the Israeli military) that routinely denies the jurisdiction of Palestinian police yet does not take on any duties itself in regard to the protection of Palestinian life, denoting in Giorgio Agamben's well-cited terms "the inclusion and capture of a space that is neither outside nor inside."[43] This was most evident in the example of the fight at a hotel where the threat to life was exacerbated by the force of denied recourse to state assistance, whether policing, military, or medical. This topological structure of *"being-outside, and yet belonging"*[44] makes for a simultaneously absolute yet indifferent form of sovereignty, a thanatopolitical space of concurrent control and abandonment, or the archetypal juridical order that renders subjects *homines sacri* or "bare life."[45] Thanatopolitics (the politics of death) aside, we might look also to elaborations on the notion of precarity as a "politically induced condition" that Judith Butler conceives as the unequal distribution of wealth, services, and rights—the "differential ways of exposing certain populations, racially and nationally conceptualized, to greater violence."[46] A particular and diagnostic bind of precarity is that those in spaces of "maximised precariousness" "have no other option than to appeal to the very state from which they need protection."[47] This was starkly illustrated during an interview with one long-term resident of the area who was trying to

FIGURE 27. Ground floor of a Palestinian house with orientations in Hebrew ("south" next to the window, "east" on the adjacent wall). Photograph by Nadir Mauge.

assist a collapsed man in the street close to the watchtower. "I called the Bethlehem hospital, the Red Cross, the Red Crescent, none of them would come because of where he was. I called the [Israeli] army, and they wouldn't come either or even allow a Palestinian ambulance to arrive." Eventually, the man had to be taken to a hospital by private car, where he recovered, but only thanks to the good fortune of an unsanctioned intervention. What we learn here is that precarity might not mean the state enacting *direct* violence on a population, but it sure is not going to prevent or remedy it, and, significantly and cruelly, it will prevent alternative attempts at prevention or remedy.

Such are the broader geographies of Checkpoint 300 in northern Bethlehem and beyond—a road and a community beleaguered by a security infrastructure that exposes Palestinians to an elevated threat of military violence. The Hebron Road area is simultaneously *unmade* and *remade,* transformed from a vibrant space of Palestinian social, economic, and political life to a nonplace of struggling or absent businesses and residents—and transformed again, periodically, into urban battle space, where an advanced military is mobilized to oppress anticolonial dissent. Within this broadened-out geography are hints of even wider spatial effects—for instance, in the proliferation of surveillance and weapons technologies and the cross-national movement of capital to purchase and sustain the complex around Rachel's Tomb—that guide us toward the global exchanges of objects, ideas, and people that contribute to and constitute the capacity of Checkpoint 300 to effect control on Palestinian people and land. It is to this geography that the next chapter turns.

5

Producing Checkpoint Space

GLOBAL FLOWS OF IDEAS AND TECHNOLOGIES

> Checkpoints are not freestanding and geographically
> discrete places and must be understood in the context of
> social relations that stretch *beyond* them and in the context of
> how the intersections of social relations function *within* them.
> They are shaped as much by events and processes that happen
> elsewhere (Knesset decisions, foreign policies in Washington
> D.C., suicide bombings in Haifa or in Baghdad) as they are by
> what happens within them (commercial activity, Palestinians
> refusing to turn back, soldiers shooting tear gas).
>
> —Helga Tawil-Souri, "Qalandia Checkpoint
>   as Space and Nonplace"

> The Israeli government was the proof of concept for everything
> we were doing globally. The technology was field-tested in one
> of the world's most demanding security environments and we
> were now rolling it out to the rest of the market.
>
> —former employee of AnyVision/Oosto

The task of this chapter is to move farther—as far as we can go—
from the city of Bethlehem and the West Bank outward to set Checkpoint 300 in a global frame, one that enables a view of the broader
flows of *ideas, objects,* and *people* that are crucial to its capacity to effect
control of Palestinian people and land. The account presented here is
concentrated on three important contexts: (1) the international networks of security technologies whose innovations (smart surveillance
systems, "nonlethal" crowd control weapons, biometric scanners) are
produced both for and through the checkpoint; (2) the wider labor
relations that govern mobilities, such as Israel's privatized domestic security market and its overseas "guest worker" programs that maintain

levels of precarity in the Palestinian labor pool; and (3) the international movements of capital and people that have enclosed and fortified the Rachel's Tomb compound around which so much security architecture is built. Theoretically, I thus set Checkpoint 300 within what geographer Doreen Massey termed the *power geometries of globalization* to show it to be a "place in which certain important elements of capitalist globalisation are organised, coordinated, produced," thereby getting at some of the global spatialities that are part of Israel's colonial project in Palestine.[1] We are from here forced to reckon with Checkpoint 300 and the Hebron Road not only as a site that "receives" global wares and capital but also as one that is integral to their production and circulation. Empirically, the chapter presents an original perspective on Israeli security infrastructure, the global geographies of which reveal new trajectories of research and targetable sites of political responsibility. We are thus brought to an understanding of Checkpoint 300 as a significant point in the global exchange of *ideas, objects,* and *people,* whereby space is produced through security commodities and rationalities, precaritized labor, and ideologized capital.

In this process, an array of international security companies come to the fore, providing hardware (biometric scanners, drones, non/lethal weapons) and software (facial recognition), along with a set of rationalities that form a part of a late-capitalist mode of security: automated surveillance practices; categorizations of the "terroristic" or "nonthreatening" body; and the prominence of nonstate, private actors. Less visibly, Israel's arranging of its labor market introduces overseas precaritized groups whose labor elevates the precarity and dispensability of Palestinian workers; wages are kept low by the presence of migrant workers, who are often prioritized over Palestinians. In addition, the fortification of the Rachel's Tomb site is produced through capital and ideological investment from overseas (chiefly the United States) that claims Palestinian land in the name of settlers and sets about denying Indigenous access. I therefore want to carefully argue that Checkpoint 300 cannot be fully understood as an entirely endogenous Israeli mechanism of control. This claim is in no way to absolve responsibility but to better apprehend the processes that enable and enhance all that we have witnessed so far. Put tentatively, Checkpoint 300 is *also* produced through ideas, objects, and people that are exogenous to the Israeli colonial state, which, in a global frame, is a coordinating but by no means determining or even wholly sovereign actor. Colonial space is formed through important *global* processes that simultaneously exceed and constitute the colonial state; Checkpoint 300 and the Hebron Road are both *produced through* and *producers of* the power geometries of globalization. The political importance of taking this broadened and dual view of a specific site of colonial control is realized, I argue toward the chapter's conclusion, in the opening of multiple sites of complicity and thus responsibility that should be identified as collaborators and profiteers in Israel's colonial project in Palestine and beyond.

The chapter once again begins inside Checkpoint 300 itself, reentering with an account of the advanced technologies that facilitate control, before—again—looking across the Hebron Road area at the hardware deployed in the spacio-cidal tactics discussed in the previous chapter. I then embark on an established geographical practice of "following the thing" to the end of "provok[ing] moral and ethical questions for participants"[2] involved in the supply of security technologies, drawing close focus on three (of many) key commodities and suppliers: tear gas, facial recognition software, and Israel's largest arms producer, Elbit Systems. The chapter then considers conditions of labor—of both those employed as private security staff and those imported as guest workers from Thailand—to show various articulations with the precaritized Palestinian labor that commutes through Checkpoint 300. Finally, I recount the international capitalist and ideological collaborations that have come together to sequester Rachel's Tomb and the area around it for exclusively Jewish Israeli use, even as it is historically recognized as a site of multifaith practice. Brought together, these empirical examples—of weapons, labor, and property—provide a vivid picture of the global geographies that implement and uphold Israeli colonialism in Palestine. I close with a political word on the anticolonial value of such a global frame and the ways it sets clear lines of accountability, identifying sites of potential disruption in the reproduction of the colonial state.

Since 2005, Checkpoint 300 has undergone extensive renovations. The two main buildings were completed toward the end of 2005, when the first turnstiles and check booths were also installed. Metal detectors arrived a year later, and airport-style bag scanners the year after that, in 2007.[3] In the years following, various changes were made to entrance routes, such as the construction of the "humanitarian lane" (in 2010) and the addition of toilets and baby-changing facilities, built in preparation for the visit of Pope Francis in May 2014 (and which have apparently been locked ever since).[4] In 2019, the checkpoint underwent a technological renovation as part of the Defense Ministry's NIS 304 million ($85 million) "border crossings upgrade," focused on the large terminals around Jerusalem. A tender was issued by the Israel Police for contracts to operate checkpoints in the "Jerusalem envelope," with Checkpoint 300 included in the southern "Cluster B" package[5] that was awarded to T&M Protection Resources Holdings Israel Ltd. (T&M Israel), a subsidiary of T&M Protection Resources LLC (T&M USA) and the largest private security company in Israel. Under the terms of its contract for operating Checkpoint 300, T&M Israel is charged with installing security guards and providing logistical and administrative services in accordance with the Israel Police's technical specifications.[6]

Checkpoint 300 is now a highly technologized security space. It is also seemingly under constant renovation. In mid-2023, the three entry lanes described in chapter 1 were out of use (though still seemingly maintained in an operational state), and arrivals entered through two turnstiles under a newly installed sign (in English): "Welcome to the Rachel's Tomb Crossing." There are then two long corridors where large screens illustrate the procedure for the 2019-installed "smart gates" ahead (Figure 28). A push through the doors at the end of the corridor leads into older parts of the checkpoint that have not changed since (at least) 2015: a hall with four more double doors that in turn lead to a set of remote-controlled turnstiles with red and green lights that indicate when to proceed. After the turnstiles are eight Garrett PD6500 metal detectors connected to Rapiscan 620XR scanners[7] and the first sign of checkpoint staff, through intervening instructions over a loudspeaker that come from a voice behind the one-way glass in a booth to the side. "Step back!" "Remove your belt!" and so forth are bellowed through the speaker, mostly in Hebrew. Beyond the scanners are sets of three smart gates under a sign that reads "For Biometric Card Holders Only," interspersed with an old-style check booth for those without biometric cards. The gates are equipped with AnyVision (recently rebranded as "Oosto"; see later) facial recognition cameras that match card data to the body to permit or deny passage using the Elbit Systems Rotem-Reut border management database. In the open space after the gates stand T&M security staff, each armed

FIGURE 28. Smart gates in Checkpoint 300. Image courtesy of imageBROKER.com GmbH & Co. KG/Alamy Stock Photo.

FIGURE 29. The Hebron Road as urban battle space (with Jacir Palace in the background). Photograph by Anne Paq/Activestills.

with a Tavor X95 (or Micro-Tavor) assault rifle manufactured by Israel Weapon Industries (IWI) (the small-arms branch of Israeli Military Industries, a formerly state-owned producer acquired by Elbit Systems in 2018). Behind them are (contextually provocative) stock images from the Israeli Tourist Board "Land of Creation" campaign.

Around the checkpoint, southward down the Hebron Road, various other technologies come to the fore, especially at times of Israeli (police and military) incursions into Bethlehem and Palestinian protest close to Rachel's Tomb. Based on media reports and conversations with residents, a "standard" response to any kind of political mobilization around the wall in the area involves the firing of tear gas and "nonlethal" rubber bullets from positions that look over the junction of the Hebron Road and Manger Street and west toward Aida Camp. Often the Gate of the Patriarchs and the gate facing the entrance to Aida are opened so that armored vehicles can pass through carrying personnel and various mounted weapons. Soldiers and Israel Border Police take cover behind the concrete blocks that mark the boundary between Areas A and C, and some of the buildings in the area—the Harb Building, for instance, and the Musallam residence (not to be confused with the Musallam Building discussed in chapter 4)—have military orders that enable soldiers to commandeer vantage points to take up firing positions. The area is very swiftly (and not infrequently) turned into an urban combat zone, where a readily mobilized advanced military fires on groups of Palestinians who are mostly young, male, and armed with stones, paint, and (less often) Molotov cocktails. Recorded incidents demonstrate a variety of hardware put to work: a Police Plasan SandCat armored vehicle fitted with a Combined Systems tear gas launcher is stationed outside the Halabi Building and fires into a dispersing crowd;[8] a heavily modified pickup truck (produced by Beit Alpha Technologies using a MAN Group chassis) sprays Odortec "skunk water" on a crowd and buildings close to Jacir Palace;[9] a drone fitted with an ISPRA Cyclone Anti-Riot Drone System[10] drops tear gas cannisters at the Hebron Road–Manger Street intersection. These are not isolated examples; the Bethlehem Municipality records one hundred "incidents" in the period 2017–22,[11] with many other, smaller operations happening almost daily at times of "elevated tensions" (Figure 29). Nor are they isolated geographies; the transformation of the area into an urban space of combat depends on much wider processes within the power geometries of globalization.

In only a two-paragraph survey of the technology deployed in and around Checkpoint 300, there is a clear sense that this particular space depends on others—spaces of research and development, of manufacture, procurement, testing, and marketing. The intellectual and material provenance of the hardware and software indicates a much broader geography of colonialism in Palestine. Inside the checkpoint, multiple suppliers are gathered: Garrett (metal detectors) is a private, Texas-based company that sells its products through an Israeli partner, Shamrad Electronics; Rapiscan is based in California, owned by OSI Systems (market capitalization $1.96 billion), and has research and manufacturing facilities all over the world (e.g., Melbourne, Johor Bahru, Hyderabad). Garrett trades on a pointedly militarized version of the American Dream: "From our humble beginnings in the Garrett family garage to today, Garrett is proud to say all of our metal detectors are made in the USA, right here in Texas. We have grown to over 300 employees, with a goal to continue to grow by offering additional cutting-edge products and technologies."[12] Rapiscan markets itself as "the world's leading security screening provider," emphasizing that its "install base includes NATO, the European Union, Manchester Airport Group, UK Customs, Hong Kong International Airport, US Department of Homeland Security (TSA, CBP), US Department of Defense, and others."[13] The Rotem-Reut database is maintained by Elbit Systems, a large, multinational weapons manufacturer, and the facial recognition software is provided by the Israeli tech firm AnyVision/Oosto, which has now expanded into markets across the world. Both Elbit and AnyVision/Oosto have, on different scales, built global markets around their products, which are "battle-tested" in Palestine (see case studies 1 and 3 later in this chapter).

The objects used by the Israeli military on the Hebron Road are produced through similar geographies. Plasan is an Israel-based military vehicle manufacturer with a subsidiary and manufacturing plant in Michigan and has sold hundreds of its models (e.g., the SandCat, Oshkosh, International MaxxPro models) to many states across the world. The SandCat is based on a commercial Ford F-Series chassis; approximately seven hundred of them are in use by at least sixteen states across five continents.[14] Combined Systems, the manufacturer whose name is printed on the spent tear gas cannisters that litter the entire area (Figure 31), is based in Pennsylvania and fulfills its NIS 4 million contract with the police through its Israeli distributor, MR Hunter. Skunk water is made operable by the cooperation of three main firms: Munich-based MAN provides the chassis, which are modified by the Israeli company Beit Alpha Technologies, from which Odortec's chemicals can be sprayed. The Cyclone Anti-Riot drones produced by ISPRA have been showcased at large, international arms fairs like Milipol (Paris) and ADEX (various cities) as part of ISPRA's range of products, which have been sold to militaries and militarized police forces in more than forty countries. The IWI-produced Tavor X95 assault rifle is standard issue for Israeli police and military—and for many private security personnel (such as those inside the checkpoint)—and is one of Israel's most lucrative small-arms exports; thousands are used by police and military in India, the United States, Ukraine, and many other states. Variants of the Tavor X95 (e.g., the Tavor TAR-21) can be fitted with a Colt-developed (United States) M203 grenade launcher produced under license by IWI, from which either explosive rounds or tear gas cannisters can be fired. As might be clear at this point, mapping the provenance of objects and the cooperation between producers is an ever-expanding task. The three case studies that follow—of AnyVision/Oosto, tear gas, and Elbit Systems—provide a representative overview of the geographical reach brought into view in this chapter.

CASE STUDY 1: ANYVISION/OOSTO

As part of an upgrade program in 2019, airport-style "smart gates" were installed at Checkpoint 300 and other major checkpoints in Palestine. The software for the gates was updated from the Basel System (a biometrics database developed by Hewlett-Packard for the Ministry of Defense and IDF) to the Better Tomorrow package provided by the Israeli company Oosto. Oosto was known as AnyVision until 2022, when it rebranded as part of an expansion into new markets and, it might be inferred, as a move to distance itself from a large amount of negative publicity it received once news of its contracts with the Israeli police and military reached the business press and investors.

Founded in 2015 by computer designers based in Tel Aviv and Belfast, AnyVision began developing the computer vision software that brought it the contract for checkpoint gates, as well as (it is widely alleged) other contracts to "upgrade" surveillance cameras in East Jerusalem and settlements with facial recognition capabilities.[15] In 2018, AnyVision won the prestigious Israel Defense Prize, awarded by the president of Israel to actors who have "significantly improved the security of the state." The award was made without naming AnyVision because its surveillance contracts were—and seemingly still are—classified. One widely referenced AnyVision project is nicknamed "Google Ayosh," a surveillance program inside the West Bank that links cameras to Big Data. "Ayosh" refers to the occupied Palestinian territories and "Google" to the capacity to search a database for people's whereabouts and activities (*not* to the American technology firm). AnyVision also attracted a $28 million injection of capital in 2018 from international investors led by the German company Bosch that increased revenues sixfold.[16] In June 2019, a larger funding package of $78 million was announced by Silicon Valley venture capitalists DFJ and Microsoft's venture capital arm, M12. Other investors that were part of the package included Californian organizations Light-Speed Venture Partners and Qualcomm Ventures and the German tech firm Bosch. This coincided with the installation of Better Tomorrow at checkpoints and subsequent scrutiny from human rights and activist organizations, such as 7amleh, the ACLU, and Jewish Voice for Peace.[17] In an investigation conducted by NBC News, AnyVision CEO Eylon Etshtein made a series of claims that aligned with Zionist visions of Palestine-Israel—there is no occupation; his was the "most ethical company known to man" (thus mirroring the famous and spurious IDF slogan of the "world's most moral army")—along with an accusation that the NBC reporter was funded by Palestinian activists.[18] Such tactics of deflection are common among Israeli political and economic elites and reveal a commitment to both entrenching and denying the extent of Israel's colonial project in Palestine. Presumably out of concern for its public image, Microsoft announced its divestment from AnyVision in May 2020.[19] None of the other investors have made public statements on their positions vis-à-vis the potential human rights violations made possible by AnyVision/Oosto products.

These international movements of capital are replicated in AnyVision/Oosto's networks of expertise and marketing. Currently, now branded only as Oosto, the company boasts of "more than 240 employees globally, with offices in Tel Aviv, New York, Mexico, London, and Singapore, and a dedicated team of over 30 PhDs in Belfast focused solely on computer vision research. AnyVision's global customers number in the hundreds, including many Fortune 50 clients."[20] Trading on this platform of international expertise and bolstered by its

Skunk weapon to go overseas

Geo-politics Israel First Responders Law Enforcement Security Military News Technology Non Lethal Jun 28, 2015

FIGURE 30. Israel Homeland Security announces the sale of skunk water to U.S. police, 2015. Screenshot of https://i-hls.com/archives/63672.

FIGURE 31. Combined Systems tear gas cannister. Photograph by the author.

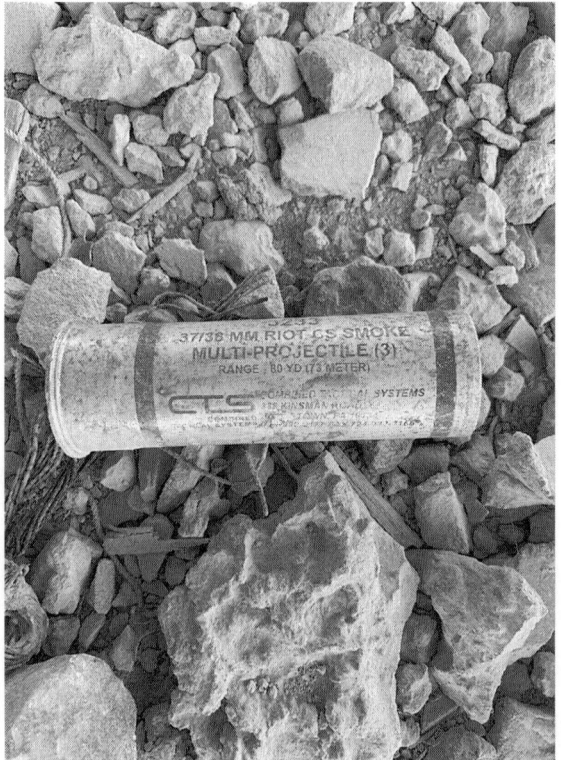

on-the-ground testing in Palestine—"20+ years of academic research and field experience"[21]—Oosto has been able to diversify. According to a Reuters report, Oosto's clients now include some very large companies—BP, Macy's, Mercedes-Benz—as well as a number of professional sports teams (e.g., the Golden State Warriors, the Houston Texans) and large casino operators in Las Vegas and London (e.g., MGM).[22] This *rooted expansion* is explicated by CEO Etshtein: "Israel was the first territory where we validated our technology. . . . However, today more than 95 percent of our revenue is generated from end customers outside of Israel."[23] I use the qualification "rooted" to hold on to the fact that the relations between domestic and international markets here are clearly codependent, that the surveillance of people, say, on the Las Vegas Strip is produced through the surveillance of people passing through sites like Checkpoint 300. As a whistleblowing former employee of Oosto put it in the NBC report, "It was heavily communicated to us [by the company's leadership] that the Israeli government was the proof of concept for everything we were doing globally. The technology was field-tested in one of the world's most demanding security environments and we were now rolling it out to the rest of the market."[24]

CASE STUDY 2: TEAR GAS

Tear gas has been deployed in policing and military operations all over the world. It has evolved over the past hundred years or so from an unreliable weapon in the World War I trenches to something of a panacea to colonial forces as a "nonlethal" tool for suppressing anticolonial groups in Ethiopia, India, South Africa, Vietnam, and elsewhere. In an archetypal example of the "boomerang" effect, tear gas has been prominent in recent decades as a tool of "domestic" control whereby heavily militarized police disperse crowds that question the actions of the state, as has happened at countless sites, including Ferguson, Hong Kong, Istanbul, and Manama. It is highly effective at disabling and dispersing groups of people in a way that allows politicians and militaries to make claims on more ethical modes of maintaining state power. This obscures the fact that the health effects of tear gas—made from synthetic chloracetophenone, 2-chlorobenzalmalononitrile gas, or naturally occurring oleoresin capsicum (the potent capsaicin in hot chili peppers)—remain largely unknown and that publications in prominent medical journals (e.g., *BMJ, JAMA, The Lancet*) have called for more research into the physiological and psychological repercussions of exposure.[25] All signs are that prolonged or repeated tear gas attacks cause significant harm to mental and physical well-being.

Palestine has been central to the historical development of tear gas from the beginning, when, in November 1933, the British high commissioner, Sir Arthur Wauchope (who, importantly, had previously served the British Empire in the Boer War and in Northern Ireland), in the context of reports of the efficacy of tear gas in India, was able to persuade the Colonial Office in London to sanction the use of British-made Lachrymatory Generators cannisters, a product that would be later withdrawn because of its deadly effects.[26] This decision was pivotal in the global proliferation of tear gas such that it quickly became widely used across the British Empire and other colonial settings, making the transition into a stock weapon in many police arsenals. Israel's use of tear gas increased massively when, in 1989, it paid $6.5 million for U.S.-produced tear gas and launchers, which have since been linked to the deaths of sixty-seven Palestinians during the First Intifada (1987–93).[27] Today, tear gas is used regularly against Palestinians in the West Bank, East Jerusalem, and (before October 7, 2023) along the Gaza border. The most teargassed place in Palestine—and reportedly the most teargassed place in the entire world—is northern Bethlehem, around the Hebron Road and the area around Aida Camp adjacent to the Rachel's Tomb cemetery. Residents routinely suffer the effects of tear gas and are quite used to taking evasive action: sealing windows, wearing masks, escaping. A comprehensive 2018 study published by the University of California, Berkeley Human Rights Center, *No Safe Space: Health Consequences of Tear Gas Exposure among Palestine Refugees,* reported that a majority of Aida residents had suffered the effects of tear gas exposure three to ten times in just the previous month.[28] Such high levels of exposure are linked, by residents and researchers, to all manner of health effects—"asthma, allergic dermatitis, headaches and neurological irritability, miscarriages, and blunt trauma from canister injuries"—and to very high levels of "worry, physiological reactivity, hyper-arousal, poor and disrupted sleep, lack of safety, and daily disruptions in basic activities of daily living—including caring for children and the sick, participating in school and work life, and engaging in basic family life activities."[29]

There are two main suppliers of the tear gas that produces these effects. The vast majority of it is manufactured by Combined Systems, a Pennsylvanian company that fulfills its multiple, multimillion-NIS contracts with the police through its Israeli distributor, MR Hunter.[30] As well as the gas itself, Combined Systems provides its handheld PENN ARMS launcher and vehicle-mounted VENOM launcher, which it markets at arms fairs around the world as battle-tested.[31] Combined Systems is majority owned by Point Lookout Capital Partners, a New York private equity firm with a broad security industry portfolio, with a minority stake held by the Carlyle Group, another U.S.-based private equity firm (with a reported $380 billion in assets). Combined Systems has leveraged the "proven" efficacy of its products by growing its sales around the world (e.g., Germany, India, Hong Kong, Argentina, Sierra Leone), sometimes by shipping through Israel, as was the case when the Egyptian Central Security Forces used Combined Systems tear gas to put down protests during the 2011 revolution.[32] In the same year, in Bahrain, Combined Systems tear gas killed fifty-four demonstrators through impact from the high-velocity launch systems or from exposure to the gas itself.[33] The second company whose tear gas products are used around Checkpoint 300 and the Hebron Road is ISPRA, an Israeli company founded in 1968 that grew on a 1970s "concerted knowledge transfer between the Israeli occupation of Palestine, the British side of the 'troubles' in Northern Ireland, and the repression of uprisings in apartheid South Africa."[34] ISPRA is today part of Taavura Holdings (a group of seventy Israeli brands) and "a global leader in developing, manufacturing and marketing of nonlethal devices for riot control" whose main involvement in the provision of tear gas in Israel is as an innovator via its Cyclone Anti-Riot Drone System, attached to a Chinese-made DJI Matrice 600 drone to drop cannisters from the air, notably around the Gaza fence and in the Rachel's Tomb area.[35] ISPRA sells its products to militaries and militarized police forces in more than forty counties.

CASE STUDY 3: ELBIT SYSTEMS

No survey of Israel's security technologies is complete without Elbit Systems, the largest arms producer in Israel and the twenty-fourth largest in the world, with a market capitalization of $9.2 billion and 2022 revenues close to $5.3 billion.[36] Elbit supplies 85 percent of the IDF's land-based equipment and 85 percent of all the drones used by the Israeli Air Force and has contracts with a reported fifty-one militaries and police forces across the world.[37] In Palestine, Elbit's products are essential to Israel's control of people and land in all areas of the West Bank, East Jerusalem, and Israel—as well as in the current military assault on Gaza[38]—and are consequently marketed as "battle-tested" or "combat-proven."[39] At Checkpoint 300 specifically, under a long-term contract with the Ministry of Interior, its Rotem-Reut database system links the permit system to biometric identification to register the movements of Palestinians (this is the case at all permit-checking checkpoints). Around Checkpoint 300, the Elbit Skylark drone is used in surveillance activities along the Hebron Road, and its flagship armored vehicle, the Musketeer, is deployed in raids on Aida Camp and farther into northern Bethlehem along the Hebron Road. Both private security staff inside the checkpoint and police and soldiers outside it regularly carry the Tavor X95 assault rifle, the standard-issue light arm of the IDF that is produced by IWI. Undoubtedly, many other Elbit products are in use around the checkpoint—from night vision and grenade launchers to radar devices and classified cybertechnologies—that are less visible. It should also be noted that Elbit was one of the main contractors for building the West Bank wall in the early 2000s and that the company is thus deeply involved in the creation and maintenance of Checkpoint 300, as it is in countless other sites across Palestine.

Though the Israeli military is its largest client, Elbit also has significant operations in the United States through its Texas-based subsidiary, Elbit Systems of America; numerous other subsidiaries (e.g., Elisra, Soltam Systems, Tadiran); and manufacturing sites in four different U.S. states (Alabama, South Carolina, Texas, and Virginia). I argue that two distinct phases built Elbit's position in the United States and the global market. It first established its reputation on a platform of "battle-proven" know-how and wares, an approach that earned it large contracts to provide drones to U.S. Customs and Border Protection, as well as a $145 million deal to build United States–Mexico border infrastructure—a "virtual wall" of surveillance towers that, not incidentally, cut across unceded Tohono O'odham land. Promoting the deal, Elbit emphasizes the mobility of ideas and know-how across space: "The talent and expertise that Elbit Systems . . . has employed for years in protecting Israel's border will now be put to use on US borders to keep Americans safe."[40] A second phase is marked by the transformation of the United States–Mexico borderlands into a complementing showroom or laboratory where Elbit has become an established part of Tech Parks Arizona (a part of the University of Arizona), whose Israel Business Initiative encourages Elbit and other companies to set up in Tucson on the promise of facilities, real-life testing grounds, and a forum of exchange in ideas and capital.[41] The American borderlands have thus become a complement for Elbit to test and sell its wares to a global market. In a telling moment in Gabriel Schivone's research on Tech Parks Arizona, he asks the mayor of Tucson (Jonathan Rothschild), "Why Israel?" The answer: "If you go to Israel and then come to southern Arizona and close your eyes and spin yourself a few times, you might not be able to tell the difference."[42] The mayor here is perhaps more insightful than he intended: while his reference is most likely to the desert conditions and a racialized threat across a border, there is a more critical likeness to be drawn between a dispossessed Indigenous population, settler colonialism, a ready testing ground for technological experimentation, and a receptive market for the extraction of profit. In other words, Elbit has graduated from its roots in the control of Palestine to a truly international actor in the globalized geographies of violence that are euphemized by the term *homeland security.*

An instructive countergeography is growing around this, however, that must also be highlighted. Such is Elbit's notoriety that it has recently drawn attention from Palestine solidarity movements. The #ShutDownElbit campaign has gained traction among activists in the United Kingdom, Australia, and the United States whereby direct action has sought to disrupt Elbit's production chain. In the United Kingdom, a group called Palestine Action has blockaded facilities run by Elbit subsidiaries across the country: UAV Tactical Systems (in Leicestershire), Elite KL (in Staffordshire), and Instro Precision Ltd. (in Kent). The Whistleblowers, Activists and Communities Alliance in Australia has blockaded the Elbit Melbourne office and campaigned for the Royal Melbourne Institute of Technology to end its collaboration with Elbit.[43] In the first weeks of Israel's 2023–25 assault on Gaza, activists in Massachusetts responded by blockading its Innovation Center in Cambridge, chanting, "War criminals work at 130 Bishop Allen Drive!" Elbit subsequently removed that address from its website, and a clear point was made: the struggle against Israeli colonial violence is a global one. This countergeography is instructive in the ways it lays bare the connections between specific spaces of colonialism—such as Checkpoint 300—and otherwise distant sites of design, assembly, testing, and training at the structural center of weapons-producing economies. As a slogan of direct action groups goes, "It is likely that the weapons used against the people of Gaza are made in a factory near you."

In these ways, Checkpoint 300 and its surroundings are produced through technologies and ideologies that come together from afar to enable control over this particular part of Palestine. But it is important to note, as I have hinted throughout, that the movement of ideas and objects does not flow only one way. Colonial space, as many have written, is often figured as a laboratory for experiments with different technologies of control that are then imported into the metropole. Historical examples of such experimentation and movements are the building of antiriot, Haussmannian-type boulevards; the militarization of policing; and the use of camps for internment. Aimé Césaire identified such movements in the 1950s, writing of *un formidable choc en retour*—translated into English as "a terrific boomerang effect"— where Europe's bourgeoisie awake to scenes of overspilling prisons and an omnipresent secret police.[44] For Césaire, fascism illustrated the constitutive force of the outside—the colonial violence distributed overseas that would eventually return home in nightmarish form.[45] Michel Foucault referred also to *un effet de retour,* similarly translated as a "boomerang effect" whereby "a whole series of colonial models was brought back to the West, and the result was that the West could practice something resembling colonisation, or an internal colonialism, on itself."[46] This outward–inward metaphor serves to conceptualize the ways colonies are used as both experimental grounds for domestic control and, more lately, as capitalist showrooms for state-of-the-art security equipment.[47] Though this first sense of boomerang technologies applies to Israel in some circumstances, for instance, in its inward use of skunk water on anti-Zionist Orthodox groups in Beit Shemesh and Bnei Brak, the movement of Israeli technologies tends outward via the use of Palestinian land as a space of historical colonial innovation that has accelerated since the turn of the twentieth century.[48] "September 11 was good for business," as Anthony Loewenstein puts it in a recent book-length account of the "Palestine Laboratory," as Israeli arms innovators were able to market their wares as "battle-tested" in a colonial "workshop."[49]

Within this global market, retaining focus on Palestinians who encounter those wares, there is an important inflection of power dynamics inside the checkpoint facility. Security staff are now charged primarily with reinforcing the nonhuman agency of the machines that perform the checks that make a modern border. They are—in important ways, if not entirely—subordinated to the decision-making function of the machines: allow unobstructed passage on a green light, take action on a red. And this is the point of automated border practices: intelligence networks are deployed to quantify risk with a higher degree of accuracy than interrogator-humans can. This carries important ethicopolitical consequences whereby, as Louise Amoore and Alexandra Hall have written on the Rapiscan scanners of the type installed at Checkpoint 300, security staff are "quite literally and physically removed from the political difficulties of decision"—that is, the conditions that make categories of colonizer and colonized— through technological abstraction: "Where border agents view their screens from a distance, seeing not 'real' people but data-based risk scores, chalk-line scans, algorithmic models, then where is a judgment actually made? What are the ethics of a decision taken on the basis of prescreened and visualised elements of data on a person?"[50] Effected by the coming together of global security innovation is a rendering of Palestinians who seek passage as legible only as data, whose admissibility/inadmissibility is determined algorithmically. Decisions are "data led," as security staff—the people, or substance of politics— "never confront the political difficulties of that which cannot be seen or resolved."[51] For Rema Hammami, this wider global trend toward such algorithmic technology solutions touches the ground in Palestine as an attempt by the Israeli military to "disembody the brutal and messy substance" of its work in controlling Palestinian movement.[52] This notion is explored specifically in Checkpoint 300 in Alexandra Rijke and Claudio Minca's insightful analysis of the "brutal materialities" of checkpoint technologies whereby "machines' 'responses' [mark] the body of the individuals subjected to their decision: from beeping to remaining silent . . . from the contact of the turnstiles' arms to their subtle but liberatory 'clicking.'"[53] From this materialist point of view, technologies at the checkpoint—conceived, designed, and manufactured all over the world—effect real consequences for people in a specific locale: they, the *ideas* and *objects* of boundless global tech capitalism, order "long and painful experiences" for Palestinians attempting to pass through.[54]

Zooming out from specific materialities to broader economic and political effects, the commodities and doctrines developed at

Checkpoint 300 and on Palestinian land more generally have enormous effects on the reproduction of the Israeli state. In economic terms, a run through the relevant financial benefits is staggering. The latest available data at the time of writing from the Stockholm International Peace Research Institute list Israel as the world's tenth largest weapons exporter in the five-year period 2018–22, with at least thirty-five countries importing Israeli weapons in deals worth $3.2 billion.[55] Over the last decade, Israel has begun to export more weapons than it imports, receiving $2.7 billion in equipment from contracts with U.S. and German arms manufacturers. This is heavily funded, of course, by Israel's massive U.S. military aid package, which is currently in the 2019–28 cycle of $38 billion over those ten years. We should recall that Israel has received more U.S. foreign aid than any other state, totaling $263 billion between 1946 and 2023 (this is a full 60 percent more than the second-largest recipient, Egypt, has received: $151.9 billion over the same period). It should also be recalled and emphasized that these vast amounts of capital move alongside—that is, both facilitate and are facilitated by—diplomatic and political alliances that significantly shape international relations. Anthropologist Jeff Halper's study of the Israeli weapons industry details how India, historically a robust critic of Israel in international political arenas, has entered into multimillion-dollar "defense" contracts with Israeli suppliers, coinciding with a right-wing political alignment between the Narendra Modi and Benjamin Netanyahu administrations and a softening of India's "traditionally pro-Palestinian position in the UN."[56] India is the world's largest importer of Israeli arms, receiving $1.2 billion in weapons between 2018 and 2022. Similar patterns of "weapons diplomacy" mark Israel's relationships with states like South Korea, Singapore, Brazil, Colombia, and Mexico, having, Halper argues, tangible results of abstentions or pro-Israel positions in UN votes.[57] In the case of Mexico, Anthony Loewenstein writes that its "voting pattern at the United Nations has shifted to a less critical stance towards Israeli politics" since a $160 million deal for the infamous Pegasus phone-hacking tool sold by the Israeli surveillance company NSO Group.[58]

From the corridors of Checkpoint 300 to international economic and diplomatic relations is quite a jump in scale, but the connections are there, and that they expand so far illustrates precisely how this and other security spaces in Palestine are importantly global. This is important for the fact that Checkpoint 300 is generative of geopolitical relations and thus not simply produced through them, as is norma-tively assumed. The methods and products that make the checkpoint and its surroundings a site of colonial control are part and parcel of a global network of security regimes whose back-and-forth trading of experience and hardware produces the desired effects of political oppression and the extraction of vast profit. It is in fact only through Checkpoint 300's connections to global geographies of the arms and security industry that everything documented in this book is made possible. To draw focus back onto the three case studies (which are included merely as illustrative; many other companies and products could be examined similarly), AnyVision/Oosto facial recognition technologies, tear gas producers, and Elbit Systems are intimately tied to intellectual labor from overseas, to international markets and investment, and to sure claims around "battle-tested" products that increase recognition and salability. They are at the same time part of a longer historical trajectory of colonial control through state-led stimu-lation of innovation in suppressing dissent and increasing surveillance. AnyVision/Oosto has established itself on the back of complicit intel-lectual work, particularly through the involvement of a U.K. university and the resources, expertise, and credibility that connection offers. Its rapid growth from checkpoint technologies in Palestine into interna-tional "civilian" markets demonstrates how porous a military–civil boundary is made through cycles of innovation and a profit incentive around the objective of control. Reemphasized particularly in this case is that no knowledge is benign and that the everyday im/mobility of a West Bank Palestinian can be tied to the research activities of faculty, staff, and PhD students at sites like Queen's University Belfast. Tear gas has been a part of the international trade in arms for more than a hundred years, developing from a chemical weapon considered too controversial by colonial authorities into a "nonlethal" stock munition in use all over the world. That it is currently supplied through both Israeli and American producers further illustrates how a globalized and competitive market in commodities cannot be overlooked in de-veloping understandings of specific sites of state and colonial violence. Similarly, Elbit Systems has built an inextricably close relationship to the Israeli state and its military as part of the military–industrial com-plex. It depends as much on the global dimensions of that complex whereby international arms deals bolster its capacities and incentive to innovate further at sites like Checkpoint 300.

Turning our focus from *ideas* and *objects* to *ideas* and *people,* I want to think now about how the labor conditions of those who are present in the checkpoint—Israeli security staff and Palestinians seeking passage—reveal the ways in which colonialism functions through a privatized domestic security market and an overseas "guest worker" program that contributes to the control of Palestinian people and land. Whereas the international exchange of weapons and security technologies has been subject to extensive scholarly and journalistic attention, the global dimensions of the labor market are seldom related to the oppressive forces that face Palestinians, as workers and (as we have seen) in Palestinian domestic and social life. Here I attempt to draw together seemingly disparate groups of workers to show how labor articulations *across space* underpin conditions *in place,* or how differently marginalized groups are deployed to maintain a system of segregated, cheap, and racialized labor.

It is perhaps counterintuitive to begin with the labor conditions of Israeli security staff, but their presence is undeniably integral to the functioning of the checkpoint, as is their differentiation from direct representatives of the state (e.g., border police and soldiers). A policy of "taking the army out of the checkpoints"[59]—or, in official terms, "the *civilianising* of the passages between Israel and Judea and Samaria [the West Bank]"[60]—was implemented during the expansion of checkpoint infrastructure around Jerusalem after 2005. The transition from police and military control to contracting private security staff wrought significant effects on the dynamics of power inside Checkpoint 300—as well as the multiple other contexts where the huge Israeli private security sector operates in Palestine (e.g., in West Bank settlements, at other checkpoints, and across East Jerusalem).[61] For Palestinians entering Checkpoint 300, where the human encounter still applies among the proliferation of security technologies, colonizers appear not as direct representatives of the state but as private security guards (who are almost always military trained) employed by whichever company holds the current contract. From the first round of tenders in 2005 until 2019, the contract for Checkpoint 300 was held by Modi'in Ezrachi, one of the largest security contractors in Israel, which—along with its competitor Sheleg Lavan—managed to grow its market share in running checkpoints around Jerusalem in successive rounds of police tender (e.g., in 2008).[62] T&M Israel won the contract in 2019 and currently provides security guards and administrative services according to Israel Police guidelines.[63] What must be acknowledged—without ever collapsing this argument into one supporting the dangerous and false narrative of the IDF's or Israel Police's greater morality[64]—is that, regardless of which company runs the checkpoint, privately employed checkpoint labor in Israel is notorious for low wages, short-term contracts, and unsocial working hours. This is work that tends to attract only "people who do not have a real alternative."[65]

In this markedly capitalist hold over the monopoly on state violence, those who are charged with enforcing the im/mobility of Palestinians are—if by entirely different degrees—embroiled in their own exploitative labor relations, and their mistreatment of Palestinians cannot be considered without referring to an articulation with the casualization of security labor and the reduced accountability of private organizations. This is not—I stress—to highlight the labor conditions for checkpoint personnel but to consider how an ideological and structural shift toward privatized security bears on Palestinians. The company that oversaw the development of Checkpoint 300 between 2005 and 2019, Modi'in Ezrachi, has repeatedly breached Israeli labor laws by underpaying and mistreating workers, yet it retains an ability to secure lucrative government contracts.[66] More importantly, and perhaps connectedly, its employees are known for a pattern of abusive behavior toward Palestinians across the Occupied Territories.[67] At checkpoints specifically, Modi'in Ezrachi has a record of distributing lethal violence: in 2016, guards shot and killed a sister and brother—their names were Maram Saleh Abu Ismail (age twenty-three) and Ibrahim Saleh Taha (age sixteen)—at Qalandia; in 2020, they shot an elderly and disabled man; and in December 2022, a motorcyclist was targeted at Checkpoint 300.[68] These are the cases that made the news; many others do not. Important to note is that these incidents pass without culpability; even when staff are investigated, they are rarely charged, and if they are charged, there has not yet been one conviction against a private Modi'in Ezrachi security guard. T&M Israel is a more recent arrival to the security market whose labor rights records and conduct of its staff are yet to reach public scrutiny, but its model is the same: recruit mostly young, military-trained Israelis whose options are limited in the labor market. As one researcher told me, "nobody *chooses* to work in checkpoint security, it's just not a nice job." It is in fact a common discourse among Israelis (the majority of whom serve in the military) that checkpoint labor is *avoda shehkora* (black work) that produces also for the colonizing population a form of "checkpoint syndrome," which forms through "the routine . . . of boredom, monotonous views (the same trees, the same rocks), monotonous work (checking IDs, asking the same questions over and over again, getting the same answers) and the same set daily programme (eight hours at the checkpoint, two hours training, six hours rest . . .)."[69]

No sympathy is called for here, but it is important to explicate the knock-on effects for Palestinians who use the checkpoint and, in particular, how Israeli security personnel who are bored, frustrated, and employed (unlike the police and military) at a remove from the state go about their work in a reconfigured relationship to colonial control. At base, this arrangement makes for an enforcing body equipped with the means of state violence but with few of its restraints. In this "lawless zone," as one human rights organization puts it, private security staff—like soldiers and police—"are equipped with IDF weapons, undergo military training, and are empowered to undertake policing actions, such as searches and detentions, and to use force," but their indirect engagement lessens accountability, both for the security personnel and for the state itself.[70] One of the main incentives for privatizing security (and other sectors) is thus realized: risk and liability are shifted from the state and its contracted proxy to the targets of security, for whom there is only ever-narrowing recourse to legal protection. In practical terms, according to the human rights researcher Iyad Haddad, the reduction of accountability coincides with an increase of violence against Palestinians; the Israeli state uses private security staff "to escape accountability, especially because the people can't recognize them, and it becomes easier for them to use force when they want [to do so] without accountability. Instructions regarding Israeli or international law are easier to escape via private forces."[71] In this way, the state's turn to a privatized labor force opens a space in which supervising or regulatory mechanisms are weak—and even weaker than the notoriously lax overseeing of Israeli soldier and police conduct toward Palestinians—such that security personnel are even freer to use unnecessary or excessive force in checkpoints.[72] These are the dynamics that enabled staff to act with impunity in the shootings at Qalandia and that underpin sustained levels of threat for all of those who pass through Checkpoint 300 and similar facilities.

This aspect of the checkpoint's capacity to impose control is tied to a global frame in the ways that the privatization of Israeli security mechanisms follows (and leads) broader trends of outsourcing formerly state-provided services, especially in the area of security and military services.[73] In 1985, at a time when the International Monetary Fund and the World Bank were enthusiastically rolling out "structural adjustment plans" to tackle public debt in poorer states, the Israeli government set in place its Economic Stabilization Plan, marking a shift from a planned market to a neoliberal policy of opening state provision to for-profit actors. This brought Israel into a broader neoliberal axis and thus the international flows of extractive capital investment, of which T&M Israel is an archetypal product, in both material and ideological terms. T&M Israel is an independent business arm of T&M USA, a U.S.-based global security, cyber, and intelligence provider that maintains a 73.5 percent controlling stake in its Israeli subsidiary. T&M USA was formed at the dawn of neoliberalism in 1981, when market deregulation enabled two New York police officers to offer security services to private contractors. In the early 2000s, T&M USA began to purchase security contracts in Israel and formed T&M Israel in 2007, continuing a neoliberal model of blending state and private operations: "T&M Israel employs highly trained agents, all of whom are former members of the Israeli Defense Forces."[74] Though this claim is somewhat tautological for the fact that nearly all Israelis are conscripted, it upholds a neoliberal mode of extracting profits from the capabilities of state-trained workers (e.g., medics, teachers, engineers). T&M Israel now operates within a network of state (the Israeli Ministry of Defense) and international corporate actors (from Hertz to Louis Vuitton), generating both capital and credibility through such partnerships. Its contract to operate Checkpoint 300 cannot be entirely separated from these broader histories and relationships; it is the outsourced, international decision-making sovereign charged by the state to uphold colonial rule in the north of Bethlehem.

The other group of people inside Checkpoint 300, permit-holding West Bank Palestinians, is situated within global geographies of labor in the ways that their working conditions articulate with those of other groups of workers in Israel's segregated economy. As I think is clear at this point, the checkpoint and wall do not simply exclude Palestinians but rather modulate the volume of crossings according to the willingness or exigencies of the Israeli state to receive cross-border workers. This works across the two separate economies, where the dominant one—that of Israel—controls movement and livelihood via a permit system designed to ensure specific sectors access to a ready pool of marginalized and securitized low-wage labor.[75] For instance, the post-Oslo construction boom in Jerusalem and Israel has been fueled by thirty-six thousand sector-specific permits for Palestinians to work on building sites in Jerusalem and Israel, and in the agricultural sector, thirteen thousand permits bring Palestinian workers into Israel's fields, where pay is far higher than it is for similar and scarce work in the West Bank. In both construction and agriculture, the working conditions for Palestinians are poor: they suffer lax health and safety regulations; undocumented and delayed pay; and very little in terms of job security, sick pay, or holiday leave—and can be paid as little as one-fifth the salary of an Israeli citizen.

One important reason for the maintenance of such low wages and poor working conditions is the presence of a global reserve army of labor. Israel's integration into the global economy has brought different waves of migrant workers, each with different relations to the ethno-nationalist project. For instance, post-1967 saw a marked increase in Mizrahi (Middle Eastern) Jews taking residence in Israel, in part to fill a requirement for low-wage labor as the economy liberalized and the Ashkenazi middle classes grew.[76] The end of the First Intifada and the breakup of the Soviet Union brought an influx of more than one million Russian Jews, which reduced the reliance—and thus bargaining power—of Palestinian labor[77] and (as importantly) facilitated the spatial partition of the Occupied Territories.[78] In addition to Jewish immigration (aliyah), the post-Oslo period saw greater numbers of "guest workers" arrive in Israel from West Africa, South America, and Southeast Asia. From these regions, 240,000 workers arrived between the mid-1990s and 2002, constituting a full 11 percent of Israel's labor force. According to the Organisation for Economic Co-operation and Development, Israel's current bilateral labor agreements are with "Thailand in agriculture (2020), Ukraine in construction (2020), Sri Lanka in home-based caregiving (2019), and the Philippines in the hotel sector (2019). In September 2020, agreements were signed with both Georgia and Nepal for auxiliary workers for work in nursing homes and institutions."[79] These labor pools are readily deported and reimported according to economic conditions; more than 140,000 were deported in the early 2000s as a response to escalating unemployment among Israel's Jewish population.[80] Such "deportability," in effect, "serves to create and sustain a legally vulnerable and precarious labour force of migrants [that] are afraid to lose their jobs" and thus enables employers to drive down wages and conditions for all cross-border workers, those from the Philippines and the West Bank alike.[81]

In recent years, one specific group of imported laborers has gained heightened attention for particularly poor working conditions. Owing to the 2011 (renewed in 2020) Thai–Israel Cooperation on the Placement of Workers, there are now more than thirty thousand Thai migrant laborers in the agricultural sector. The workers have been subject to high-profile investigations by Human Rights Watch (HRW) and the BBC's Thai language news outlet.[82] HRW reports substandard living conditions, working days of up to seventeen hours, as few as four rest days per year, payment below the legal minimum wage, and a lax enforcement of labor laws. Under these conditions, 122 Thai migrant workers died in the period 2011–15, including, the HRW report documents, "Praiwan Seesukha [who] worked in a moshav [farm cooperative] in central Israel, for two years and eight months until his death in May 2013 at the age of 37."[83] Before his death, Seesukha "was planning to return within a couple of months to Thailand, where he had a wife and a son in his late teens and also supported his wife's parents."[84] The BBC's 2018 report—three years later—shows no improvement and highlights the case of Wicha Duangdeegaew, who died at the age of thirty-six after long working days and exposure to harmful pesticides. Focusing on the wife he left behind, the report explains, "She will never know why her husband died, he worked hard all his life because his family is poor."[85] The two cases in the HRW and BBC reports are tragic extremes of labor exploitation and indicative of a broader logic of labor relations whereby the power geometries of Israeli capitalism extend into Thai domestic spaces. Of the thirty thousand workers, 95 percent are male, and most leave families and children at home for the duration of the five-year guest worker permits provided for in the bilateral agreement.[86] Though it is yet to be documented, the articulations with women's labor at home in Thailand are likely to differ only by degree and not by quality with those discussed in chapter 3; the exploitation of cheap male labor in Israel coincides with women's increased domestic burden, from Bethlehem to Bangkok.

None of these spatial connections are tenuous; the exploitability of one rests on that of another—this is the base tenet of wage compression and trade unionism. These relations extend also to the unwaged labor of social reproduction that sustains the workforce and thus its capacity to produce a surplus. Although there is a notable cross-border effect of this from the West Bank through Checkpoint 300, a global frame provides a fuller view of the ways in which Israel's segregated economy both produces and depends on a marginalized, securitized, and ultimately racialized population.[87] Attending to geographies of guest labor agreements, international development, and cross-border care shines new analytical light on both the Palestinian workers who pass through Checkpoint 300 (i.e., the focus of chapter 1) and their families at home (chapter 3) that brings into view other cross-border workers alienated from their homes, even ones as far away as Thailand. If it were not for those migrant agricultural workers, and for their networks of social reproduction at home, their function as a competing and replacement workforce would not enable the wage suppression and scarcity available to Palestinian workers. It goes without saying that this is not to direct culpability at guest workers but simply to explicate how Israel's policy of importing international labor contributes to the control of Palestinian life. Another study would take in the surely significant repercussions for Thai families of labor conditions in Israel in a way that draws together the women and children "left behind" in al-Walaja with those with similar domestic duties in Thailand. The conditions of Palestinian workers who use Checkpoint 300 are *codependent* on those who arrive from Thailand to work in agriculture, and the gendering of the homes of overseas guest workers is very likely parallel with the experiences of Palestinian families. Resources of colonial control are thus drawn from Thailand to Bethlehem, from the peripheries of capitalist empire to the Palestinian core, a space where Israel's advantageous position within skewed global labor markets upholds a system of Indigenous exploitability.

A third important aspect that comes into view through a global frame is the space-making processes that form through international movements of ideology and capital that have enclosed and fortified the Rachel's Tomb compound. Aside from the tomb itself, whose importance to European proto-Zionists is addressed in the previous chapter, the Musallam Building is key to understanding these processes. Built in the 1950s as a residential and commercial unit that was used by three Palestinian brothers for their pottery and restaurant business, the building became a frontier, the final point of Israel's incursion into northern Bethlehem as the wall was erected in the early part of 2005. As each slat was lowered, the Musallam's exclusion eventually became total; its resident businesses were forcibly folded with no recourse to pathways—as Palestinians—of legal contestation or state compensation. The Musallam Building now forms part of the Bnei Rachel complex, one of Israel's more particular settlement projects, which has turned a Palestinian building into a yeshiva and accommodations for Orthodox families. This conversion, like most processes of contemporary Israeli settlement in Palestine, was typically convoluted and is subject to speculation and hearsay in Bethlehem. What is sure is that three brothers owned the building and that two of them sold and emigrated to Chile; the other did not sell. Details of the purchases around who and how are more complicated. A 2012 *Haaretz* investigation[88] into the acquisition of the Musallam Building reported that the purchase was made by a Tzahi Mamo working with a leader of the settler movement, Benny Elon, using a "series of nonprofit organisations and Israeli and American companies" (posing as Arab purchasers)[89] largely funded by a $500,000 investment by Evelyn Haies, a Jewish woman from New York. The investigation conveys something of the convoluted relationships between these parties: "In the first years after 2000, three companies were registered in New Jersey with the aim of purchasing the property. The first, Bnei Rachel, was established by Haies and the American Friends of Beit Orot in Jerusalem, and it paid for the purchase of the first part of the structure. The two other companies, Chearland and Homebred III, which were funded by various individuals, including Haies, paid for the rest of the property. At present, both companies are registered in Delaware."[90]

Perhaps inevitably, a legal dispute followed that led to an agreement between Haies and Beit Orot on shared control of the site. From here, I think, the details of ownership and control are less important than the largely shared visions of these main protagonists. On an ideological level, the claim on the land for exclusively Jewish use is realized through investment from overseas. It is important to emphasize that this is entirely consistent with the form of settler colonialism in Palestine, which is not replicated elsewhere. Unlike in other settler colonies (e.g., Australia, the United States, South Africa), the Zionist movement, from the beginning, did not depend on a "mother country," nor was it driven primarily by economic expansionism. This is not to separate entirely Zionism from European or Enlightenment roots in terms of property rights and enclosure—those logics also underpin Zionist land acquisition[91]—but to situate the current arrangement of space around Checkpoint 300 and Rachel's Tomb within broader patterns of colonialism in Palestine. Uniquely, from the beginning of the twentieth century, without the military or political means to displace the Indigenous population, Zionist settlement plans took shape in capitalist fashion whereby privately owned land was purchased rather than conquered or expropriated. Colonial primitive accumulation thus was premised not on extracting capital from land but rather on acquiring land through capital and turning it over for exclusively Jewish use and inhabitation.[92]

The gradual and purposeful process of purchasing the Musallam Building marks a continuation of this colonial practice, as does its later development into a kollel and, eventually, a yeshiva and attached compound for resident families. Today the compound is home to "11 families, and 24 lovely children living all year round, 24/7," the organization American Friends of Yeshivat Bnei Rachel reports. This specific organization is registered in Brooklyn and is exempt from U.S. taxes because of its charitable activities of funding scholarships for "needy" students at the yeshiva.[93] Numerous other organizations (e.g., Rachel's Children Reclamation Foundation) seem to form and re-form through U.S. registered offices, each using the marketing material of the Bnei Rachel Yeshiva to generate publicity and raise funds. A post during the military assault on Gaza after October 7, 2023, appealed for "life-saving equipment for the Jewish settlement of Bethlehem" and had raised (as of December 2023) $10,000 toward "essential" supplies, including a "security vehicle for the emergency vehicle . . . 3 electric shockers, 5 pepper spray guns, 5 tear gas spray . . . guns, weapons and ammunition."[94] Such is the shopping list of a civilian and religious community on stolen land at a time when the children of Gaza are trapped, starving, or dead. Other appeals over recent years have seen the movement of funds from U.S. private and civil society institutions, which has had the effect of entrenching the Israeli presence at Rachel's Tomb. A 2020 campaign run through Bruriah High School in New Jersey[95]—one whose mission statement is premised on "recognising the historic, national and spiritual significance of the State of Israel . . . [and] develop[ing] an attachment to Israel and its people as well as a sense of shared responsibility and destiny"[96]—raised just under $5,000 for an indoor playground at the

Rachel's Tomb complex. A general campaign to enable Bnei Rachel teachers "to tell the people of Israel about Rachel's legacy in a Zionist spirit" stands (at the time of writing) at $54,000, also comprising mostly donations from the United States. These smaller amounts—of which there are surely many more—are bolstered by more significant sources of capital. For instance, the Kever Rachel Fund Inc., a charity registered in Pikesville, Maryland,[97] reports revenues totaling $1.76 million between 2011 and 2022 that have been used for "protecting, maintaining, and encouraging all Jewish people to visit Rachel's Tomb to ensure a constant Jewish presence at this biblical site."

Edward Said once wrote that to understand the production and maintenance of colonial space, "one must always remember that in America, Palestine and Israel are regarded as local, not foreign policy, matters."[98] In the seamless movement of capital and ideology from numerous states (Delaware, Maryland, New York, New Jersey), in its seemingly organic roots in educational and cultural activities, and in the deeper shared ideologies of settler colonialism and destiny, this sense of proximity to and ownership of Palestinian land delivers multiple spatial materialities. As we critique Israeli colonialism, therefore, room must be given for these wider alliances—ones that act as guarantors of the right to colonize—so that we can fully reckon with, for instance, the U.S.-based campaigners and donors who have played an integral role in reshaping a part of northern Bethlehem.

In this chapter, I have sought to map out the international geographies of Israeli colonialism that come into view through a global frame. Rather than concluding with a rerun of the main points of the chapter, I close with two points. First, the global frame here is necessarily selective in what is brought into view. Left out are multiple other connections between Israel's presence in northern Bethlehem—and Palestine more generally—and global movements of *ideas, objects,* and *people.* I do not here address the hugely important issue of the provenance of raw materials, especially in the proliferation of advanced weaponry, such as drones, that depends on "technologically critical elements" that can be traced back to other sites of occupation or war (e.g., the Democratic Republic of the Congo).[99] Though part of a much wider research project, it must be noted that the networks of production I reference here extend to extraction: the copper, tantalum, cobalt, lithium, tin, and so forth that are mined from the ground at countless sites across the world. I also provide only a partial account of the full range of companies, subsidiaries, and "downstream" suppliers whose labor and profits depend on end users like the Israeli police and military. For sure, there are further articulations with both the management classes and the low-paid workers in components and munitions production facilities. AnyVision/Oosto, Combined Systems, and Elbit are but three examples of vast international operations that are built on low-skilled labor and thus on the exploitation and—indications are—compromised health of munitions factory workers across the world.[100] It is important to recognize that none of that documented in this book would be possible without, for instance, a readily exploitable workforce of factory workers at sites in Leicestershire, Staffordshire, and Kent. And this is just a small number of those made visible by the #ShutDownElbit campaign in the United Kingdom; hundreds of others are implicated across the world. Similarly, I only scratch the surface of "weapons diplomacy" here, especially the notable development in recent years of the Abraham Accords, or the normalization of Israeli relations with a number of powerful Arab states that in 2022 received 24 percent of all "defense exports" from Israel (a 50 percent increase from the time of the Accords).[101] I also provide only a cursory analysis of perhaps the most significant global geography of Israel: its historic and strategic importation of international capital and Jewry that is its existential substance. Without an importable land-purchasing class and citizenry coupled with an exclusion of Indigenous Palestinians, Israel would not be possible. This is beyond all right-minded dispute, and careful and detailed accounts of this are plenty; I would direct any reader interested to know more to consider Palestine through a global frame of a highly selective yet ideologically pliable policy of attracting different populations to live in the State of Israel in a way that continually—and strategically—redefines the state's idea of Jewishness itself.[102]

A second point on which to close is cautionary. The analysis presented here is vulnerable to a contingent argument that places accountability on a nebulous vision of globalization—or global capitalism—that works to exonerate the Israeli state. As prominent commentators have warned, drawing connecting lines between Israeli militarism and militarism elsewhere can bring Israel into a category of "liberal democracy"—that is, alongside allied security states and blocs, the United States, the United Kingdom, the European Union, and so forth—in a way that flattens difference and thus reduces accountability.[103] This is empirically evident in, to give just one example relevant here, AnyVision/Oosto's insistence that its "ethical" stance rests on a liberal worldview: "No one in the world does mass surveillance other than China, and I don't operate in China. I also don't sell in Africa or Russia. We only sell systems to democratic countries with proper governments."[104] My approach here seeks to refute such continuities by naming specific sites and cases that emphasize the particular within the general. Nothing happens without the wider context, but the specific must not be consumed by meta-analysis; the more Checkpoint 300 is recognized as the product and producer of global patterns, the more contestable sites are opened for the types of action we have seen recently against Elbit and other profiteers of colonialism. Rhys Machold makes this point very clearly in his insightful critique of the "laboratory thesis," urging close attention to "*what* travels, *how* the global transmission of Israeli knowhow takes place and the practical consequences of these transactions."[105] By naming and tracing movements of technology and capital, I have sought to retain a specificity within global geometries—the international making of Israel (and vice versa) as it unfolds in a contested field of capitalist innovation. A necessary conclusion is thus that Israel is a nameable and identifiable colonial force among many others, both historical and contemporary, from which it both draws and departs. So although Israel should not be collapsed into broader colonial patterns, we must fully reckon with the fact—perhaps by employing all our capacities of dissonance—that there is an ideological contiguity between the United Kingdom's, the United States', and Europe's support for Israeli colonialism, because it is, after all, a colonialism born of nineteenth-century empire, long-held designs on the "Holy Land," and a shared know-how in displacing and replacing Indigenous populations.[106] Add to this more recently grown alliances among the international right wing, such as between Netanyahu's Likud government and those of Modi and (until 2023) Bolsonaro in India and Brazil, respectively—as well as the various agreements and exchanges with authoritarian Persian Gulf states—and a fuller (and fully dreadful) schema of global support and complicity comes into view. Critique is thus weaker for not recognizing that the colonization of Palestine is an importantly international project, the ills and gains of which are not entirely reducible to the Israeli colonial state.

Such an assertion demands a final political word: a global frame does not deflect criticism of Israel's oppressive security infrastructures, nor does it blur or reduce the object of politics into a vague and inevitable "global capitalism." Setting Checkpoint 300 within the power geometries of globalization, instead, as Doreen Massey has put it, "open[s] up to the very sphere of the political" by "rais[ing] questions of the politics of those geographies and of our relationship to and responsibility for them."[107] By excavating the connections between the restrictions placed on Palestinians' lives and global actors, the possibilities for critique and action are opened to the security hardware companies, policymakers, and national governments whose complicity consists in entrenching Israel's occupation of Palestine. These are importantly *global* trajectories that cannot be overlooked when addressing Israeli colonialism; the challenge is not to allow them to be reduced to helpless opposition to a nebulous form of power or an un-sited mechanism of capitalism or ideology. As I have shown here, the movements of *ideas, objects,* and *people* can be traced and thus obstructed. The spirit of this is carried into the final chapter of this book, in which I draw focus onto Palestinian agency and politics in the re/making of colonial space in and around Checkpoint 300.

6

Re/making Colonial Space

REFUSAL, ADAPTATION, SURVIVAL

> There is a collective understanding that the checkpoints are there to stop life, to destroy livelihoods and education and ultimately defeat the will of a nation. Thus, simply continuing to cross them becomes encoded not as an individual experience of victimisation but as part of a collective act of defiance and ultimately national resistance.
>
> —Rema Hammami, "Qalandiya: Jerusalem's Tora Bora and the Frontiers of Global Inequality"

> When there are times of tear gas and clashes and whatnot . . . we have our emergency situation, we get out, we take care of ourselves, we take care of our artists, but the next day we're back in, we clean up, and we continue.
>
> —Aline Khoury, Dar Yusuf Nasri Jacir for Art and Research on the Hebron Road

In this final chapter, I want to cut across the geographies discussed in this book to address an obvious and important gap in the story so far: Palestinian agency and the possibility of politics. While previous chapters are focused mainly on Israeli attempts at colonial control and their damaging effects on Palestinian life, in this chapter, Palestinian political agency, in both strong and subtle forms, is brought to the fore. This is not an addendum to the story of Checkpoint 300 but a central part that comes through a dual ethics of retaining focus on Israel's pernicious colonial project while recognizing a meaningful counterpolitics, a politics in which Palestinians and solidaristic movements re/make colonial space. It is to this crucial aspect of colonial space that this chapter is dedicated, revisiting Checkpoint 300 and the Hebron Road with close attention to Palestinian practices of maintaining Palestinian cultural, economic, and political presences on the land. In doing so, space is re/made in multiple forms, from the artistic (e.g., the repurposing of security hardware for politicized art) and the adaptive (the evolution of economic endeavor in strangulated space) to the strategic (such as the tactics of coping and countering adopted by West Bank Palestinians in everyday life) and a politics of refusal (to normalize Israeli mechanisms of control in Palestine). Across these examples—which I document in detail here—emerges a topology of specifically *Palestinian* space that teaches us valuable lessons about relations between colonial power and space. We learn that even in and around Checkpoint 300, a space marked by Israel's thanatopolitical logics of governing, Palestinian political life endures and that a part of this is owed to "ungovernability" or that quality of life that simultaneously calls forth and evades attempts to govern. The chapter addresses such abstract notions of power while keeping them fully grounded in empirical examples that point toward a material vision of a decolonized Palestine. The first section surveys examples of Palestinian space-making practices in the checkpoint and its surroundings; the second builds theory around those examples that conceptualizes relations between governing and the governed. The chapter concludes by sketching out the decolonial promise that consists in the endurance of Palestinian political life in the context of Israeli colonial control.

Within, despite, or even *outwith* the colonial space-making practices discussed so far, Palestinian life persists. It even grows as spatio-cide opens ground to reassertions and reconfigurations of cultural, economic, and political expression. Everywhere around the entrance to Checkpoint 300 and along the Hebron Road are signs that Israel's colonial project is incomplete, that it can never be complete precisely because Palestinian agency holds on to or remakes space. For instance, at the southern limit of the boundary between Areas C and A, the Jacir residence (built circa 1880) aside the closed-down hotel is known as Dar Jacir and is now one of Bethlehem's most vibrant centers for arts and research. For the last ten years, Dar Jacir has hosted educational, cultural, and agricultural activities designed "to dream and grapple with our contemporary situation."[1] One such activity, to draw from many examples, is an urban farm on the building's grounds that was created by the permaculture expert Mohammed Saleh to showcase sustainable agricultural methods with which residents of Aida Camp can engage and from which they can learn. Another project is the "traveling kitchen," built by Ayed Arafah and Leila Sansour, who aimed to educate residents in the area about Bethlehem's agricultural heritage "with the goal of 'agri-resistance': growing as a political act and form of remembering."[2] Dar Jacir, in addition, hosts artists and researchers who give performances and public lectures that both grapple with and present something of a solution to the issue of how to foment creative and critical thought in a context of political oppression. At the heart of these activities are questions of lost and reclaimed land, sustenance and survival, control and subversion—and a deeply political commitment to re/making space. For Emily Jacir, the center's director, hosting artists and local residents, especially in a location "at the forefront of clashes between the youth and the Israeli army," is "representative of the local and general Palestinian struggle; it acts as an important reminder that Palestinians have agency and continue to produce and engage with creative processes, even in the direst of situations."[3] In a *New York Times* profile of Dar Jacir, artist-in-residence Dima Srouji describes her work there as "occupying" Palestinian space as "a defender of and cultural actor within that space."[4]

A similar act of respacing is taking shape across the road, aside the Palestinian Heritage Center, where Omar (pseudonym), a Palestinian who grew up in California, has cultivated a lush "secret garden" with an open-air dining area. The greenery is a striking contrast to the grays of the wall and watchtower over the road, and this is precisely the point, according to Omar: "The project is about creating the opposite energy, we need some balance against the tower." He describes his move from California as "partly a sacrifice to keep this area Palestinian." In practical terms, the garden—whose greenness is matched in the West Bank only, tellingly, by gardens in Israeli settlements[5]—is made possible because it straddles Oslo designations: "being across Areas A and C means my water is never cut off." The vision for the garden is to provide a calming antidote to the oppressive atmosphere of its surroundings, a place of Palestinian hospitality that counters Israeli hostility in the area. Across the road and into Aida Camp is Akram al-Wa'ra's former blacksmith's workshop, which has reopened as a popular arts studio and shop. In 2014, as Gaza again was being bombarded and parts of the West Bank came under frequent attack, al-Wa'ra recalls, "I was forced to close my workshop, my only source of income, to protect myself from the tear gas falling down on us." He then attended courses to learn how to clean and recycle spent tear gas cannisters and eventually repurposed his smithery tools to produce arts and crafts with the military metals gathered from around the wall. Al-Wa'ra has claimed in interviews with journalists that through his modified line of work, he has "transform[ed] the Israeli killing tool into antiques that carry the message of our people, and replaced it with artifacts that make people happy and convey reassurance and peace instead of fear and killing."[6]

Back at the intersection and the by now familiar Sansur Building, a Jerusalemite businessperson is in the process (at the time of writing) of renovating for a cultural center directly under the watchtower. The building is significant—as I discuss in chapter 4—because of its proximity, and on the upper floors, in a symbolic reversal of Israel's surveillance regime, one can peer into the watchtower through one-way glass and observe soldiers as they look down on the intersection below. Visiting this building is one of the most vivid memories of the research; the urban intimacy between colonizer and colonized is striking. Though the watchtower is designed to look down on Palestinians, such are the politics of verticality in security that, at this unique site, Palestinians are able to peer downward into military infrastructure and the yeshiva compound beyond (Figure 33). The cultural center will, to use the new owner's words, "build bridges of peace" by establishing a space for Palestinian cultural expression specifically here: "I wanted this place *because* it's in Area C. . . . We want to show that we're human and to live in dignity . . . this is the perfect place to do that." These new initiatives complement more established cultural institutions in the area, such as Wi'am on the intersection (see chapter 4) and the Arab Educational Institute (AEI; discussed later) closer to the checkpoint, both of which provide educational programs that aim to empower Palestinians and provide critical materials for international visitors.[7]

This second focus is important because the area has become a hot spot for solidarity tourism, which in its more critical iterations performs a mind-opening pedagogical role for international visitors to Palestine. A number of large hotels and smaller guesthouses in the area cater mainly to pilgrims, who tend not to visit "political" sites (though they are all political, of course), but others—notably, the Anastas Walled-In guesthouse and the Walled Off Hotel—present a highly politicized account of Israeli colonialism (on these hotels, see chapter 4). There is, in addition, as in many other parts of Palestine (especially Jerusalem and Hebron), a ready army of (qualified or not)

FIGURE 32. The secret garden close to the wall. Photograph by Nadir Mauge.

FIGURE 33. View from the new cultural center at the Sansur Building. Photograph by Nadir Mauge.

tour guides who will walk groups or individuals around sites for a fee. This economy is one of both necessity and opportunity: a need to generate income in a limited labor market and a chance to provide a Palestinian view of life under Israeli colonial rule, often placing visitors in situations that expose Israel's discriminatory security regime. In her detailed ethnography of solidarity tourism, Jenny Kelly recounts the following, which occurred at Checkpoint 300:

> Here, organisers make sure that tourists understand that their Palestinian guide, who has facilitated their movement around the Bethlehem area thus far, cannot go with them. Tourists walk through the labyrinthine corrals of the checkpoint and wave their international passports in front of the bulletproof glass while the Palestinians next to them have to show their wrinkled permits and ID cards and place their fingers in the biometric scanner. Armed teenagers serving in the Israeli military sit behind the bulletproof glass or pace above and around the tourists and workers corralled within the walls of the checkpoint. Palestinian workers often hurriedly try to get through, while tourists sometimes slow down the process, marvelling at the cage they—only momentarily— find themselves in. . . . Palestinians subject to Israeli rule crossing the checkpoint know that their entry is contingent on permits and the arbitrary permission granted by the soldier, a humiliation further exacerbated by the presence of tourists, who have unfet- tered access to all those spaces. This experience of the checkpoint demonstrates the ambivalent role of the solidarity tourist as one who both challenges and affirms racial and spatial inequalities in Palestine.[8]

For Kelly, this and other activities on solidarity tours constitute a "fraught anticolonial strategy" that narrates colonialism on Palestinian terms by putting space to work toward growing international solidarity and activism.[9] In this particular case, tourists are "invited to witness" Checkpoint 300, then "invited to go home," carrying a responsibility to challenge international complicity in the reproduction of the Israeli colonial state. I cite Kelly's account at length because it is elegantly written and theorized and also because it strongly resonates with my own experiences of political tours of Bethlehem over the last de- cade, where a typical itinerary passes through much of the geography

FIGURE 34. One of Bethlehem's most lucid political activists and tour guides, Baha. Photograph by Nadir Mauge.

described in chapter 4, emphasizing stories of dispossession, colonial violence, and resistance. Guides point out Rachel's Tomb (recalling also that it is known to many as Bilal bin Rabah Mosque) and the Mus-allam Building, the shuttered shops and unfinished buildings, giving accounts of colonial spacio-cide while simultaneously breathing new life into the space, mobilizing it as pedagogical space. This is aided by a complementing practice of adding printed text and infographics to buildings, particularly to the wall, that provide information to visitors with or without a guide. An important initiative in this respect is the AEI's Wall Museum, "a series of posters with true stories written by Palestinian women. The stories of suffering and oppression as well as 'sumud' (steadfastness or resilience), inner strength and cultural identity are here to bring out the truth of Palestinian life, which this wall tries to hide and kill." The museum now comprises 270 exhibits (posters) that bring contexts and testimonies to visitors on many different themes. Some posters are aimed at providing the most basic information to newer visitors: "Queuing: During weekly early mornings, Palestinian workers make long queues in front of Checkpoint 300 located in occupied territory"; "Occupation: This wider Hebron Rd, and also other streets along the Wall, are Area C, under direct Israeli military occupation." Others give details of different aspects of life under colonial military rule: house demolition, nighttime military raids, Israeli prisons, land confiscation, bureaucratic restrictions, and martyrdom.[10] This is all a project, Fuad (pseudonym) at the AEI explains, of "trying to own the space," wresting it both from the Israeli state and also from the artists (international and Palestinian) who have used the wall as a canvas in the last two decades: "Our project is not to beautify the Wall, not to accept it, but to re-make it as a space of information—one where people can learn about life under occupation."

The reference to beautification takes aim at the famous artworks and graffiti that cover the Bethlehem side of the wall around the Rachel's Tomb compound. They are painted, repainted, and modified by a range of Palestinian and international artists, as well as by tourists and activists. Thousands of contributions are now present on the wall, ranging from simple statements of solidarity from different parts of the world to pasted-on infographics, advertisements for taxis and restaurants, and large artworks that commemorate prominent Palestinian figures like Shireen Abu Akleh, Leila Khaled, and Ahed Tamimi. Many works are pointedly political, such as those painted by the Palestinian artist Taqieddin Sabatin: an image of Rouzan al-Najjar, a paramedic who was killed on June 1, 2018, by an Israeli sniper during the Great March of Return in Gaza, and one of Iyad Hallaq, an autistic man who was unarmed and shot dead by Israeli police in Jerusalem on May 30, 2020—whose face is flanked by a call for international solidarity: "Not only Floyd, Iyad Hallaq too" (a reference to George Floyd and the Black Lives Matter movement). Other works, such as the well-known ones by the U.K.-based artist Banksy and the now-famous "Make Hummus Not Walls" graffito by the Palestinian artist known as Issa, are characterized by a whimsical postmodern politics of irony and wordplay that, nonetheless, takes an aesthetic position that can be read (at least superficially) as variously anticapitalist, anti-imperialist, and anticolonial. There is also a proliferation of Instagram-influenced pastiche, such as the pieces by the Australian meme artist Lushsux, which would not be worth mentioning but for their (undue) prominence on the wall and their vacuous politics that manage to be both anti-Semitic and demeaning to Palestinians.

An expansive body of scholarly commentary on the various art-works ranges from the broadly celebratory, for instance, that they transform a "traumascape" into a "resistancescape,"[11] to more critical views of international appropriation, normalization, and depoliticiza-tion. Writing in *Mondoweiss,* Tamara Nassar contends that the works, especially those by non-Palestinians, make Palestinian suffering an "exhibit to a very specific class of tourists who are able to enter the West Bank . . . essentially reproducing the image of struggle in land-scape and completely robbing it of its ability to speak for itself."[12] I would not argue against this but would add that this critique applies only to that which is most prominent to the (often Western) eyes that produce and consume online photo galleries of headline works (e.g., those by Banksy and Lushsux, even as their respective politics are importantly different). For instance, a proliferation of resistance slo-gans (written mostly in the collective grammar of "we") that are re-peated along the wall and have been cataloged by Ibrahim Fraihat and Hamid Dabash—"We are here to stay," "We die standing and will not kneel," and, most explicitly in a project of reclaiming narrative space, "We want to scream and break this wall of silence"—"effectively detail the vocabulary of what sustains Palestinians' self-consciousnesses as a people."[13] In addition, an active and evolving tagging and defacing movement (re)politicizes existing work. The "Make Hummus Not Walls" graffito, one that is now reproduced on "alternative" souvenirs in Palestine and internationally, was defaced by the original artist him-self with the words "welcome to the shopping mall" as a reaction to the opening of the Walled Off Hotel and "growing concern over the small but dangerous industry of commercialising apartheid, and the fear that it might have a vested interest in actually maintaining the wall."[14] On a Lushsux play on an internet meme that attributes Nelson Mandela quotes to the actor Morgan Freeman—the racial politics of which are symptomatic of that artist's problematic outputs—Palestinian activist-defacers wrote over in red Arabic text "Palestine is not a draw-ing board" (Figure 35). They also tagged other Lushsux works with "alt-right propaganda," referencing his tendency to reproduce alt-right memes in his images. These interventions, as the visual anthropolo-gist Connie Gagliardi has argued, claw back ownership over narration; they are a "testament to a moment of collective Palestinian reckoning with the force of the Wall's fetish-power in Bethlehem."[15]

FIGURE 35. "Palestine is not a drawing board." Photograph by Connie Gagliardi.

FIGURE 36. Wall images on a (less touristic) section across from Aida Camp. Photograph by Nadir Mauge.

A less overtly politicized but no less important aspect of Palestinian space making around the checkpoint is the emergence of an adaptive economy that mitigates (and occasionally thrives on) urban spacio-cide in northern Bethlehem. In addition to the more creative economies of Dar Jacir and Omar's secret garden, these changes in the commercial landscape of the area are born of necessity and opportunity created by closure and movement restrictions. As discussed in chapter 4, a now mature yet still largely informal economy of vendors and transportation has formed around the entrance to Checkpoint 300, one whose rhythms and goods are tied to commuter schedules and exigencies and whose viability depends on the tax gray zone of Area C. For some, being part of this economy is a practice of getting by in pronouncedly precarious conditions, as it is for Abed Abu Shiera, a coffee seller who has served workers at the checkpoint's entrance for more than ten years: "My main source of income is here, I have seven children and my wife, they all need to live off this. . . . This is my job, I don't have an alternative, the workers know me, I know them. I got used to this."[16] For others, such as the fruit and vegetable vendors, the choke point created here presents a critical mass of potential custom whose volume coincides with mealtimes in a space where standing permits and fees are not applicable, as they are in the center of Bethlehem and in Area A in general (Figure 37).

The Christmas Restaurant, a few meters down the Hebron Road, has also adapted: it might have lost its middle-class Sunday afternoon clientele, but it now serves "faster" food for checkpoint commuters and for those who work in the checkpoint economy. Another restaurant, the Bahamas Seafood Restaurant, attracted international attention when its owner, Joseph Hazboun, went so far as to paint the menu on the wall and even projected football matches onto it during the men's football World Cup in 2010. "They put up this wall thinking they can suffocate us, but we are not going to suffocate—we are determined to make something nice out of this," Hazboun told a BBC reporter.[17] Owners of two of the large villas at the top of the street (the Kawas house, closest to the checkpoint, and another across from the AEI that belongs to the Anastas family) have paved over approximately seven dunams of olive groves to create space for parking. A porta cabin at the entrance to these parking spaces houses the keys of those who park a car before crossing Checkpoint 300 at a cost of fifteen shekels per day (Figures 38 and 39). If we leave aside for a moment the important fact that spacio-cide connects to ecocide in this development, this is an important repurposing of space according to the needs of Palestinians, even within quite narrow parameters.

Helga Tawil-Souri has argued that such activities and developments indicate an "ever-unfolding" dialectical colonial struggle in which the Israeli state builds and continually modifies checkpoints and terminals and "Palestinians [turn] the Israeli-created landscape of checkpoints into a battlefield where everyday life continues to exist."[18] Those who work around the checkpoint may not have "overthrown the checkpoint, but they are contesting it and recreating it as a centre rather than a 'boundary.'"[19] Rema Hammami describes similar economic forms at the Surda Checkpoint (between Ramallah and Birzeit) as the production of a "liminal zone" that has taken "men [workers around the checkpoint] from the margins and allowed them a role that [is] fundamentally and publicly important for the entire society's survival" by turning "a source of dispossession into a living."[20]

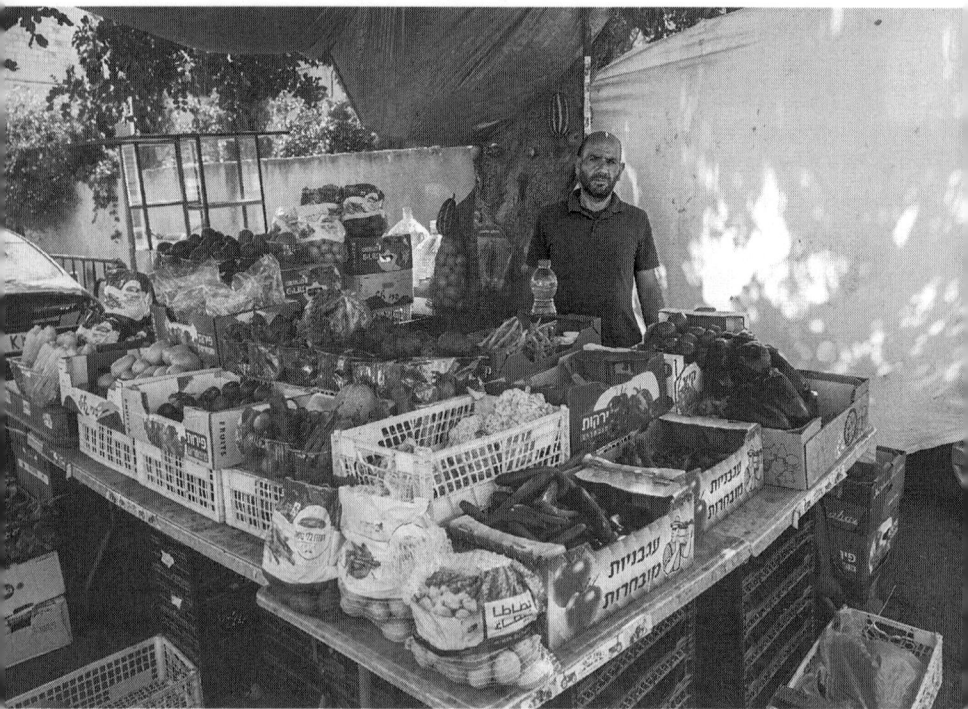

FIGURE 37. Fruit and vegetable stands outside Checkpoint 300. Photograph by Nadir Mauge.

FIGURE 38. Parking lot close to Checkpoint 300. Photograph by Nadir Mauge.

FIGURE 39. Keys at the lot attendant's desk. Photograph by Nadir Mauge.

Hammami makes the following estimation: "There were roughly 25 porters, 18 horse carriage drivers, as many as 400 transit vans, as well as another 30 small taxis working at Surda. Added to this were the peddlers, whose numbers averaged about 30 in good weather, and rose to as many as 70 during the last Ramadan. In sum . . . as many as 540 people made a living from this checkpoint on any given day."[21] Both Tawil-Souri and Hammami caution against celebratory or normalizing accounts of this aspect of checkpoints yet stress that Palestinian life—social, economic, cultural, religious, political—continues; sometimes diminished, often adapted, yet always agential, the colonized population is central to colonial space-making processes. This tells us, at the very least, that analyses of colonial power must extend to the political agency of the colonized and that spatial struggle is never resolved. Indeed, it might be said that there is an *ungovernable* aspect to Palestinian persistence that remakes space as *Palestinian*: "Through both necessity and ingenuity, [Palestinians reclaim] the space of the checkpoint from being purely a site of oppression and brutality into one where livelihood, social life and even sociability could be recovered," in Hammami's words.[22]

This political agency is carried also by many who pass through or around the checkpoint. It is important here not to disclose specific tactics that are shared in confidence, but a survey of existing literature on the strategies used by Palestinians in negotiating checkpoints and the wall gives a clear idea of how movement restrictions are countered. This is another key theme of Hammami's work on checkpoints, where she writes of the ways that Palestinians adopt normalizing narratives as a psychological coping strategy against Israeli violence to enable regular passage through checkpoints. In the face of a mechanism that makes mobility "arbitrary, chaotic, and uncertain," some Palestinians conceptualize political violence as *aadi* or "normal," a countermechanism that evades the checkpoints' (and soldiers') capacities of subjectivization as a mode of "getting by."[23] This is, according to Hammami, a deeply self-conscious strategy of "reconstitut[ing] agentic selves capable of creating a liveable world within an on-going structure of colonial violence."[24] Nadera Shalhoub-Kevorkian has similarly documented the tactics that young people use to confuse or distract checkpoint staff, recounting an array of behaviors that counter or re-form colonial power in ways that ease crossings, or at least make them more bearable.[25] Writing of her own experiences of checkpoints, Shalhoub-Kevorkian portrays a subtle but purposeful persistence of Palestinian agency, for instance, on one occasion, with a group of women at a checkpoint near Esaweyyeh in Jerusalem: "We communicated to each other without words, through facial and hand gestures, and eyes that were asking 'When will this uncertainty be over?' In silence we helped each other to find our place within the confusion of militarised space as we were forced to co-operate with the soldiers. . . . Our bodies were used to draw lines between men and women and also between the ones with power—the soldiers—and those lacking it—us Palestinians; but our minds and souls created a new kind of solidarity—a collective marginality that survived the coldness of the space and weather."[26] Resistance comes in many forms, and this is a powerfully embodied yet understated mode of feminist "getting by" that makes spatial contestations; it effects Palestinian mobility, presence on the land, and even agency in the supposedly Israeli sovereign space of the checkpoint itself, as Shalhoub-Kevorkian concludes, "by reappropriating our oppression and aligning our oppositional energies and powers to create new patterns of survival."[27]

It is also important to note a politicized move among those who decide not to cross, either by staying in place or by opening networks that bypass checkpoints. On the latter, since the building of the wall and the network of checkpoints, Palestinian taxi and minibus drivers have sought to circumvent blockages in mobility, charging fees to navigate the hills around Jerusalem. This practice originated around Qalandia Checkpoint but spread through the West Bank in the mid-2000s and was nicknamed "Tora Bora," in reference to the shared evasive function of a quarry close to Qalandia and the cave complex in Afghanistan used by the Mujahidin and later by Osama bin Laden. For every new section of the wall, the routes changed, taking new roads and new risks to move Palestinians from one part of Palestine to another, thus circumventing Israeli organization of space. Once the quarry was closed off, a road via Rafaat, a village that borders Qalandia, was used; when that was blocked, more circuitous routes were devised, all in the name of holding on to the right to move. By "refusing to be imprisoned behind physical barricades, hiking and driving through anything to 'get there,'" Helga Tawil-Souri writes of the "Tora Bora method": "Movement becomes central in the resistance against the spatial manifestation of Israeli domination."[28] Taxi drivers, like in many parts of the world, are also key sources of up-to-date and localized information that can be used to move around with a lower profile, for instance, where people want to cross with less chance of detection. A taxi driver who uses checkpoints between Jerusalem and Bethlehem daily explained to me, "This checkpoint is a private one, it's easy to pass here [in a car] because they don't even look so if I have time to drive this way, I do"; a second one he described as "a lot more difficult" but with the important detail that "there was a squad change [military staff rotation] so for the next three months there is a new commander and we don't know how it will be." At a third checkpoint, he recounted, "They know me here and even with passengers they never check anything." In this case, the arbitrary and privatized aspects of security infrastructure are known and turned against the project of restricting movement; in the words of that particular taxi driver, "there is usually a way—and we find it."

Then there are those who stay in place, not (only) because their movement is restricted but out of a principle of not recognizing the right of the Israeli state to control Palestinian mobilities. This is particularly true among activists in Bethlehem who refuse to apply for a permit because of the normalizing function of engaging with Israeli bureaucracy in Palestine. A friend in Beit Sahour once told me, "If I apply for a permit I legitimise the right of Israel to decide, I legitimise the racist regime that allows a settler—probably from Brooklyn or Russia or France—to travel around this place freely while I have to go through processes just to visit Jerusalem, where my family is from." It cannot be said that this view is widespread, but it is not unusual that people take such a stance, with a particular objection to the underlying racist logic that Palestinians are automatically subjects of suspicion who must prove innocence to the colonizer: "It is intentionally humiliating to make people declare they are not terrorists just so they can go to work or pray or visit family." While there is a certain privilege to such an ethical stance, for instance, not having dependents or having connections to creative industries and remote working, a political stance of refusal is one that should also be recognized as a counter to Israeli spatial control. Staying in place in this case is not merely passive immobility but a political choice to evade the common tactics of limited recognition and conditional integration of settler states.[29] In more practical and visible terms, certain circles of activists remain, and that remaining involves a level of underemployment and precarity: there is a vibrant leftist and artistic scene in Bethlehem and its adjacent villages, Beit Jala and Beit Sahour. Dar Jacir is just one key part of this scene—others are the Citadel in Beit Sahour and the Singer Café in Beit Jala—where Palestinians gather, often also with internationals, to create, collaborate, debate, organize, and educate around issues to do with life in the context of Israeli colonial rule. These are sites, therefore, where refusal to move precipitates a refusal to succumb to Israeli space-making tactics; attempts at spacio-cide are met with the vibrancy of Palestinians' creative and political life.

This survey of the persistence of Palestinian life in and around Checkpoint 300 is instructive on the relations of space and colonial power. It shows that even against a technologically advanced, entrenched, and violent spatial ordering, control over the colonized population is always incomplete. On one hand, this is a fairly simple observation; on the other, it has important implications for the ways in which we understand not only Palestinian political agency but also the dynamics of colonial power more generally. In this final section of the chapter—and final substantial section of the book—I want to bring together some threads with the account of Palestinian life here to build critical interventions into notions of colonial power, governing, and governability. I first set what is detailed earlier in a consideration of spatial exception, spacio-cide, or the politics of death ("thanatopolitics"), which are key theoretical frameworks for explicating the ways that Israeli security infrastructure organizes Palestinian space, before then zooming out to address a more fundamental conceptualization of governing and (un)governable life. As I show, this intervention has important implications for our understandings of colonial power in Palestine and beyond.

   An important starting point is to develop an analytic of the logics of Israeli colonialism without transposing those logics onto a theory of power. What I mean by this, straightforwardly, is that a spacio-cidal or thanatopolitical force does not—even *cannot*—produce a *total* spacio-cide or *totalizing* politics of death. By "politics of death," I refer both to Giorgio Agamben's account of "thanatopolitics"[30] and to Achille Mbembe's "necropolitics,"[31] widely cited in the study of Palestine for their insight into the ways modern states—and especially colonial states, in Mbembe's case—mobilize exposure to death in the (re)production of state power, and thus in complementing contrast to Michel Foucault's notion of biopolitics (the politics of life).[32]

Throughout this book, these exegeses on power are the tempting interpretive frames that would set Israeli colonialism in northern Bethlehem within a broader geography of the liberal state and the erosion
of protective mechanisms availed to (non)citizen-subjects. It is evi-
dently the case that a thanatopolitical logic of exception consists in
the ways that legal rights are withheld from Palestinians at Checkpoint 300 (and also in the West Bank more generally), yet the de facto
suspension of law remains within the juridical domain of the state. To
readers of Agamben, this spatiolegal arrangement will appear as a paradigmatic "state of exception," whereby sovereign power is expressed
by the suspension of the law within sovereign space to produce a legal
"threshold" between "inclusion and exclusion."[33] In this spatial modality of state power, in the maintenance of total control without the
encumbering deference to (its own) legal safeguards, the sovereign
produces "bare life" (or what the Greeks termed *zoē*) as distinct from
communal or political life *(bios)*, a distinction that is marked by the
exposure to the punitive mechanisms of state power without recourse
to any of its protective functions. Turning to Roman law, the figure
Agamben evokes as bare life, the subject within exception, is *homo
sacer* (sacred man), who is "included in the juridical order solely in the
form of its exclusion (that is, of its capacity to be killed)."[34]

Given the absoluteness of Israel's position as sovereign decision
maker, the exceptional juridical status of the Palestinian territories it
occupies, and the impunity with which Palestinians are incarcerated,
exiled, and killed, thanatopolitics has become a persuasive conceptual
framework to take to Palestine generally and checkpoints specifically.[35]
In the oppressive checkpoint or depressed borderlands around it, a
thanatopolitical framework enables a clearer articulation of the ways
in which space can be sequestered without responsibility and in which
Palestinians are denied rights—or are legally dehumanized, reduced
to "bare life" or *zoē*—such that harm can be distributed with impunity. This is all part of Israel's wider thanatopolitical "management of
death and destruction," writes the Palestinian sociologist Honaida
Ghanim, by which Palestinians "are exposed to the continual threat of
death that becomes a permanent shadow accompanying them. Death is
just on hold again and again, from moment to moment."[36] At the wall,
and at the checkpoint specifically, a thanatopolitical frame enables an
examination of a "genuine space of exception: a sovereign act of land
appropriation and delimitation produced via a strategy of inclusive ex-

clusion" and a vocabulary to articulate the ways that this spatial strategy renders Palestinians an "urban *homo sacer* . . . the paradigm of an exceptional production of space by decree—a member of a largely waste, invisible, poor marginalised subpopulation whose rights are potentially suspended."[37] However, an important qualification is needed, one that places limits on the drive of theory in such conclusions. A focus on sovereign decision and a state politics of death tells us only of *attempts* to govern, *designs* on control—the logics of state power. It does not guarantee that subjects are produced through that logic; that they appear "invisible" or "waste" is quite probably owed to an analytical frame not suited to (or indeed never intended for[38]) assumptions around a corresponding sociological—locatable, nameable, actually existing—figure of *homo sacer*. All of this is to say that the logics of state power cannot be coterminous with a theory of power; as we see around Checkpoint 300 and the Hebron Road, amid an extensive architecture of colonial control, Palestinian communal life persists within exception.

With this corrective, something of a qualified account of spatial exception can be developed from northern Bethlehem. It is surely significant that inside the checkpoint facility, Palestinians' subordination to sovereign decision, a looming potential of banishment, and the threat of corporeal violence indicate, very strongly, a stripping away of Palestinian political life *(bios)*. It is also significant that the area around the checkpoint is transformed into something of an urban wasteland precisely because it is both claimed and abandoned by the colonial state with the result that essential services, planning, and policing are absent, exposing the resident population to elevated threats of harm without recourse to mechanisms of protection. But it is as significant that Palestinians are able to mitigate threats of violence inside the checkpoint and that urban life endures, and even thrives in some spaces. In the "dead" zones of spacio-cide springs new life: a profitable parking lot, a vibrant cultural center, an entire class of checkpoint vendors whose livelihoods grow out of a mobility bottleneck. Inside the checkpoint, the thanatopoliticial denial of rights and communicability is countered by often subtle but nonetheless agential strategies of coping, distracting, or camaraderie. Political agency in this sense is immanent to the lives and activities of those who are subjected to the logics of exception without ever being completely subsumed by it. Palestinian political and social life persists; Israeli processes of spatial control are incomplete—and there are no signs that it ever *can* be complete.

Without lingering too long on the idea of exception and connected concepts of bare life and *homo sacer,* there is a broader lesson here. In the final analysis, there is a clear delineation between state practices of control and the lived lives of those for whom state control is to be negotiated, evaded. Or if not evaded, state control is a *response* to the fact of politics and sociality and is thus a *retroactive* formation around a complex of inherently unknowable or unpredictable forms of life. What cannot be known or predicted cannot be governed, and it is this *ungovernability* that holds the key to a fuller understanding of power in this and other contexts. At first cut, then, we are led to an explication of conceptual limits and a skepticism toward totalizing accounts of power (and accounts of totalizing power). This is not to say that we cannot develop sophisticated understandings of state expressions of power, but it is to caution against consequential claims of the ways that state mechanisms "touch the ground." Clear here, at and around Checkpoint 300, is that "lived space" emerges in tension with "bare space"[39] via collective politics within exception that, to draw on Hammami's words once more, "*make liveable lives* against and in resistance to its necropolitical logics."[40] Crucial for a wider discussion is that a thanatopolitical frame enables an understanding of the power of the state to mobilize death to the ends of governing yet struggles to address that which emerges alongside and exceeds it, such as a willful "show that we're human" or a resilient economy of necessity: "I have seven children and my wife, they all need to live off this." These Palestinian perspectives challenge us to think dually: of simultaneously threatened yet durable political agencies; of both an awesome state power and an element of life that remains ungovernable; and, ultimately, of a never-fixed tension between the governing and the governed.

Within this tension lies a truth about power that is frequently overlooked or turned to only as an appended unit of analysis. In the works of Foucault, perhaps the person who has taught us most about the workings of power,[41] there is a consistent corrective to recall that "where there is power, there is resistance";[42] "it is not that life has been totally integrated into techniques that govern and administer it; it constantly escapes them."[43] Though of course Foucault was one of the great students of the state and its institutions (as is Agamben, who sees his project as a "completion" of Foucault's[44]), his conclusions were never drawn by state-centrism: "Power is not monolithic. It is never entirely controlled from a certain point of view by a certain number of people. At every moment it is in play in little singular struggles, with local reversals, regional defeats and victories, provisional revenges."[45] It is this corrective that both precedes and illuminates this chapter, where a state's attempt to be monolithic is undermined by local reversals and provisional revenges. But what do sites of "constant escape" tell us about the ways we can conceptualize relations between the colonizer and the colonized? Given that that relation is one of governing, there is much to be learned about the abilities, possibilities, and limits of attempts to govern and the constitutive roles of "the governed." Under a regime of colonial governing, as is clear from this chapter's account of Checkpoint 300 and its surroundings, an unreachable element of Palestinian life is produced or maintained by either a *responsive* counterforce (e.g., resistance, activism) or a *preceding* condition of life that is irrecuperable. In less abstract terms, attempts to govern are always precisely *attempts* and, as such, are met with both that which resists and that which it tries to "fix" in the first place: *governing is always necessarily at a step behind the object of governing*. In this sense, the object or target of governing is the existential condition of governing itself, and this conditional relationship has implications for the ways we understand colonial power.

Whatever the investments of colonial power—in terms of capital, infrastructure, bureaucracy, violence, or ideology—the targeted population breathes life into spaces of legal exception, deploys evasive and distracting tactics inside the checkpoint, and sustains cultural expression against a dehumanizing force. These counters reveal the failure of governing's pretensions to control in complete form. Although this can be read as a "failure" of state or colonial power, an emphasis can also be placed on the incapacity to grasp that which always *exceeds* and remains beyond the claims of governing: ungovernable life. As an idea, ungovernability is something of a slippery concept that has been instrumentalized to various nefarious ends, most obviously as a rationale of governing that justifies political and colonial interventions under the pretext of "ungovernable" territories and populations. This iteration of ungovernability is worth pausing with for a moment: it is an underlying logic of a performative discourse from the British Parliament and Colonial Office on the "Palestine Problem"[46] in which the "Arab States" were figured as "absolutely free from control," whose people "have not for hundreds of years had control of these States. . . . ['The Arabs'] are not a coherent people, they are tribal," as Prime Minister David Lloyd George put it in 1921.[47]

Contemporaneously and in concert, a key rhetoric of the Zionist

Organization was to accentuate the trope of Palestine as a land "free from control," as is evident from Chaim Weizmann's 1918 correspondence with the British foreign secretary Arthur Balfour, in which he warns of the "treacherous nature of the Arab" and that "the Arabs have to be 'nursed' lest they should stab the Army in the back."[48] Weizmann repeats over and over that "the Arabs" are given to treachery and therefore must be governed ("nursed") most assertively. This version of ungovernability was addressed via the British Mandate for Palestine (1918–48), whose advanced colonial structures of government would govern a population that was, in the eyes of the League of Nations, "not yet able to stand by themselves under the strenuous conditions of the modern world."[49] Checkpoint 300 is a contemporary product of this logic, not only by way of historical and material trajectories of spatial division in Palestine but also as a reinvigorated rationale for managing an "ungovernable" population. Israel's entire infrastructure of security and surveillance is premised on a set of justifications that renders Palestinians a constant security threat where the "security fence" (West Bank wall), "check terminals" (checkpoints), and the vast permit bureaucracy are built, to use the words of the Israel Ministry of Foreign Affairs, for one specific reason: "It is Palestinian terrorism . . . that is the threat and the catalyst of conflict in the region. Terrorism has forced Israel to take the defensive step of building an anti-terrorist fence."[50]

But while Israel imagines the ungovernable as "the masked Arab, the Kufiyya, the stone-throwing Palestinian," as Edward Said put it,[51] the more readily observable version of ungovernability on the ground is something very different and politically consequential. In the counters, negotiations, refusals, distractions, persistence, adaptation, and so forth lies a deeper revelation in the relations between governing and ungovernable life. Rather than a condition of governing (i.e., "governing is necessary because of ungovernability"), a subtle but consequential reformulation is made necessary to do with the longevity and endurance of Palestinian life before and under Israeli colonialism. In Agamben's writing on the topic, which should be considered here as separate to his works on thanatopolitics, he locates ungovernability "beyond states of domination and power relations,"[52] where in the governmental processes of "subjectification" there necessarily remains an ungovernable irreducibility that constitutes "the beginning and, at the same time, the *vanishing point* of every politics."[53] Though I am keen not to be tethered too tightly to European political philosophy, or to weigh down a vibrant politicized site with abstractions, this can form an important critical intervention. For Agamben, an analytical attachment to the functioning of the state's mechanisms of governing forecloses the potential of a "zone of ethics entirely subtracted from strategic relationships, of an *ungovernable* that is situated beyond states of domination and power relations."[54] From here, much of that documented in the first section of this chapter is theoretically unlocked: the ungovernability of life is revealed as that which exceeds aims to govern; it is a "vanishing point," because, ultimately, ungovernability will never be entirely subsumed within formations of power. Here ungovernability is not *produced* discursively (for instance, in the Arab figure evoked by Said), it is not something that gains *form* in governing but something that remains on the point of *excess*. Ungovernability is, instead, a condition that *exceeds* mechanisms of control, importantly also *preceding* them to the extent of forming their irresolvable source of impotency and incapacity.[55]

To bring us back from abstraction, evident in the preceding account is a back-and-forth in which the vast asymmetries that constitute colonial state power—access to resources, the permissibility of mobility, military violence with impunity, the sequestering of Indigenous land—remain incapable of fulfilling Israel's designs on total domination. Faced with an architecture of awesome physical barriers and surveillance, mobility is not entirely subordinated but is supplemented by tactics of distraction and bypassing; against the "dead-zoning" of the areas around the checkpoint, cultural and economic life emerges renewed, without the benefits of municipal services but also free of the municipality's regulation and taxation. These apparently resistant counters to colonial power, crucially (and aside from debates around "resistance" as an idea and practice), coincide with a community's base needs for sociality, for sustenance—for survival. Seen from those needs, the entire security architecture put in place by Israel appears quite differently: as an after-the-fact response to the activities (mobility, exchange, consumption) that fulfill the conditions for survival. The checkpoint can thus be read with fidelity to conditions on the ground as an expression of power that responds to life's inherent vulnerability to, in the first instance, physical and mental harm and, more subtly in the second (and in a particular order), stasis, isolation, hunger, malnutrition, starvation. Palestinian responses, in turn, express not only courage or a certain ingenuity (it is not my interest to buttress or glorify responsive "resistance") but—again in quite base terms—the need to survive and sustain life against the harm to which it is exposed. Sustaining life against harm is thus not merely reactive but the root of an ungovernability that always remains beyond the grasp of power and thus always exceeds it. It is in this way that Palestinian life *(and all life)* remains irreducible to techniques of control. Accepting of this, once we note the incapacity of power to grasp the ungovernable life that always *exceeds* it—that is, via a focus on what power *does* or *attempts*—there can be a full reckoning with that which *precedes* power and thus that to which it can only be an *inadequate response*: the life that is already there, exposed and vulnerable.

To conclude, I want to address the signs and possibilities of decolonized space around Checkpoint 300. An important step in doing so is to take what we are witness to "on the ground" as instructive to our examination of colonial power. This brings us to an understanding of power that is not reduced to cycles of domination–resistance but instead consists in life and spaces of living as always irreducible to governing. As we have seen, this stands in even the most oppressive conditions: in the hypermilitarized and juridical exception that Israel has created in northern Bethlehem. The prospect of decolonized space appears remote when seen through these colonial mechanisms of control, yet that Palestinians are able to respatialize, in whatever form, and within sometimes the narrowest of parameters, tells us of an "otherwise." This goes beyond the metaphor of, for example, an aesthetics of solidarity in the artworks on the wall or the ideals of activism in solidarity tourism and toward a materiality of practice that realizes *(makes real)* that "this is Palestinian land where Palestinian life *goes on.*" It matters, ethically and politically, that against a regime of control and dehumanization, people remain and reproduce life (e.g., most literally in the "agriresistance" initiative) with an insistence that "we want to show that we're human and to live in dignity." This is just one example of many that gesture toward a decolonial praxis of living that is already and always prevalent among Palestinians under Israeli rule.

For interpretive practices, we are thus called on to modify theoretical approaches, recognizing the provenance of conceptual frameworks and explicating analytical limits so as not to foreclose a decolonial politics. On the level of epistemology, it must be recalled that the theoretical logics of exception, bare life, thanatopolitics, and so forth are firmly situated within a European history of sovereignty (Agamben himself does the genealogical work, beginning with the originary Roman figure of *homo sacer*)[56] and may not apply so readily across space. It is an indictment of the skewed geographies of the "permission to narrate" Palestinian realities[57] that an Aristotelian distinction between *bios* and *zoē* underpins so much scholarship in a non-European context[58] but struggles to account for political agency, especially as it forms through the gendered and racial politics of the body.[59] While it is obviously significant that Palestinians are figured as an uncivilized/terroristic Other in order to justify occupation, and a thoroughgoing analysis of the governing logics and structures that result is crucial, it is as significant that a racialized state thanatopolitics comes up against a politics of refusal, adaptation, or survival. As I have argued, it is imperative not to reduce one to the other; it is not that the lives of "the governed" correspond to the claims of governing. Pushing further, it can even be said that one is derivative of the other: that modes of governing exist precisely because of the persistence of refusal, adaptation, survival, and so forth; Palestinian political agency is the existential condition of the entire Israeli security state. This is not merely a theoretical curiosity; it is a view onto new horizons of decolonial presents and futures in Palestine and beyond.

These are big claims, certainly, but they bring into view the ways that a decoloniality is already rooted in Palestinian praxis, that decolonial forms of life persist in and beyond colonized space. There lie the irremovable roots that wait to grow in a better future. This claim is based not in romanticism or vitalism but rather on a political surety from a view of colonial power as inherently derivative and incapable of total domination. If decolonizing is partly about "decolonizing the mind,"[60] or wresting Indigenous culture from colonial subsumption, then the preservation of Palestinian cultural, economic, and political life at a front line of Israel's colonial project is surely significant. But decolonizing is of course centered on the repatriation of Indigenous land—"all of the land, and not just symbolically," as Eve Tuck and Wayne Yang famously put it—and here we can only be ambivalent in our conclusions.[61] That Palestinian life remains, and in often creative and vibrant forms, *but* under Israeli sovereignty over the land, reduces decolonial space-making claims to the symbolic; the land is not in any meaningful sense returned to Indigenous control. It would be both an overstatement of ungovernable life and a dilution of decolonial politics to make any sort of confident proclamation of decolonial space in and around Checkpoint 300. Yet—*yet*—it cannot be denied that a decolonial praxis makes space anew, or maintains space *as was*, as avowedly decolonized. It would take a very heavy hand of cynical theory making to dismiss Palestinian life here as entirely unsuccessful in reclaiming the land, in retaining the land for Indigenous purpose. To mind here, not uncoincidentally, is an ethical and political drive of Said's connection between the discursive and the material, whereby the Oriental "vision and material reality propped each other up, kept each other going."[62] Something of this performative energy might persist here: as we recognize and foment Palestinian political agency, it more fully recognizes itself, foments itself, and accumulates as an immovable presence on Palestinian land. This is a call not to the legitimizing politics of colonial recognition but to a wider practice of recognizing not only Palestinian claims over space but Palestinian *claim-making spatializing practices*. From the cultural and artistic centers to the business gray zones and paved-over orchards, this is Indigenous land put to Indigenous use; that it is not formally recognized in the international system of statehood is simultaneously everything and nothing. And here lies the ambivalence: yes, the colonizing state holds ultimate control, and yes, the "controlled" are not entirely controlled; they live a life beyond coloniality.

It is without glorifying sentiment that this decolonial view is presented. There is clearly nothing to be triumphant about; but there is also no place for defeatism. Clearly Palestine is not decolonized, and nor is there currently a realistic prospect of decolonizing processes of territory, yet there are decolonial practices that should not be foreclosed. Understanding and platforming political agency and decoloniality in a context of political oppression builds the awareness and solidarities that are undoubtedly necessary for the fracturing of colonial power and Israel's apartheid regime, which segregates or exiles all Palestinians. The possibility of politics is made urgent here; where, from one perspective, colonial space is made through practices of state control and violence, from that explicated here, it is produced through a never-resolved dialectic led by a population steadfastly holding on to political agency. That which exceeds the colonial state and yet dictates the very conditions of governing could then be crucial for its undoing.

Conclusion

Geographies for a Decolonized and Free Palestine

A point not touched on in any of the chapters is the issue of non-Palestinian mobility and Checkpoint 300. While the Hebron Road in northern Bethlehem was part of the main north–south road that stretches from Beersheba to Nazareth—the historic Way of the Patriarchs and designated "Route 60"—Israelis now bypass Bethlehem altogether through the Tunnels Highway to the west. Opened in 1996 and expanded in the years since, this section of road passes around and under Beit Jala and the Har Gilo settlement for 900 meters underground (the longest tunnel in the West Bank), across a bridge over the al-Walaja Valley (the longest and tallest bridge), and through a second tunnel (approximately 270 meters) under the Gilo settlement and northward toward Jerusalem (see Figure 40). This is a massive infrastructure project that was built with a vision of making Jerusalem, as the city's mayor, Ehud Olmert, put it in 1996, "a metropolitan centre that is connected to the region south of the capital, as far as Gush Etzion." The tunnels and bridge have been expanded over the past decade to cope with the increase in traffic volumes as the settler population of the West Bank grows such that Israeli citizens can drive the twenty-eight kilometers between Jerusalem and Hebron in less than thirty minutes. As we know, for a West Bank Palestinian, that journey is possible only with an Israeli-issued permit, a journey along the original section of Route 60 inside Bethlehem, passage through the corridors and checks of Checkpoint 300 on foot, and public transport from the other side of the wall. The differences in terms of time, stress, cost, reliability, safety, and dignity between Palestinians and Israelis are constitutive of an apartheid spatial regime in which a metropolitan connectedness from Jerusalem outward is the privilege of only some who make claims on that city. Aside the colonial spaces discussed in this book is this one: a network of convenient infrastructures bur-rowed under or erected above a complementing network of choke points and checkpoints of which Checkpoint 300 is an important and archetypal part. This might seem an obvious context, but it is a point worth emphasizing to set the preceding chapters into sharp relief.

A similar analysis of the Tunnels Highway would present a diamet-ric account of colonial space in Palestine. Passage is possible only in an Israel-registered vehicle (identifiable by a yellow license plate; West Bank Palestinians can only drive cars with white or green plates), and a notoriously light-touch and low-tech checkpoint stops very few cars as they drive northward through the tunnels. There are cameras and some speed bumps but no traffic arms to stop drivers from proceed-ing; most cars do not come to a stop but decelerate for long enough to receive a nod from the attending soldier. It is a safe bet that the time saved for settlers can be dedicated to social or domestic activi-ties in a way that is not possible for the families of al-Walaja whose breadwinners pass through Checkpoint 300. It is also true that the surrounding technologies (traffic cameras, standard-issue weaponry carried by the soldiers, and the security overhangs around the high-way) are deployed to protect commuters rather than to control or harm. It should be added, too, that the international collaborations that make the tunnels possible (the Swiss engineering firm PINI Group won an award for its design and construction, and the Spanish mining company OSSA was contracted for excavations) bring in civil partners to Israel's colonial project, whose work on occupied land should be brought under the same critical light as that of military contractors. As the architects Rafi Segal and Eyal Weizman documented more than two decades ago, such projects bring a "different kind of warfare" to the people of Palestine, in which "the mundane elements of planning and architecture have been conscripted as the tactical tools in Israel's state strategy . . . [that] further[s] national and geopolitical objectives in the organisation of space and the redistribution of its population."[1] With the doubling of capacity effected by the latest upgrade to the Tunnels Highway section of Route 60 (scheduled to be complete in 2025), this is by now a mature tactic that has entrenched Israeli settler colonial society in the heart of Palestine. Checkpoint 300 should be understood against this backdrop, as not only a stand-alone border crossing, or one that is part of the much larger network of Israeli mili-tary infrastructure that controls Palestinians, but also the existential

FIGURE 40. The Tunnels Highway under Beit Jala and the Har Gilo settlement. Photograph by Nadir Mauge.

counter to the compression of time-spaces for the colonizing population. So far as Checkpoint 300 connects to the Tunnels Highway section of Route 60 just two kilometers away, one space creates a demonized other, while the other affirms an idealized self.

Brought into sharp focus in northern Bethlehem, this underlying dynamic of simultaneously segregated yet intimately connected populations becomes more readily detectable in different renderings of colonial space across Palestine and farther afield. The State of Israel's Orientalist evocations of a violent or uncivilized Palestinian society are integral to its projected image of a liberal democracy, a progressive and tolerant civil society, and the heightened morality of its military forces. No informed view can take these claims seriously; it is in the detail of settings such as Checkpoint 300 and its multiple spatial resonances—from the Hebron Road and Palestinian homes in al-Walaja to the tunnels of Route 60 and research laboratories in Belfast and Arizona—that a politics of counter takes shape. This book does not, of course, *begin* this process, but it contributes to one that is already in train, where scholars and activists continue to build a robust body of evidence that documents and critiques Israel's colonial project in Palestine. Here I have attempted to take the detail of one site whose significance in and of itself is great but by no means extraordinary; there are many other checkpoints (Helga Tawil-Souri's extensive work on Qalandia is an important predecessor and companion to this work[2]) and multiple other sites of spatial struggle: the cycles of settlement expansion and Palestinian house demolition in the Naqab (Negev), center-of-life policies and dispossession in Jerusalem, and the confiscation of agricultural resources (land and water) in the Jordan Valley. This is to name but three examples of too many where the underlying power dynamics documented here are at play. Local struggles connect to multiple colonial geographies on different scales, from the intimate to the geopolitical; the challenge is to connect the dots, to relate the marginalized and quotidian to the colonial state and its profiting accomplices. This is the account of Checkpoint 300 I have attempted here.

By way of a brief recap, very much the primary scene of the book is the checkpoint itself in the early hours of the morning, when thousands of permit-holding Palestinian men are corralled through its corridors and vetted by the colonizing state. Immediately to view is thus a disciplinary function of Checkpoint 300 to sift for able-bodied, politically compliant, male subjects to provide low-wage labor for Israel's economy. Given that the checkpoint and permit system are designed to facilitate and control this particular type of mobility, an obvious question follows: how does the checkpoint affect people who do not fit that profile? For women, permission to cross Checkpoint 300 is less frequently given and is tied mostly to gendered roles of care and piety. Faced with this discriminatory system of permission and a record of gendered humiliation and violence of staff inside Checkpoint 300, women tend to remain in place, taking on more homemaking duties than their husbands who pursue work in Jerusalem and beyond. From the checkpoint, we are thus led to the Palestinian homes where the wives and children of the thousands of permit-holding men pick up surplus domestic physical and emotional labor. Partnering and parenting are strained; women fill the gaps—cooking more, caring more, and worrying more—all as a traceable result of the family's reliance on checkpoint permit–enabled wage labor. Residential and economic space is also considerably affected by Checkpoint 300 and the wall into which it is built as the northern part of Bethlehem is rendered a colonial borderland that is marked by de-development, exception, and the ready transformation into urban battle space. This is made possible, following the trail, via an even wider geography of exchange in ideas, objects, and people; Checkpoint 300 is both *produced through* and *producer of* the power geometries of globalization. And yet, amid these multiple levels of spatial control, Palestinian political agency persists and consists in the re/making of space via artistic, adaptive, or strategic means. Colonial space is thus both multiple and contested, produced not only by the colonizer but also by the colonized, whose presence on the land remains a steadfast gesture toward a decolonized future.

This is not therefore the story only of Checkpoint 300, nor solely an account of a particular colonial space; it is also an exegesis of colonial space across Palestine and beyond. From the racialized permit system and architecture of the border resonate structural and gendering impositions on the household, as well as spacio-cidal effects across northern Bethlehem and into the southern West Bank. It is from this perspective a sure claim that hundreds of thousands of Palestinians are, at different removes and by various degrees, brought within the checkpoint's extensive spatial reach. This reach extends much farther: into Israeli and overseas research and development laboratories, Zionist philanthropic and donor activities, and even the lives and families of guest workers who are imported as an alternative pool of low-wage labor to serve Israel's economy. We thus learn that colonialism in Palestine forms through a great many figures, from the more visible (low-wage Palestinian laborers, Israeli soldiers and private security staff) to the less visible (their families, local business owners and residents, Israeli settlers) and those who tend to be out of view altogether yet are instrumental in producing colonial space (software developers, munitions manufacturers, donors, guest workers, university and private researchers). This is to name but a few of the many actors who are brought into view in the details of Checkpoint 300 and its surroundings.

It is crucial to concede, however, that this is still only a partial account that opens as many paths of research as it treads. Obviously missing here is an ethnographic engagement with the men who cross Checkpoint 300 in the crowded mornings. As I touched on in the book's introduction, I excuse this for two reasons. First, this approach is most readily taken in existing literatures on checkpoints,[3] a fact that provides much of the rationale for the more holistic account provided here, and second, my positionality (white, non-Arab) simply does not lend itself, for example, to walk-through interviews in a highly racialized setting. There is a discomforting ethics around an outsider peering into the humiliating and violent experience of checkpoint crossings during the morning's commute; my sense is that men who cross would not want accompaniment, nor would they want to return home to revisit their checkpoint experiences in an interview during precious free time. Additionally, the issue of marginalized groups who are not routinely brought into consideration of restricted mobilities in Palestine is only partly addressed by attending to the accounts of women and their families at home. As I have mentioned at points, there is an alternative pool of labor, the thirty- to fifty-five thousand workers who are unable to gain permits (often because of blacklisting) and take great risks to find weaker points in the wall to pursue (mostly informal) wage labor. These workers are also part of the checkpoint's regulation of Palestinian movement. So, too, are differently abled groups for whom crossing is difficult for obvious reasons; as one wheelchair user from Bethlehem put it in an interview, "Checkpoint 300 is barely accessible for those who are 100 percent fit, so how can I use it?" It is also important to mention that, as any Bethlehemite knows, checkpoint permits for cultural or religious activities are more readily given to Christians than they are to Muslims, a fact that can exacerbate existing divisions in Bethlehem. Add to this, too, the surely prevalent fallout of Israel's heteronormative conditions on laborer permits (married with at least one child) that make exclusions along lines of sexuality and fertility. There is thus work to be done to better understand the intersections of marginalization within Palestinian society and Israeli colonialism. All signs are that the unevenness of class, race, religion, gender, sexuality, able-ness, health, and so forth are amplified by a regime of mobility and spatial control.

Also missing is a full account from an Israeli perspective. By this, if it needs explicating, I do not mean a "both sides" approach but rather a deeper understanding of how two groups live so closely together in terms of geometric space but are topologically worlds apart. Often no more than ten meters away as one walks around this part of Bethlehem are hundreds of settlers going about their lives: studying, praying, socializing. Settlers in the Bnei Rachel complex also live in the shadow of the checkpoint and wall, albeit in a very different relation;

their ideological commitment and presence represent the existential condition of this particular case of land grabbing. Were it not for interventions by the Sons of Rachel organization, much of the security infrastructure that reaches south into Bethlehem may not exist at all. As with all Israeli settlers, it would be instructive to know the drivers of relocation to this specific and somewhat unusual settlement. Among the approximately seventy residents of the compound and a hundred students of the yeshiva, what are their paths to *aliyah*? Taking for a moment that it would be possible (and ethical) to gather such information, there would be value in knowing the global drivers of migration to Israel and the lands it occupies. Anti-Semitism is a major factor, as are others, such as geopolitical rupture (war in Ethiopia, regime change in Russia) or deep-set cultural mores (e.g., so-called Israelism in the United States)[4] that premise birthright tours, citizenship, and settling. Is it possible that Palestinians like Omar, who returned from California and built a garden café close to Rachel's Tomb, "partly a sacrifice to keep this area Palestinian," is neighbored by settlers coming from similar directions with parallel designs on the land? It is possible and even probable; Americans make up a full 13 percent of settlers in the West Bank (approximately 60,000 of 450,000) and are known as pioneers of both land grabbing and settler violence.[5] Omar's claim, of course, is rooted in the substance of his birth in Bethlehem, his family's home, and we cannot lose perspective on how unjust it is that his and all Palestinians' rights to reside are so gravely threatened by the ethnonationalist project of planting settlers in contested areas. Until we know more about the ideas, objects, and people on the other side of the wall, we miss crucial aspects of the formation of colonial space in northern Bethlehem and in Palestine more generally.

What we do know, as I hope is clear from the preceding chapters, is that colonial space is formed through a bureaucratic and material security architecture that is both the product and the producer of wider geographies of oppression, complicity, and counter. After many drafts and redrafts, this is as succinct and representative a formulation as possible offered on the question of Checkpoint 300 and colonial space. But as I have argued, this is about more than Checkpoint 300; the lessons here can shine new light on a range of contexts across Palestine and beyond. To elaborate on those mentioned earlier, the cycles of settlement expansion and Palestinian house demolition in the

Naqab can be considered through the confluence of state, private, and civil society actors that prize Indigenous life apart from the land, the deployment of hi-tech drone surveillance techniques, and the intractable resistance of resident communities; the use of center-of-life policies to remove Jerusalemites from their homes should be connected to wider geographies of Zionist philanthropy and real estate purchase in and around the old city, the instrumentalization of archaeology as a legitimizing discipline, and the various tactics deployed by Palestinians to retain the right to remain in the city; the confiscation of agricultural resources in the Jordan Valley might be set in a context of Oslo-derived land designations, migrant seasonal pickers, lost Palestinian livelihoods, and a focus on the ways that alternative food supply chains form through and around Israel's restrictions. Not all approaches need to be holistic, of course, but if colonial space forms though the intersection of local and wider geographies, then a more effective vantage point looks across different scales, recognizing "space as the product of interrelations . . . from the immensity of the global to the intimately tiny," as Doreen Massey put it.[6] A broad lesson from this is that Palestinian struggles are at once local and global, simultaneously endogenous and exogenous, and resulting strategies take on the task of holding in view the tiny, the immense, and all else in between.

This ethos, I think, can be taken to four key aspects of colonial space that merit emphasis beyond the pages of this book to do with borders, feminist approaches to geopolitics, less spectacular geographies, and the ethics of research at sites of pronounced political oppression. To be clear, I am not making discipline-changing claims here but rather suggesting incremental checks and tunes to the end of producing a fuller and *actionable* account of contemporary colonialism. On the theme of borders, for instance, there is by now a vast literature, especially in my own discipline of political geography. For the context to hand, the clear connections between, say, family lives in al-Walaja and the checkpoint 3.4 kilometers away disclose a capillary-like dispersal of core functions of borders (e.g., profiling, movement control, and general subordination to the state) in ways that suggest a certain ubiquity of the border or of processes of *bordering*. We can thus, following the border scholars Sandro Mezzadra and Brett Neilson, "separate the border from the wall" in our analysis, in this case doing away with the idea that the border begins and ends at the checkpoint (which is anyway the case, because *both* sides of Checkpoint 300 are on Palestinian land).[7] From here spaces and objects that are constitutive of border infrastructures become part of the border (e.g., the DCO office, a permit application form), as do subjectivizing or psychological effects whereby the border is "internalised by individuals, as it becomes a condition, an essential reference of their collective, communal sense, and hence, once again, of their identity."[8] It is readily claimed in border studies that "the border is everywhere" to refer to the ways that border infrastructures permeate society in terms of visa checks and requirements (e.g., by employers and universities), constant informal and formal verification processes faced by "outsiders," and the levels of uncertainty and precarity maintained by incomplete processing.[9] Bordering, as an idea, encompasses borders *and* life lived in the context of border functions—and thus the extensive spatial reach of borders.

Gloria Anzaldúa's notion of "borderlands" captures these dynamics in a settler colonial setting through a frequently cited but always powerful metaphor: "an open wound . . . where the Third World grates against the first and bleeds. And before a scab forms it haemorrhages again, the lifeblood of two worlds merging to form a third country—a border culture."[10] Without reduction or overdetermination, if we draw lines between the clearly significant role of borders and any sense of Palestinian-ness,[11] how far can we understand *all* Palestinians as inhabitants of such a borderland? In Jerusalem, the West Bank, Gaza, the diaspora, and Israel, Palestinians are in a continuous struggle for rights and recognition against the colonial state, and that, in itself, becomes a part of Palestinian-ness, or the culture of a "third country" in Anzaldúa's terms. Palestine *is* a borderland insofar as it is an "undetermined place created by the emotional residue of an unnatural boundary. It is in a constant state of transition. The prohibited and forbidden are its inhabitants."[12] To briefly and tentatively turn to contemporary Gaza, this indeterminacy manifests in extremis as the Gazan people are thrust into a violent space in which competing claims clash: Israeli, Egyptian, and international political and capitalist interests uproot Palestinian belonging to the land through periods of occupation, siege, and now colonial warfare. All to which we are witness in Bethlehem is amplified to terrifying levels where the simultaneous inclusion within Israeli (aerial and terrestrial) sovereignty and exclusion from a national or international juridical order has compounded humanitarian crisis. As I preface in the introduction to this book, the current suffering of the people of Gaza is significantly a product of spatial control effected by checkpoint border crossings—chiefly at Beit Hanoun (Erez) and Rafah—that deny both the respite of exit and the succor of aid delivery. Without overstating the importance of the research presented here (because nothing is as important or as urgent as Gaza as this book goes to press—and for some time to come), the patterns documented are shared with the colonial dynamics that have made Gaza such a violent borderland that bleeds so profusely.

Attending to lives lived in colonial borderlands—in Bethlehem in the case at hand, in Gaza when that is possible—necessarily inflects or disrupts normative framings of geopolitics. In broad sweeps, we are drawn away from a state-centric form of geopolitics and security and toward a question at the center of feminist geopolitics as formulated by Rachel Pain and Lynn Staeheli: "how is intimacy wrapped up in national, global and geopolitical processes and strategising, international events, policies and territorial claims"?[13] For another key thinker in feminist approaches to geopolitics, Jennifer Hyndman, beginning in the intimate, "traversing scales from the macrosecurity of states to the microsecurity of people and their homes," takes us "from the disembodied space of neorealist geopolitics to a field of live human subjects with names, families, and hometowns."[14] Set back in the context to hand, Israel's territorial claims are drawn down from state-level abstraction into grounded and nameable Palestinian homes as sites of geopolitical spatialization.[15] We thus come to know geopolitics from the most important perspective: that of the targets and victims of the neorealist (or colonial) security state. Questions that are most obviously raised in this book have to do with groups of people (predominantly women) whose conditions of labor articulate, even at great distance, with those of Bethlehem. As I point out in chapter 5, it is not inconceivable that, given the significantly global dimension of Checkpoint 300, there is a codependency between the domestic labor that supports Palestinian low-wage labor and that which supports guest workers imported by Israel from states like the Philippines, Sri Lanka, and Thailand. This relationship can be read also between the families of manual workers all along the vast production chains that supply military hardware, from those of miners charged with extracting raw materials to those who sit on munitions factory assembly lines. A sustained feminist geopolitics of Checkpoint 300 would attempt to track and document this distant and intimate fallout of Israel's security infrastructure on homes across the world, and especially in working-class homes of the Global South.

Such a project would align with an emerging body of work that in recent years has sought to emphasize "less spectacular" geographies of Palestine whose violence may not take eventful shape in, say, a military raid or checkpoint but whose effects are nonetheless integral to colonial violence. This move recognizes that a large part of "canonical" literature on Palestine, as Saree Makdisi has written, remains focused on "those forms of violence that lend themselves in one way or another to televisual spectacle," which has the effect of "overshadowing, even displacing, the much less visible but equally deadly effects of the Israeli apparatuses of bureaucracy and control in the occupied territories, which by its nature does not lend itself to televised images (unless you can imagine a five-hour sequence of a man standing in line)."[16] A less spectacular scholarship, it follows, one located in the details of bureaucratic queues, forms, requirements, obfuscations, and deterrence, can reveal equally (or perhaps, for their subtlety, *more*) effective technologies of control that inflect the lives of targeted populations. We see this especially for women and their experiences of being denied permits and the intimidating conditions of the permit-issuing office (the DCO), as well as for residents and business owners around the Hebron Road, where the details of land designations underlie a slow but definite process of depopulation and economic decline. There is nothing less spectacular than nothing happening at all, and this is the case where the checkpoint and permit system fulfill a deterrent function such that women do not even attempt to claim rights to movement, choosing instead to remain home. Then there are dull but consequential details, such as that the municipal government in Bethlehem is unable to control unauthorized parking on the streets around Checkpoint 300, and businesses (the larger hotels and souvenir shops) lose revenue because tourist coaches are not able to park in the area. In this sense, removing the check *point* from the checkpoint reveals the more mundane registers of colonial control. For every house demolition in the West Bank, many more Palestinian homes are subject to military orders that threaten dispossession;[17] for each bomb that is dropped on Gaza is a military lawyer deliberating (and skewing) international humanitarian law,[18] and as we find here, before and around checkpoints is an extensive permit bureaucracy that controls movement outside of the border crossing itself. In many respects, the "paper wall of bureaucracy" is as strong and restrictive as the more spectacular and thus more widely studied West Bank wall itself.[19]

This links to the issue of research ethics at sites of pronounced political oppression, such as Palestine. Aside from the usual and important concerns around practicalities and positionality, and beyond a discomforting sense that there is a certain voyeurism to concentrating on the spectacular, a crucial element of ethical engagement in Palestine is keeping in view a pernicious colonial regime without foreclosing the presence and possibilities of Palestinian politics. An important step to this end is to hold up our own theoretical frameworks (to name prominent ones in this book, biopolitics, necropolitics, settler colonialism, and thanatopolitics) to critical light, taking seriously the ethics of interpretive and representative practices. One way toward this is via an interrogation of the "ontological lock-ins" of (pre-)given theoretical frames "that narrow down what the political can mean" to build, as geographers Mikko Joronen and Jouni Häkli argue, a "politicised ontology" founded in the *taking place* of "events and situations as always emerging and constituting in multiple ways."[20] I read this as a practice of taking the conditions on the ground to the frame, testing and modifying the frame where necessary, and at all times avoiding an approach of imposing theory on the field. This is not to deny that theoretical preconceptions can provide a helpful lens *during* fieldwork but to carefully position analytical frameworks as somewhat after the fact, a tool that enables us to understand the social conditions that precede them. In the case of Palestine and other colonial settings, the point is precisely that the Israeli state and its partners (private contractors, settlers) operate at and contend with different scales of complementing or countering arrangements of power, giving cause to qualifying understandings of the colonial state's centrality to the making of space and control of life within that space. In J. K. Gibson-Graham's writing on what they term "performative ontology," ethical research works to an analytical principle of "difference not dominance," whereby interpretive practices seek to give "what is nascent and not fully formed some room to move and grow."[21] To take such a position is to recognize that interpretation is never innocent[22] and thus the ethical dues owed to the political life that is the target of attempts to control. As long as Palestinians and others living in politically oppressive conditions are denied the "permission to narrate,"[23] it is on all those who interpret and represent (academic and otherwise) to remain open to (and, in an important sense, *write into being*) the possibilities of political struggle. Besides, what is the point of studying colonial power if it is not to the end of understanding it from the perspectives of targeted colonized populations?

A final reflection motions from understanding to changing. The detail included in this book is angled toward an *actionable* knowledge of colonialism. Writing against a strong critique of disembodied, theory-driven accounts of Palestine, and toward a broader material promise of decolonizing, the vision of Checkpoint 300 and Palestine offered here aims at uncovering trajectories of power and thus sites of accountability. This is not overstated: books like this one do not decolonize, but they can be invested in a decolonizing politics that turns toward a restitution of Indigenous land. And though "turning toward" is precisely the kind of equivocal language that takes decolonization to the plane of metaphor, there are material gains to be made by acting on some of the spatial relations set out here. Documenting and naming specific actors in the formation of these relations arouses a "discomforting" decolonial politics that "implicates" and "unsettles,"[24] a politics that is not subordinated to theory but constitutes "a way, option, standpoint, analytic, project, practice, and praxis."[25] The tangibility of power relations is what marks out the project of decolonization: "we cannot just think, write or imagine our way to a decolonised future," writes Leanne Betasamosake Simpson.[26] From the symbolic domains of language and metaphor, therefore, we are brought to the materiality of land, and *understandings* of colonial space are made servants to *strategies* of its unmaking. Such an approach takes seriously an instrumental notion of "decolonizing the mind" that will undo deepset colonial normalizations[27] toward a base objective of repatriating Indigenous land—"all of the land, and not just symbolically."[28] The dual task, then, is to traverse colonial delimitations of Indigenous possibility to an end of restoring Indigenous cultural and material stewardship of land; decolonizing knowledge is but a preliminary step toward decolonizing structures and institutions.[29] To counter that a vision of decolonized structures or repatriated land is "unworkable" or "unrealistic," the response is emphatic: decolonizing is an inherently "discomforting" process, "a programme of complete disorder," as Frantz Fanon famously put it.[30] The ordering of Palestinian land and population by the Israeli state must be traced in all its spatial breadth (a project to which I hope to have contributed here) to the end of dismantling the current regime. Where order is colonially produced, disorder is the only proper response.

In an important sense, this response is already in formation. Palestinian life endures, and even prospers, in ways that signal a certain decoloniality of living. A moment or space of defying or not recognizing the colonial regime is not only a prospectus of a decolonial future but a decolonial present in itself. As long as Palestinian life is not entirely subsumed by Israeli attempts at control, a decoloniality of living persists and haunts the colonial regime. It is coiled, in other words, to spring into the spaces of a decolonized Palestine. Bringing that about is an international effort of solidarity and action against the political and economic support structures of Israel's colonial project. From so-called defense contractors (weapons producers) to diplomatic allegiances, the everyday realities of occupation are tied to networks of ethically corrupt deals for ideological and material support. Precisely because these networks extend beyond the hypersecuritized Israeli state, they are knowable as they traverse scales into sites of potential political intervention: traceable production chains, image-aware suppliers, accessible manufacturing sites, systems of ethical procurement, and democratically accountable decision makers. These wider geographies of oppression, complicity, and counter are the key to unlocking Israel's bureaucratic and material security architecture of control in Palestine. Knowledge of this wider geography of colonial space must found an agenda that works toward a decolonized and free Palestine.

Acknowledgments

This book would not have come together without a great deal of support from many, many colleagues and friends. At Newcastle I am able to think and write thanks to a departmental culture created and protected by some brilliant people, Stuart Dawley, Kyle Grayson, Al James, and Rachel Woodward in particular. Thanks especially to Rachel for sage and selfless mentoring. Newcastle is a vibrant space of critical thought and teaching on Palestine thanks also to the work of Mohamed El-Shewy, Olivia Mason, Una McGahern, Silvia Pasquetti, Mori Ram, Jemima Repo, Rob Shaw, Burak Tansel, and Lewis Turner. My PhD students at Newcastle are an equally excellent source of intellectual and political strength: Zena Agha, Daoud Ghoul, Omar Hmidat, Anas Ismail, Ichamati Mousampruti, and Ishraq Othman. James Riding has given important advice on writing and framing; Craig Jones has read drafts and provided general support, as he always does. I am very fortunate to work with such people.

I am grateful also to a wider network of scholar-friends whose ideas and comradery are very important to me: Kate Baker, Christine Barnes, Oliver Belcher, Lisa Bhungalia, Desirée Cappa, Rachel Clarke, Alice Cree, Muna Dajani, Sol Gamsu, Wassim Ghantous, Katharina Grueneisl, Toufic Haddad, Tiina Järvi, Jessi Lehman, Noam Leshem, Jessa Loomis, Rhys Machold, Lauren Martin, Francis Massé, Aya Nasser, Jesse Proudfoot, Henry Redwood, Matt Richmond, Kali Rubaii, Arun Saldanha, Oscar Schiavone, Omar Shweiki, Alex Tarr, Ali Wedderburn, and Harry Weeks.

I have presented parts of this work to responsive audiences at various universities: Cambridge, Glasgow, King's College London, Newcastle, Northumbria, Portsmouth, and Tampere. Thanks especially to Jacob Fairless Nicholson, Emma Laurie, Jon Phillips, and Faith Taylor for invitations and warm hospitality. At the University of Minnesota Press, Jason Weidemann and Zenyse Miller showed enthusiasm and provided clear guidance from the beginning of the publication process; thanks go to both. I must also thank Holly Monteith for very attentive copy editing and two reviewers for comments that were humbling and improved the final manuscript.

A major part of this study was undertaken with Jemima Repo on a project funded by a British Academy/Leverhulme Small Research Grant, "Checkpoints beyond the Checkpoint: The Implications for Women Left at Home" (2018-19 SRG/170330). Jemima is a brilliant feminist and anticolonial scholar of biopolitics and gender whose influence will be obvious in the first chapters and therefore throughout the entire book. I am indebted to her determination and ethnographic nous, especially in the details of chapters 1, 2, and 3, which are rewritten and refocused versions of our coauthored work. I am grateful to the British Academy and the Leverhulme Trust for financial support and to Jeremy Crampton for providing a reference for that grant. Further financial support was provided via my NUAcT (Newcastle University Academic Track) Fellowship; thanks to Candy Rowe for showing faith in my project.

Andrew Brooks is a friend and colleague whose thought bears on the book, especially in chapter 5 and in the insight gained from focusing on articulation and labor. I always look forward to meeting with Andrew and flailing at his challenging questions around comparison, political economy, and apartheid. Parts of chapter 5 are rewritten and refocused from our collaborative writing. Another significant influence is Mikko Joronen. Over almost ten years, we have collaborated extensively and become close friends; I cannot now think without his insight bearing on my own formulations and writing. Mikko is humble and generous, while also being a geographer of great political and ethical force. His work informs many of the arguments of the book, especially the reflections on "ungovernability" in chapter 6. Thank you, Mikko—ten more years!?

There are so many people in Palestine, most importantly, to acknowledge and to thank. My work there over many years has been facilitated by the fearless Lara Kilani, the best researcher I have ever been able to formally involve on a project. Dina Yatim helped a lot in the early stages of the study with women in Al-Walaja, as did Lamees, a member of the Women's Group whose ethnographic skills bear significantly on chapters 2 and 3. Without Lamees's dedication and unique positionality, none of what follows would have been written. Daniela Freund—via the always-collegial Merav Amir—completed, with great efficiency and professionalism, commissioned research into Israeli and international arms companies that informs the analysis provided in chapter 5. Kate Khair, a skilled linguist based in Beit Sahour, transcribed and translated interviews conducted for chapter 4. Mohammad Alyan drove me around, taught me about the road system, and made me laugh. Ala' Hilu has been a friend for a decade now and was kind enough to provide drone footage (at some personal risk), which appears in chapter 4. I owe you all a lot—*shukran*.

There are two really special people without whom the book would not be a book. Nadir Mauge is a talented and courageous filmmaker whose documentary, *My Tomb, Your Tomb, Rachel's Tomb*—funded through Newcastle University's NUAcT Fellowship scheme—is integral to chapters 5 and 6. Not only is Nadir a warm and kind person but he is a meticulous and critical researcher with a great future ahead. Thank you, Nadir, for everything you have done—this is just the beginning! Baha Hilo is a person who does not take compliments, but I cannot express enough gratitude for his friendship and guidance. Baha was the first person I met in Bethlehem on my first visit in 2015, and since then, he has welcomed and facilitated research—for me and for *many* others—in Palestine, on condition that it works against Israeli colonialism. Above all else, I hope I have met this criterion. Thank you, Baha—I think you are wonderful!

Beatriz and Heimo have become a second family in Helsinki, whose home is always welcoming. Rachel knows—reluctantly—that I hold her on a pedestal; she is a sister who I admire and am always cheering on in her ever more varied pursuits. I am so proud of you, Rachel. This book is dedicated, if I may, to my late mother, Jean, and to my dad, Paul, without whom nothing would be possible. Jemima and Niko, lastly, are everything to me. I love you both without bounds.

Notes

INTRODUCTION

1. By "historic Palestine," I refer to the land between the Jordan River and the Mediterranean Sea that preexists the declaration of the State of Israel in 1948. The Green Line refers to the 1949 Armistice Agreements between Israel and its Arab neighbors (Egypt, Jordan, Lebanon, and Syria) that were signed after the 1948 Arab–Israeli War and Palestinian Nakba. The Green Line (sometimes also referred to as "pre-1967 borders") demarks the West Bank (including East Jerusalem) and Gaza and is recognized by the United Nations as Palestinian territory.

2. As an essential part of the bureaucratic management of Palestinians, Israel issues ID cards in a blue casing to Palestinian residents of East Jerusalem and green ones to West Bank Palestinians. These designations dictate in very strict terms where people can live and travel. West Bank Palestinians need to apply for a permit to cross the West Bank wall into Jerusalem and do not have access to the range of services that are conceded to blue ID holders, or provided to Israelis, including those who live in West Bank settlements. For a detailed study of ID cards in Palestine, see Helga Tawil-Souri, "Uneven Borders, Coloured (Im)mobilities: ID Cards in Palestine/Israel," *Geopolitics* 17, no. 1 (2012): 153–76.

3. It is always striking to read Edward Said's recollections of his family's summer holiday trips: "We usually travelled by train from Cairo to Lydda with at least two servants, a large amount of luggage, and a generally frenetic air . . . boarding the luxury Wagons-Lits train in Cairo's Bab-el-Hadid Station for the twelve-hour overnight journey to Jerusalem." Said, *Out of Place: A Memoir* (London: Vintage, 1999), 25.

4. Most people in Bethlehem make this reference. One man, in an interview, explained, "There was a carob tree that everybody knew, as it was a landmark between Bethlehem and Jerusalem. You would say 'I'll wait for you at the carob tree.' This tree was big and famous around there. . . . When you reached the carob tree [from the north], it meant that you reached Bethlehem."

5. The Israeli Ministries of Defense and Foreign Affairs quoted in Mikko Joronen and Mark Griffiths, "Ungovernability and Ungovernable Life in Palestine," *Political Geography* 98 (2022): 1–10, and Daniela

Mansbach, "Normalizing Violence: From Military Checkpoints to 'Terminals' in the Occupied Territories," *Journal of Power* 2, no. 2 (2009): 255–73. The original online statements are no longer available.

6. Hebron is subject to spatial designations outlined in the Hebron Protocol (1997) and is often not part of UN-provided statistics.

7. For an up-to-date OCHA map, see https://www.ochaopt.org/2023 -movement.

8. Laura Robson, *States of Separation: Transfer, Partition, and the Making of the Modern Middle East* (Berkeley: University of California Press, 2017); Joseph Massad, *The Persistence of the Palestinian Question: Essays on Zionism and the Palestinians* (Abingdon, U.K.: Routledge, 2006).

9. Important sources on the Nakba are Nahla Abdo and Nur Masalha, eds., *An Oral History of the Palestinian Nakba* (London: Bloomsbury, 2019); Ghazi Falah, "The 1948 Israeli–Palestinian War and Its Aftermath: The Transformation and De-signification of Palestine's Cultural Landscape," *Annals of the Association of American Geographers* 86, no. 2 (1996): 256–85; and Ilan Pappé, *The Ethnic Cleansing of Palestine* (London: OneWorld, 2016).

10. Amy Kaplan, *Our American Israel* (Cambridge, Mass.: Harvard University Press, 2018).

11. As of August 2024, the United States had vetoed forty-two resolutions on Israel (this is more than half of all vetoes used by the United States in Security Council resolutions).

12. Israel's U.S. military aid package for the period 2019–28 totaled $38 billion. Israel has received more U.S. foreign aid than any other state, totaling $263 billion between 1946 and 2023 (this is a full 60 percent more than the second-largest recipient, Egypt, which received $151.9 billion over the same period).

13. This comes through a range of historical and contemporary discursive and material formations. Indicative examples include the characterization of Israel as "a fortress of the West" and similar such expressions of military alliance (see Daniel Marwecki, *Germany and Israel: Whitewashing and Statebuilding* [Oxford: Oxford University Press, 2020]); the historical inclusion of Israel and occupied Palestine in the U.S. military's U.S. European Command Area of Responsibility and not in U.S. Central Command (a status that changed in 2021) (see Derek Gregory, "Middle of What? East of Where?," an essay curated for *Safar/Voyage: Contemporary Works by Arab, Iranian and Turkish Artists*, Museum of Anthropology at UBC, 2012, https://geographicalimaginations.files.wordpress.com/2012/07/gregory -middle-east1.docx); and Israel's standing as a prominent import/export partner in the global trade in "homeland securities" (important sources of information here are Jeff Halper, *War Against the People* [London: Pluto

Press, 2015]; Antony Loewenstein, *The Palestine Laboratory: How Israel Exports the Technology of Occupation around the World* [London: Verso, 2023]; and Rhys Machold, *Fabricating Homeland Security Police Entanglements across India and Palestine/Israel* [Stanford, Calif.: Stanford University Press, 2024]).

14. See, e.g., "Public Statement: Scholars Warn of Potential Genocide in Gaza," *Third World Approaches to International Law Review,* October 17, 2023, https://twailr.com/public-statement-scholars-warn-of-potential-genocide-in-gaza/, and Office of the United Nations High Commissioner for Human Rights (OHCHR), "Gaza Is 'Running Out of Time' UN Experts Warn, Demanding a Ceasefire to Prevent Genocide," 2023, https://www.ohchr.org/en/press-releases/2023/11/gaza-running-out-time-un-experts-warn-demanding-ceasefire-prevent-genocide.

15. For the ICJ's ruling, see https://www.icj-cij.org/case/186.

16. Vetoed UN Security Council resolutions include S/2023/773 (October 18, 2023), S/2023/792 (October 25, 2023), S/2023/970 (December 8, 2023), S/2024/173 (February 20, 2024), S/2024/239 (March 22, 2024). Resolution S/RES/2728, ordering a ceasefire, passed on March 25, 2024.

On the U.S. ambassador to the UN, see Abbie Llewelyn, "UK Minister Insists UN Gaza Ceasefire Resolution 'Is Binding' in Contrast to US," *Independent,* March 26, 2024, https://www.independent.co.uk/news/uk/un-security-council-linda-thomasgreenfield-gaza-john-kirby-foreign-office-b2519108.html.

17. For an autoethnography of the Rafah crossing from this time, see Abdalhadi Alijla, "Palestine and the Habeas Viscus Borders an Autoethnography of Travel, Visa Violence, and Borders," *Borders in Globalization Review* 1, no. 2 (2020): 1–15.

18. Although this is a feature specifically of Israeli settler colonialism, it is important to note the involvement of USAID in the "apartheid road" network. See Omar Salamanca, "Assembling the Fabric of Life: When Settler Colonialism Becomes Development," *Journal of Palestine Studies* 45, no. 4 (2016): 64–80.

19. For accounts of the permits scheme, see Yael Berda, *Living Emergency: Israel's Permit Regime in the Occupied Territories* (Stanford, Calif.: Stanford University Press, 2017), and Mark Griffiths, Yael Berda, Mikko Joronen, and Lara Kilani, "Israel's International Mobilities Regime: Visa Restrictions for Educators and Medics in Palestine," *Territory, Politics, Governance* 12, no. 7 (2024): 891–909.

20. Mikko Joronen and Mark Griffiths, "The Affective Politics of Precarity: Home Demolitions in the Occupied West Bank," *Environment and Planning D* 37, no. 3 (2019): 561–76.

21. Anne Meneley, "Blood, Sweat and Tears in a Bottle of Palestinian Extra-Virgin Olive Oil," *Food, Culture, and Society* 14, no. 2 (2011): 275–92.

22. Mark Griffiths and Mikko Joronen, "Marriage under Occupation: Israel's Spousal Visa Restrictions in the West Bank," *Gender, Place, and Culture* 26, no. 2 (2019): 153–72.

23. To use Israeli military nomenclature, Operation Cast Lead (2008–9), Pillar of Defense (2012), Protective Edge (2014), and Breaking Dawn (2022). The ongoing operation (2023 to present) is termed Operation Iron Sword.

24. Jennifer Hyndman, "What Feminist Geopolitics Do: A Nonmanifesto," *Dialogues in Human Geography* 8, no. 1 (2018): 77–79.

25. For a profile of al-Walaja, see UN Relief and Works Agency, "Mini Profile: Al-Walaja," 2013, https://www.unrwa.org/userfiles/image/articles/2013/The_International_Court_of_Justice_AlWalaja_mini_profile.pdf. For a study of the effects of the wall, see Mikko Joronen, "Negotiating Colonial Violence: Spaces of Precarisation in Palestine," *Antipode* 51, no. 3 (2019): 838–57.

26. For information on the activities of the al-Walaja Women's Group, see Natalie Alz, "Carving Sumud out of Wood," +972, December 31, 2021, https://www.972mag.com/rweisat-wood-art-walaja/, and "The Palestinian Women of Walaja . . . a Small Project That Tells Their Story to the Germans" (in Arabic), *Al Jazeera*, September 2, 2019, https://www.aljazeera.net/women/2019/2/9/ نساء-الولجة-الفلسطينيات-مشروع-صغير .

1. THE PUNITIVE COMMUTE

1. Using figures from the Palestinian Bureau of Statistics, Andrew Ross reports that in 2017, an estimated "139,600 [West Bank Palestinians] were working, with or without permits, in Israel and in Israeli settlements (and a further 10,000 without permits in the latter): almost 60 percent of these were in construction." Ross, *Stone Men: The Palestinians Who Built Israel* (London: Verso, 2019), 230.

2. Ross, 11.

3. In 2016, Human Rights Watch reported that most settlement companies pay Palestinian workers less than Israel's minimum hourly wage of twenty-three shekels ($5.75), with most of these workers receiving eight to sixteen shekels per hour ($2–$4). Human Rights Watch, "Occupation, Inc.: How Settlement Businesses Contribute to Israel's Violations of Palestinian Rights," 2016, https://www.hrw.org/report/2016/01/19/occupation-inc/how-settlement-businesses-contribute-israels-violations.

4. For a detailed explication of ID cards, see Tawil-Souri, "Uneven Borders."

5. This policy is documented and discussed in Mansbach, "Normalizing Violence," and Eyal Weizman, *Hollow Land: Israel's Architecture of Occupation* (London: Verso, 2007), 139–60. See also Mark Griffiths and Jemima Repo, "Biopolitics and Checkpoint 300 in Occupied Palestine: Bodies, Affect, Discipline," *Political Geography* 65 (2018): 17–25.

6. There are no official statistics; fifteen thousand is the most widely reported number. See, e.g., Al Jazeera, "Commuting through Israeli Checkpoints, a Photo Essay by Activestills," 2018, https://interactive.aljazeera .com/aje/2018/commuting-through-israeli-checkpoints/index.html.

7. "Gilo Checkpoint: What the Pope Won't See . . . ," *Belfast Telegraph*, May 4, 2019, http://www.belfasttelegraph.co.uk/news/world-news/gilo -checkpoint-what-the-pope-wont-see-28478030.html.

8. For a cinematic representation from a Palestinian viewpoint, see Farah Nabulsi, dir., *The Present* (2020).

9. William Booth and Sufian Taha, "A Palestinian's Commute through an Israeli Checkpoint," *Washington Post*, 2017, https://www.washingtonpost .com/graphics/world/occupied/checkpoint/.

10. Some caution is needed around such characterizations in the context of a recurrent trope in Israeli political discourse of referring to Palestinians as animals.

11. Nasser Abourahme, "Spatial Collisions and Discordant Temporalities: Everyday Life between Camp and Checkpoint," *International Journal of Urban and Regional Research* 35, no. 2 (2011): 453.

12. Weizman, *Hollow Land*, 151.

13. B'Tselem, "Inhuman Conditions in Checkpoint 300," 2016, http:// www.btselem.org/video/20170731/20160731_inhuman_conditions_in _checkpoints_300.

14. Mikko Joronen, "Spaces of Waiting: Politics of Precarious Recognition in the Occupied West Bank," *Environment and Planning D* 35, no. 6 (2017): 1002.

15. David Bissell, "Animating Suspension: Waiting for Mobilities," *Mobilities* 2, no. 2 (2007): 285–86.

16. For a clear discussion of affect and difference, see Divya Tolia-Kelly, "Affect—an Ethnocentric Encounter? Exploring the 'Universalist' Imperative of Emotional/Affectual Geographies," *Area* 38, no. 2 (2006): 213–17.

17. Jaclynn Ashly, "Israel's Checkpoint 300: Suffocation and Broken Ribs at Rush Hour," *Al Jazeera*, March 13, 2019, https://www.aljazeera.com /features/2019/3/13/israels-checkpoint-300-suffocation-and-broken-ribs -at-rush-hour.

18. Ashly.

19. See the report by the WAFA News Agency, "Palestinian Worker

Dies in Slip Accident at Overcrowded Checkpoint near Bethlehem," 2018, https://english.wafa.ps/page.aspx?id=foCdyka104036120430afoCdyk.

20. Bissell, "Animating Suspension," 282.

21. Brian Massumi, "Fear (The Spectrum Said)," *Positions* 13, no. 1 (2005): 31–48.

22. For work on uncertainty and governing, see Mark Griffiths and Mikko Joronen, "Governmentalizing Palestinian Futures: Uncertainty, Anticipation, Possibility," *Geografiska Annaler, Series B* 103, no. 4 (2021): 352–66; Nadera Shalhoub-Kevorkian, *Security Theology, Surveillance and the Politics of Fear* (Cambridge: Cambridge University Press, 2015).

23. Mikko Joronen, Helga Tawil-Souri, Merav Amir, and Mark Griffiths, "Palestinian Futures: Anticipation, Imagination, Embodiments," *Geografiska Annaler, Series B* 103, no. 4 (2021): 280.

24. Hagar Kotef and Merav Amir, "Between Imaginary Lines: Violence and Its Justifications at the Military Checkpoints in Occupied Palestine," *Theory, Culture, and Society* 28, no. 1 (2011): 59–60.

25. Kotef and Amir, 60.

26. Booth and Taha, "A Palestinian's Commute."

27. Tawil-Souri, "Qalandia Checkpoint," 11–12.

28. Rashid Khalidi, *Palestinian Identity: The Construction of Modern National Consciousness* (New York: Columbia University Press, 2010), 1.

29. Helga Tawil-Souri, "Qalandia Checkpoint as Space and Nonplace," *Space and Culture* 14, no. 1 (2011): 23.

30. Abourahme, "Spatial Collisions," 453. Many similar and important reflections attest to the prominence of checkpoints in making Palestinian subjectivity under Israeli occupation; see, e.g., Mourid Barghouti, *I Saw Ramallah* (London: Bloomsbury Press, 2008); Emile Habibi, "Your Holocaust, Our Catastrophe," *Politica* 8 (1986): 26–27; Laila el-Haddad, "The Quintessential Palestinian Experience," *Electronic Intifada*, April 14, 2009, https://electronicintifada.net/content/quintessential-palestinian -experience/8183; Edward Said, *The Question of Palestine* (London: Vintage, 1979).

31. EAPPI, "Bethlehem Checkpoint 300 Humanitarian Situation Deteriorates," 2014, https://www.scribd.com/document/223491540 /Bethlehem-Checkpoint-300-Humanitarian-Situation-Deteriorates.

32. "How This Israeli Checkpoint Turns Morning Commute into 5-Hour Ordeal," *Al-Monitor,* March 2016, https://www.al-monitor.com /originals/2016/03/bethlehem-palestinian-laborers-checkpoint-300 -danger.html.

33. Irus Braverman, "Checkpoint Watch: Bureaucracy and Resistance at the Israeli/Palestinian Border," *Social and Legal Studies* 21, no. 3 (2012): 312.

34. Kate, "Israeli Soldiers Held Gun to Palestinian Teen's Head, Made Him Say 'Mohammed Is a Pig,'" *Mondoweiss,* June 16, 2017, https://mondoweiss.net/2017/06/soldiers-palestinian-mohammed/.

35. Rema Hammami, "Destabilizing Mastery and the Machine: Palestinian Agency and Gendered Embodiment at Israeli Military Checkpoints," *Current Anthropology* 60, no. 19 (2019): 93.

36. B'Tselem, "Inhuman Conditions in Checkpoint 300."

37. Giorgio Agamben, *State of Exception* (Chicago: University of Chicago Press, 2005), 35.

38. Giorgio Agamben, *Homo Sacer: Sovereign Power and Bare Life* (Stanford, Calif.: Stanford University Press, 1995), 171.

39. For a review and critique of thanatopolitical approaches to Palestine, see Mark Griffiths, "Thanato-geographies of Palestine and the Possibility of Politics," *Environment and Planning C* 40, no. 8 (2022): 1643–58.

40. Silvia Federici, *Caliban and the Witch: Women, the Body and Primitive Accumulation* (New York: Autonomedia, 2004), 16. See also Ann Laura Stoler, *Carnal Knowledge and Imperial Power: Race and the Intimate in Colonial Rule* (Berkeley: University of California Press, 2002); Alexander Weheliye, *Habeas Viscus: Racializing Assemblages, Biopolitics, and Black Feminist Theories of the Human* (Durham, N.C.: Duke University Press, 2014).

41. Michel Foucault, *Discipline and Punish* (London: Penguin, 1991), 153.

42. Michel Foucault, *The History of Sexuality, Volume 1: The Will to Knowledge* (London: Penguin, 1978), 145.

43. Foucault, *Discipline and Punish,* 25.

44. Timothy Mitchell, *Colonising Egypt* (Berkeley: University of California Press, 1991), 93–94.

45. Foucault, *History of Sexuality, Volume 1,* 123.

46. Foucault, 139.

47. Michel Foucault, *The Punitive Society: Lectures at the Collège de France, 1972–1973* (Basingstoke, U.K.: Palgrave Macmillan, 2015), 211.

48. Foucault, *Discipline and Punish,* 143.

49. Foucault, 152, 201.

50. Michel Foucault, *Psychiatric Power: Lectures at the Collège de France, 1973–1974* (Basingstoke, U.K.: Palgrave Macmillan, 2006), 40.

51. Foucault, *History of Sexuality, Volume 1,* 139.

52. Ben Anderson, "Affect and Biopower: Towards a Politics of Life," *Transactions of the Institute of British Geographers* 37, no. 1 (2012): 31.

53. Diana Coole, "Rethinking Agency: A Phenomenological Approach to Embodiment and Agentic Capacities," *Political Studies* 53, no. 1 (2005): 129.

54. Coole, 129–30.

55. Mika Aaltola, "The International Airport: The Hub-and-Spoke Pedagogy of the American Empire," *Global Networks* 5, no. 3 (2005): 270.

56. William Connolly, *Neuropolitics: Thinking, Culture, Speed* (Minneapolis: University of Minnesota Press, 2002), 71.

57. Khalidi, *Palestinian Identity*, 1–2.

58. Tawil-Souri, "Qalandia Checkpoint," 13.

59. Note that this category is not "having served a prison sentence," because a great many Palestinian men are not sentenced but detained without charge. See Human Rights Watch, "Occupation, Inc."

60. Andrew Ross documents this age as twenty-two, while the *Washington Post* reports it as twenty-three. As is quite common in Israeli bureaucratic mechanisms for Palestinians, written requirements are not provided, but the general understanding of everyone with whom I have spoken during this research is that thirty is the minimum age for most permits. See Ross, *Stone Men*, 9; Booth and Taha, "A Palestinian's Commute."

61. "According to the Israeli state comptroller, more than 50,000 [Palestinians work] without permits every day inside the Green Line." Ross, *Stone Men*, 230. For a narrative account, see Suad Amiry, *Nothing to Lose but Your Life: An 18-Hour Journey with Murad* (London: Bloomsbury, 2010).

62. Foucault, *History of Sexuality, Volume 1*, 141.

63. Foucault, *Discipline and Punish*, 138.

64. Lauren Berlant, "Unfeeling Kerry," *Theory and Event* 8, no. 2 (2005): 8.

65. Tawil-Souri, "Qalandia Checkpoint," 18.

66. Israel Ministry of Foreign Affairs, "Security Fence," 2019. No longer available.

67. Yasmeen Abu-Laban and Abigail Bakan, *Israel, Palestine and the Politics of Race: Exploring Identity and Power in a Global Context* (London: Bloomsbury, 2019), 29.

68. On "ungovernability," see Joronen and Griffiths, "Ungovernability and Ungovernable Life."

69. Mitchell, *Colonising Egypt*, 79.

70. "A Gruelling Life for Palestinian Workers in Israel," *Al Jazeera*, February 6, 2016, http://www.aljazeera.com/news/2016/01/gruelling-life -palestinian-workers-israel-160124130049349.html.

2. WOMEN AT THE CHECKPOINT

1. Key literature on the theme of gender and security that relates to this chapter includes Victoria Basham and Nick Vaughan-Williams, "Gender, Race and Border Security Practices: A Profane Reading of 'Muscular Liberalism,'" *British Journal of Politics and International Relations* 15, no. 4 (2012): 509–27; Cynthia Enloe, *Maneuvers: The International Politics of Militarizing*

Women's Lives (Berkeley: University of California Press, 2000); and Lauren Martin, "The Geopolitics of Vulnerability: Children's Legal Subjectivity, Immigrant Family Detention and US Immigration Law and Enforcement Policy," *Gender, Place, and Culture* 18, no. 4 (2011): 477–98. See also Mark Griffiths and Jemima Repo, "Women and Checkpoints in Palestine," *Security Dialogue* 52, no. 3 (2021): 249–65.

2. E.g., Rema Hammami, "On (Not) Suffering at the Checkpoint: Palestinian Narrative Strategies of Surviving Israel's Carceral Geography," *Borderlands* 14, no. 1 (2015): 1–17; Hammami, "Destabilizing Mastery and the Machine"; Nadera Shalhoub-Kevorkian, *Militarization and Violence against Women in Conflict Zones in the Middle East: A Palestinian Case Study* (Cambridge: Cambridge University Press, 2009); Shalhoub-Kevorkian, *Security Theology.*

3. Jennifer Hyndman, "Feminist Geopolitics Revisited: Body Counts in Iraq," *Professional Geographer* 59, no. 1 (2007): 35–46; Natalie Koch, "Security and Gendered National Identity in Uzbekistan," *Gender, Place, and Culture* 18, no. 4 (2011): 499–518.

4. DCOs (also known as district coordination and liaison offices [DCLs]) were established during Oslo negotiations for cooperation between the Palestinian Authority and the Israeli Civil Administration. DCOs function less as sites of bilateral cooperation than as permit processing offices. Like most West Bank Palestinians, I use "Civil Administration" as shorthand to refer to COGAT.

5. Judith Keshet, *Checkpoint Watch: Testimonies from Occupied Palestine* (London: Zed Books, 2006), 20.

6. The Etzion DCO is subject to sustained attention from the Israeli women's human rights organization Machsomwatch, whose regular reports provide accounts of seemingly deliberate slowness and specific cases of arbitrary administrative decisions, accompanied by intimidation by its various personnel. See https://machsomwatch.org/en/taxonomy/term/891.

7. See B'Tselem, "Restrictions on Movement," November 11, 2017, https://www.btselem.org/freedom_of_movement; Berda, *Living Emergency*; Joronen, "Spaces of Waiting."

8. Julie Peteet, *Space and Mobility in Palestine* (Bloomington: Indiana University Press, 2017), 85.

9. OCHA, "Some 320,000 West Bank ID Holders Permitted into East Jerusalem for Ramadan Friday Prayers," 2019, https://www.ochaopt.org/content/some-320000-west-bank-id-holders-permitted-east-jerusalem-ramadan-friday-prayers.

10. Most interviewees refer to checkpoint staff as *jundiun*. I keep this in the transcription, even though Checkpoint 300 is staffed by private security contractors (see chapter 5).

11. On "petty sovereigns," see Judith Butler, *Precarious Life: The Powers of Mourning and Violence* (London: Verso, 2004), 56.

12. The critical language here draws on Gayatri Spivak, "Can the Subaltern Speak?," in *Marxism and the Interpretation of Culture*, ed. Cary Nelson and Lawrence Grossberg, 271–313 (Champaign: University of Illinois Press, 1988).

13. Lauren Wilcox, *Bodies of Violence: Theorizing Embodied Subjects in International Relations* (Oxford: Oxford University Press, 2015), 15.

14. Iris Jean-Klein, "Into Committees, out of the House? Familiar Forms in the Organization of Palestinian Committee Activism during the First Intifada," *American Ethnologist* 30 (2003): 556–77; Julie Peteet, *Gender in Crisis: Women and the Palestinian Resistance Movement* (New York: Columbia University Press, 1991).

15. Jamileh Abu-Duhou, "Motherhood as 'an Act of Defiance': Palestinian Women's Reproductive Experience," *Development* 46, no. 3 (2003): 85–89.

16. Hannah Rought-Brooks, Salwa Duaibis, and Soraida Hussein, "Palestinian Women: Caught in the Cross Fire between Occupation and Patriarchy," *Feminist Formations* 22, no. 3 (2010): 124–45; Spivak, "Can the Subaltern Speak?"

17. Polly Pallister-Wilkins, "How Walls Do Work: Security Barriers as Devices of Interruption and Data Capture," *Security Dialogue* 47, no. 2 (2016): 151–64.

18. Hammami, "On (Not) Suffering at the Checkpoint"; Hammami, "Destabilizing Mastery and the Machine"; Shalhoub-Kevorkian, *Militarization and Violence*; Shalhoub-Kevorkian, *Security Theology*.

19. Berda, *Living Emergency*, 45.

20. Hammami, "On (Not) Suffering at the Checkpoint," 5.

21. Hammami, "Destabilizing Mastery and the Machine," 88. See also Étienne Balibar, *Politics and the Other Scene* (London: Verso, 2002).

22. Michel Foucault, *Security, Territory, Population: Lectures at the Collège de France, 1977–78* (New York: Palgrave Macmillan, 2007), 99.

23. Thomas Lemke, "New Materialisms: Foucault and the 'Government of Things,'" *Theory, Culture, and Society* 32, no. 4 (2015): 3–25.

24. Michel Foucault, "The Subject and Power," in *Power: Essential Works of Michel Foucault* (New York: New Press, 2000), 340–41.

25. Foucault, 341.

26. See also Griffiths and Joronen, "Governmentalizing Palestinian Futures"; Stephen Legg, "Subject to Truth: Before and after Governmentality in Foucault's 1970s," *Environment and Planning D* 34, no. 5 (2016): 858–76.

27. Further research is needed to do with anticipation, self-governing, and longer-term futures—especially where this has to do with reproduction

and thus demographics. In one group interview in al-Walaja, conversation turned to the checkpoint as a marker of worsening conditions for Palestinians that prompt reflective life decisions: "There are many thoughts that come into our minds for having babies, wondering if the situation will be safe on a financial and security basis. . . . It's even too much now to have two or three babies. This is not enough for the Palestinian family" (Lamees).

28. Nadera Shalhoub-Kevorkian, "Palestinian Women and the Politics of Invisibility: Towards a Feminist Methodology," *Peace Prints: South Asian Journal of Peacebuilding* 3, no. 1 (2010): 14.

29. Peteet, *Space and Mobility in Palestine,* 60–61.

30. See Geoffrey Boyce and Samual Chambers, "The Corral Apparatus: Counterinsurgency and the Architecture of Death and Deterrence along the Mexico/United States Border," *Geoforum* 120 (2021): 1–13.

31. For more on bureaucracy and "making nothing happen," see Griffiths et al., "Israel's International Mobilities Regime."

3. BEYOND THE CHECKPOINT

1. Sandro Mezzadra and Brett Neilson, *Border as Method; or, The Multiplication of Labor* (Durham, N.C.: Duke University Press, 2013), 8.

2. Spivak, "Can the Subaltern Speak?"

3. Ilan Pappé, *The Idea of Israel* (London: Verso, 2014), 305–13; Shalhoub-Kevorkian, *Militarization and Violence.*

4. On accelerating processes, see Wassim Ghantous and Mikko Joronen, "Dromoelimination: Accelerating Settler Colonialism in Palestine," *Environment and Planning D* 40, no. 3 (2002): 393–412.

5. On purposeful delaying processes, see Joronen, "Spaces of Waiting"; Anne Meneley, "Time in a Bottle: The Uneasy Circulation of Palestinian Olive Oil," *Middle East Report* 248 (2008): 18–23.

6. Peteet, *Space and Mobility in Palestine,* 139–68.

7. Ghassan Hage, *Waiting* (Carlton, Vic.: Melbourne University Publishing, 2009), 2.

8. Pierre Bourdieu, *Pascalian Meditations* (Stanford, Calif.: Stanford University Press, 2000), 228.

9. Helga Tawil-Souri, "Checkpoint Time," *Qui Parle* 26, no. 2 (2017): 400.

10. el-Haddad, "Quintessential Palestinian Experience."

11. Tawil-Souri, "Checkpoint Time," 398.

12. Tawil-Souri.

13. Tawil-Souri, 399–400.

14. See Rachel Pain and Lynn Staeheli, "Introduction: Intimacy-Geopolitics and Violence," *Area* 46, no. 4 (2014): 344–47.

15. See, e.g., Christine Sylvester, *War as Experience: Contributions from IR and Feminist Analysis* (London: Routledge, 2013).

16. Hyndman, "Feminist Geopolitics Revisited," 36.

17. Christopher Harker, "Precariousness, Precarity, and Family: Notes from Palestine," *Environment and Planning A* 44, no. 4 (2014): 854.

18. Harker, 861.

19. Nancy Chodorow, *The Reproduction of Mothering: Psychoanalysis and the Sociology of Gender* (Berkeley: University of California Press, 1978).

20. Ellen Fleischmann, *The Nation and Its "New" Women: The Palestinian Women's Movement, 1920–1948* (Berkeley: University of California Press, 2003).

21. Peteet, *Gender in Crisis*.

22. Jean-Klein, "Into Committees, out of the House?"

23. Simona Sharoni, *Gender and the Israeli–Palestinian Conflict: The Politics of Women's Resistance* (New York: Syracuse University Press, 1995).

24. Shalhoub-Kevorkian, *Militarization and Violence*.

25. Shalhoub-Kevorkian, 13–16.

26. Julie Peteet, *Landscape of Hope and Despair: Palestinian Refugee Camps* (Philadelphia: University of Pennsylvania Press, 2005), 89,

27. Peteet, 89.

28. Katherine Brickell, "Geopolitics of Home," *Geography Compass* 6, no. 10 (2012): 576.

29. Nicholas De Genova, "Spectacles of Migrant 'Illegality': The Scene of Exclusion, the Obscene of Inclusion," *Ethnic and Racial Studies* 36, no. 7 (2013): 1183.

4. AN URBAN GEOGRAPHY OF CHECKPOINT 300 AND THE HEBRON ROAD

1. Genesis 48:7: "As for me, when I came from Paddan, to my sorrow Rachel died in the land of Canaan on the way, when there was still some distance to go to Ephrath, and I buried her there on the way to Ephrath (that is, Bethlehem)" (ESV). There is debate on the location of Rachel's burial site, with some philological arguments indicating a site to the north of Jerusalem at modern-day Al-Ram (biblical Ramah). See Tom Selwyn, "Tears on the Border," in *Contested Mediterranean Spaces: Ethnographic Essays in Honour of Charles Tilly*, ed. Maria Kousis, Tom Selwyn, and David Clark, 276–98 (Oxford: Berghahn Books, 2011); Fred Strickert, *Rachel Weeping: Jews, Christians, and Muslims at the Fortress Tomb* (Collegeville, Minn.: Liturgical Press, 2007).

2. Helga Tawil-Souri, "New Palestinian Centers: An Ethnography of

the Checkpoint Economy," *International Journal of Cultural Studies* 12, no. 3 (2009): 217–35.

3. It must be highlighted that this five-hundred-meter stretch traveled by the Patriarch and functionaries to Bethlehem moves between Israeli-controlled Jerusalem (which is not considered by the UN as part of Israel), into Area C of Bethlehem, and back into (again unrecognized) Israel before reentering Area C in Bethlehem and moving up the hill into Palestinian Authority–administered Area A.

4. I take "inside" here to mean the side assigned to Palestinians at the 1949 Armistice—that is, internationally recognized Palestinian territory.

5. Rafi Segal and Eyal Weizman, *A Civilian Occupation: The Politics of Israeli Architecture* (London: Verso, 2003).

6. For plans announced by the Jerusalem Municipality, see https://www.jerusalem.muni.il/en/newsandarticles/parkingmesseges/hebron-road-construction/.

7. The demonyms "Bethlehemite" and "Jerusalemite" have taken on new resonance in the post-Oslo period that, in an important way, defers to Israeli spatial delineations. For instance, a Palestinian from Beit Safafa—now part of the Jerusalem Municipality—would previously have more closely identified with Bethlehem, as it is the closest urban center, but is now considered a Jerusalemite because of the blue ID card given to residents and the corollary benefits that brings in terms of mobility and municipal services. As one person put it, "Bethlehem was always a southern extension of Jerusalem, so there was no need for the idea of 'Bethlehemite' before they built the wall."

8. The problem is obviously rooted in Israel's land grabbing, but residents point also to a request to the governor of Bethlehem made by Yasser Arafat in 2003 that read, "I hope that your honours will consider the [Rachel's Tomb region] as economically stricken and therefore that stores are exempted from taxes on income and property to help the people of the area cling to their land and their shops" (trans. Nadir Mauge). The request was accepted but, according to some (not all) residents, not evenly applied.

9. From personal correspondence with a Bethlehem Municipality official and resident of the area.

10. E.g., "Living in the Shadow of the Wall," *Al Jazeera*, December 28, 2011, https://www.aljazeera.com/opinions/2011/12/28/living-in-the-shadow-of-the-wall; "Walled Off Hotel: Not All Palestinians Are Happy with Banksy's Bethlehem Hotel," *Independent*, March 8, 2017, https://www.independent.co.uk/travel/middle-east/walled-off-hotel-banksy-guesthouse-palestinians-bethlehem-israel-separation-barrier-graffiti-artist-a7617391.html; "Palestinians Fear Being Trapped by Israeli Wall,"

New York Times, February 18, 2003, https://www.nytimes.com/2003
/02/18/world/palestinians-fear-being-trapped-by-israeli-wall.html.

11. The family and the house are also subjects of countless rumors of
and speculation about deals made with Israel to gain favorable conditions
(e.g., Jerusalem IDs) in exchange for negotiating the route of the wall. One
person told me that the family "capitalized on the misery" of the area by
saving their own property, while other families' properties were destroyed
or brought within total Israeli control. It is not my concern to verify this but
to report a repeated perspective. It must be contextualized with the following: one member of the family spoke out in favor of Israel's wall and is now
making a career in the United Kingdom as a spokesperson for "peace," a role
that most Bethlehemites would dismiss as normalizing Israeli colonialism.

12. https://tinyurl.com/4uatpk4u.

13. Mark Stone, "Bethlehem: The Town That Symbolises the Stalemate
in the Israel–Palestine Conflict," *Sky News,* December 25, 2019, https://
news.sky.com/story/bethlehem-the-town-that-symbolises-the-stalemate
-in-the-israel-palestine-conflict-11894471. A longer interview with Claire
Anastas is Toine van Teeffelen, "The Writing on the Wall: Claire Anastas,"
Electronic Intifada, December 23, 2005, https://electronicintifada.net
/content/writing-wall-claire-anastas/5820.

14. Scholarly writing includes Jamil Khader, "Architectural Paral-
lax, Neoliberal Politics and the Universality of the Palestinian Struggle:
Banksy's Walled Off Hotel," *European Journal of Cultural Studies* 23, no. 3
(2020): 474–94, and Tommaso Milani, "Banksy's Walled Off Hotel and the
Mediatization of Street Art," *Social Semiotics* 32, no. 4 (2022): 545–62. Two
examples of journalism on the Walled Off are "'Worst View in the World':
Banksy Opens Hotel Overlooking Bethlehem Wall," *Guardian,* March 3,
2017, https://www.theguardian.com/world/2017/mar/03/banksy-opens
-bethlehem-barrier-wall-hotel, and "Banksy Puts Mark on Bethlehem Hotel
with 'Worst View in the World,'" *New York Times,* March 3, 2017, https://
www.nytimes.com/2017/03/03/world/middleeast/banksy-hotel-bethlehem
-west-bank.html.

15. https://walledoffhotel.com/questions.html.

16. After many inquiries, I am still not sure why this was built into the
wall; watchtowers and cameras provide surveillance capacity.

17. It was at the gate and under the watchtower that Pope Francis made
an unscheduled and widely covered stop to pray at the wall for peace. See
the video published on the *Guardian* website, "Pope Francis Prays at the
Separation Wall during West Bank Visit," May 25, 2024, https://www
.theguardian.com/world/video/2014/may/25/pope-francis-prays
-separation-wall-west-bank-visit-video.

18. Soldiers also use live fire from positions at the top of the wall and from

the watchtowers; see Activestills, "Israeli Army Increasing Use of Live Fire at West Bank Protests," +972 *Magazine,* January 19, 2015, https://www.972mag .com/israeli-army-increasing-use-of-live-fire-at-west-bank-protests/.

19. On the use of tear gas in the area (discussed at length in chapter 5), see Jess Ghannam and Rohini Haar, *No Safe Space: Health Consequences of Tear Gas Exposure among Palestine Refugees* (Berkeley: University of California, Berkeley School of Law, Human Rights Center, 2018), https:// humanrights.berkeley.edu/programs-projects/past-projects/no-safe-space. A reference to "the camp's 'death row'" appears in Gideon Levy and Alex Levac, "An Israeli Sniper Shot Me," *Haaretz,* October 16, 2015, https:// tinyurl.com/4b8abb2p.

20. Levy and Levac.

21. There is a widely circulated image of the banner, but I was not able to obtain permission to publish it here.

22. There is an image of Stock, but I was not able to obtain permission to publish it here.

23. *Abu* is a *kunya,* the teknonymic practice in Arabic of referring to a person according to their eldest child (e.g., *abu* means "father of"). *Abu* and *umm* (mother of) signify confidence and respect.

24. Quoted in Brett Kline, "Welcome to Bethlehem, Where 'Teargas Has Become Our Perfume,'" *Haaretz,* November 11, 2015, https://tinyurl.com /bdhtjc5x.

25. There is also a case made by philologists and theologians that the site of Rachel's burial place is in modern-day Ramah, close to Ramallah. See Strickert, *Rachel Weeping,* 61–69.

26. Glenn Bowman, "Israel's Wall and the Logic of Encystation: Sovereign Exception or Wild Sovereignty?," *Focaal* 50 (2007): 127–35.

27. This account is presented (in a somewhat glorified form) in the video by Yeshivat Bnei Rachel, "Yeshivat Bnei Rachel Kever Rachel Beit Lechem," YouTube video, 5:51, https://www.youtube.com/watch?v=0vy_1PI2428. Another account is Nadav Shragai, "Rachel's Tomb: Beyond or Within?," *Haaretz,* July 22, 2022, https://tinyurl.com/579awm8m.

28. Lior Lehrs, "Political Holiness: Negotiating Holy Places in Eretz Israel/Palestine, 1937–2003," in *Sacred Space in Israel and Palestine,* ed. Marshall Breger, Yitzhak Reiter, and Leonard Hammer (Abingdon, U.K.: Routledge, 2013), 237.

29. Oslo II Accord, annex I, article V, part 7.

30. Quoted in Nadav Shragai, "Rachel's Tomb to Be Annexed—De Facto," *Haaretz,* September 12, 2002, https://tinyurl.com/3p46j9e9.

31. A 2005 report by the OHCHR special rapporteur John Dugard reads, "The monstrous Wall around Rachel's Tomb . . . has killed a once vibrant commercial neighbourhood of Bethlehem. Although Rachel's

Tomb is a site holy to Jews, Muslims, and Christians, it has effectively been closed to Muslims and Christians. Moreover, 72 of the 80 businesses in the neighbourhood have been compelled to close." See https://www.un.org /unispal/document/auto-insert-181826/.

32. Some news outlets refer to it as Beit Hamakolot or (mostly by settlers) Beit Midrash.

33. See the Bnei Rachel website: https://bneirachel.com/en/.

34. Nadav Shragai, "Back from the Grave," *Israel Hayom,* September 6, 2021, https://www.israelhayom.com/2021/09/06/back-from-the-grave/.

35. https://bneyrachelmm.com/index.php/about/.

36. The renovation of Rachel's Tomb was designed by the architectural firm of Kalman Katz Yaron Katz. The firm's website includes before-and -after photos: https://katz-arch.com/portfolio/rachels-tomb-bethlehem-2/.

37. Sara Roy, "The Gaza Strip: A Case of Economic De-development," *Journal of Palestine Studies* 17, no. 1 (1987): 56–88; Roy, *The Gaza Strip: The Political Economy of De-development* (Beirut: Institute for Palestine Studies, 1995).

38. Sari Hanafi, "Explaining Spacio-cide in the Palestinian Territory: Colonization, Separation, and State of Exception," *Current Sociology* 61, no. 2 (2012): 192.

39. See Dorota Golańska, "Slow Urbicide: Accounting for the Shifting Temporalities of Political Violence in the West Bank," *Geoforum* 132 (2022): 125–34.

40. See Mikko Joronen and Wassim Ghantous, "Weathering Violence: Atmospheric Materialities and Olfactory Durations of 'Skunk Water' in Palestine," *Environment and Planning E* 7, no. 3 (2024): 1122–41.

41. Stephen Graham, "The Urban 'Battlespace,'" *Theory, Culture, and Society* 26, no. 7–8 (2009): 278–88; Graham, *Cities under Siege: The New Military Urbanism* (London: Verso, 2011).

42. Griffiths, "Thanato-geographies of Palestine."

43. Agamben, *State of Exception,* 35.

44. Agamben.

45. Agamben, *Homo Sacer.* For further discussion, see chapter 6.

46. Judith Butler, *Frames of War: When Is Life Grievable?* (London: Verso, 2009), 28.

47. Butler, 26. See also Hammami, "Precarious Politics."

5. PRODUCING CHECKPOINT SPACE

1. Doreen Massey, *For Space* (London: SAGE, 2004), 12.

2. Ian Cook, "Follow the Thing: Papaya," *Antipode* 36, no. 4 (2004): 642.

3. Much of this information is owed to the research organization Who

Profits and to other investigative sources (e.g., Corporate Occupation and
the Database of Israeli Military and Security Export, the mapping project
Campaign against the Arms Trade), company websites (whose pride in
their products is never not shocking), and research I commissioned specifically for this chapter by a Hebrew-speaking expert.

4. B'Tselem, "Inhuman Conditions in Checkpoint 300."

5. Cluster B comprises Checkpoint 300 (Rachel), a-Sheikh Sa'ed,
Mazmoriya, Ein Yael (al-Walaja), a-Sawahrah, a-Za'ayem, Mazmuriyeh,
the Tunnels (Bayt Jala), Anata (Ring Road), and a-Zaitun Checkpoints.
Another company, Sheleg Lavan, won the operation of the other six checkpoints in Cluster A, around northern Jerusalem.

6. In May 2016, the Crossing Points Authority (part of the Ministry
of Defense), the Ministry of Defense Finance Department, the Ministry of
Finance, and COGAT signed an agreement titled "The Crossings Upgrade
Plan 2016–2017: Memorandum of Understanding" (in Hebrew, "תכנית
מסמך :2017–2016 המעברים לשדרוג תכנית"). The agreement is mentioned
in the State Comptroller report 61/a (2011) titled "The Activity of the
Crossings between Israel and the Judea and Samaria Area" (in Hebrew,
"דוח שנתי 61א (2011) פעילות המעברים בין ישראל ובין אזור יהודה ושומרון").
See "The Activity of the Crossings between Israel and the Judea and
Samaria Area—Follow-up Findings—Cross-organizational Issues // 1797"
(in Hebrew), 18–19. According to an Israeli media article from January
2022, the Checkpoint 300's upgrade was completed in April 2019: https://
www.inn.co.il/news/399436. The amount allocated to redeveloping
Checkpoint 300 was NIS 25 million ($7 million): https://m.news1.co.il
/Archive/001-D-448705-00.html?t=110210&AfterBan=1. See also a
report in the *Washington Post*: "A High-Tech Facelift Takes the Sting out
of an Israeli Checkpoint—but Not out of the Occupation," June 11, 2019,
https://www.washingtonpost.com/world/israels-high-tech-face-lift-takes
-the-sting-out-of-checkpoints--but-not-of-the-occupation/2019/06/11
/3bda3690-78bf-11e9-a7bf-c8a43b84ee31_story.html.

7. I gathered information on hardware in Checkpoint 300 during many
crossings by foot and by memorizing details of the equipment inside.

8. See Corporate Occupation, "Combined Systems Tear Gas Launcher
Deployed at Gaza Fence," May 19, 2018, https://corporateoccupation
.org/2018/05/19/combined-systems-tear-gas-launcher-deployed-at
-gaza-fence/.

9. See Robert Cusack, "Israeli Soldiers Fire Live Ammunition at Civilian Crowd in Bethlehem," *New Arab,* July 28, 2017, https://www.newarab
.com/news/israel-fires-live-ammunition-civilian-crowd-bethlehem.

10. Josh Breiner, "Israel Using Drones to Tear Gas Palestinian Demonstrators in West Bank," *Haaretz,* April 28, 2021, https://tinyurl.com/485fhcec.

11. From personal correspondence with a Bethlehem Municipality worker.

12. https://garrett.com/careers.

13. https://www.rapiscansystems.com/en/company/about.

14. https://dimse.info/sandcat/.

15. Amnesty International, "Automated Apartheid: How Facial Recognition Fragments, Segregates and Controls Palestinians in the OPT," May 2, 2023, http://www.amnesty.org/en/documents/mde15/6701/2023/en/.

16. Amitai Ziv, "This Israeli Face-Recognition Startup Is Secretly Tracking Palestinians," *Haaretz*, July 15, 2019, https://tinyurl.com/2wc46nwr.

17. See 7amleh, "Facial Recognition Technology and Palestinian Digital Rights," 2020, https://7amleh.org/storage/Research%20and%20Position %20Papers/Facial%20Recognition%20Technology%20&%20Palestinian %20Digital%20Rights%20-%207amleh.pdf.

18. Olivia Solon, "Why Did Microsoft Fund an Israeli Firm That Surveils West Bank Palestinians?," NBC News, October 28, 2019, https:// www.nbcnews.com/news/all/why-did-microsoft-fund-israelifirm-surveils -west-bank-palestinians-n1072116. This article is also the source of the quote from an employee of AnyVision/Oosto in the chapter's epigraph.

19. Olivia Solon, "Microsoft Sells Stake in Israeli Facial Recognition Company," NBC News, March 27, 2020, https://www.nbcnews.com/tech /tech-news/microsoft-sells-stake-israeli-facial-recognition-company -n1170781.

20. Business Wire, "AnyVision Closes $74 Million Series A with New Participation from M12 and DFJ Growth," June 28, 2019, https://www .businesswire.com/news/home/20190618005250/en/.

21. https://www.anyvision.co/.

22. Paresh Dave and Jeffrey Dastin, "Why a U.S. Hospital and Oil Company Turned to Facial Recognition," Reuters, April 20, 2021, https://www .reuters.com/world/middle-east/exclusive-why-us-hospital-oil-company -turned-facial-recognition-2021-04-20/.

23. Solon, "Why Did Microsoft Fund an Israeli Firm?"

24. Solon.

25. See, e.g., Howard Hu, Jonathan Fine, Paul Epstein, Karl Kelsey, Preston Reynolds, and Bailus Walker, "Tear Gas—Harassing Agent or Toxic Chemical Weapon?," *JAMA* 262, no. 5 (1989): 660–63; Patricia Alejandra Huerta, Manuel Cifuentes, Marcelo González, and Tamara Ugarte-Avilés, "Tear Gas Exposure and Its Association with Respiratory Emergencies in Infants and Older Adults during the Social Uprising of 2019 in Chile: An Observational, Longitudinal, Repeated Measures Study," *BMJ Open* 13, no. 6 (2023): e067548; Rex Pui Kin Lam, Kin Wa Wong, and Chi Kin Wan, "Allergic Contact Dermatitis and Tracheobronchitis Asso-

ciated with Repeated Exposure to Tear Gas," *The Lancet* 396, no. 10247 (2020): e12.

26. Anna Feigenbaum, *Tear Gas: From the Battlefields of World War I to the Streets of Today* (London: Verso, 2017), 59–60.

27. Feigenbaum, 149

28. Ghannam and Haar, *No Safe Space.*

29. Ghannam and Haar, 3.

30. Who Profits reports that Combined Systems was awarded in September 2021 an NIS 4 million contract with the Israeli police forces to supply tear gas cannisters. This is in addition to its NIS 2.6 million contact with the Ministry of Interior to supply VENOM tear gas launchers. See Who Profits, *Israeli Repression of the Palestinian May Uprising: Suppliers of Crowd Control Weapons* (Tel Aviv: Who Profits, 2021), https://www.whoprofits.org//writable/uploads/old/uploads/2022/01/Israeli-Repression-of-the-Palestinian-May-Uprising-Final.pdf.

31. Shrimrit Lee, "Simulating the Contact Zone: Corporate Mediations of (Less-Lethal) Violence in Israel, Palestine, and Beyond," *Jerusalem Quarterly* 75 (2018): 24–47.

32. Jack Shenker and Luke Harding, "US Firm's Teargas Used against Tahrir Square Protesters," *Guardian,* November 21, 2011, https://www.theguardian.com/world/2011/nov/21/tahrir-square-us-teargas-used-egypt.

33. Who Profits, *Proven Effective: Crowd Control Weapons in the Occupied Palestinian Territories* (Tel Aviv: Who Profits, 2014), 17, https://www.whoprofits.org//writable/uploads/publications/1668627954_45a9756927392d533f0e.pdf.

34. Feigenbaum, *Tear Gas,* 149.

35. Josh Breiner, "Israel Using Drones to Tear Gas Palestinian Demonstrators in West Bank," *Haaretz,* April 28, 2021, https://tinyurl.com/485fhcec; Nick Waters, "First ISIS, Then Iraq, Now Israel: IDF Use of Commercial Drones," *Bellingcat* (blog), June 18, 2018, https://bellingcat.com/news/mena/2018/06/18/first-isis-iraq-now-israel-idf-use-commercial-drones/.

36. Stockholm International Peace Research Institute, "Trends in International Arms Transfers, 2022," SIPRI Fact Sheet, March 2023, https://www.sipri.org/sites/default/files/2023-03/2303_at_fact_sheet_2022_v2.pdf.

37. https://investigate.afsc.org/company/elbit-systems.

38. See Mohamed El-Shewy, Mark Griffiths, and Craig Jones, "Israel's War on Gaza in a Global Frame," *Antipode* 57, no. 1 (2025): 75–95.

39. Romana Rubeo and Ramzy Baroud, "'Combat Proven': Israel's Thriving War Business in Europe," *Al Jazeera,* December 21, 2018, https://

www.aljazeera.com/opinions/2018/12/21/combat-proven-israels-thriving -war-business-in-europe.

40. Quoted in Kaplan, *Our American Israel*, 267.

41. Brittany Dawson, "U.S.–Mexico Border: An Israeli Tech Laboratory," Institute for Palestinian Studies, December 6, 2018, https://www.palestine -studies.org/en/node/232052.

42. Quoted in Dawson.

43. Andy Park, "Pro-Palestine Activists around the World Protest Israeli Weapons Manufacturer Elbit Systems," *Honi Soit*, October 25, 2023, https:// honisoit.com/2023/10/pro-palestine-activists-around-the-world-protest -israeli-weapons-manufacturer-elbit-systems/.

44. Aimé Césaire, *Discourse on Colonialism*, trans. Joan Pinkham (1950; repr., New York: Monthly Review Press, 2001), 36.

45. For a discussion of Aimé Césaire and the boomerang effect and boomerang-as-metaphor, see Nasser Abourahme, "Of Monsters and Boomerangs: Colonial Returns in the Late Liberal City," *City* 22, no. 1 (2018): 106–15.

46. Michel Foucault, *Society Must Be Defended: Lectures at the Collège de France, 1975–1976* (Basingstoke, U.K.: Palgrave Macmillan, 2003), 103.

47. See Naomi Klein, *The Shock Doctrine* (London: Penguin, 2007), 435.

48. Stephen Graham, "Laboratories of War," in *Surveillance and Control in Israel/Palestine: Population, Territory and Power*, ed. Elia Zureik, David Lyon, and Yasmeen Abu-Laban, 133–52 (Abingdon, U.K.: Routledge, 2010); Laleh Khalili, "The Location of Palestine in Global Counter-insurgencies," *International Journal of Middle East Studies* 42, no. 3 (2010): 413–33.

49. Loewenstein, *Palestine Laboratory*, 45–68.

50. Louise Amoore and Alexandra Hall, "Taking People Apart: Digitised Dissection and the Body at the Border," *Environment and Planning D* 27, no. 3 (2009): 461.

51. Amoore and Hall.

52. Hammami, "Destabilizing Mastery and the Machine," 96.

53. Alexandra Rijke and Claudio Minca, "Inside Checkpoint 300: Checkpoint Regimes as Spatial Political Technologies in the Occupied Palestinian Territories," *Antipode* 51, no. 3 (2019): 984.

54. Rijke and Minca, 986.

55. Stockholm International Peace Research Institute, "Trends in International Arms Transfers."

56. Halper, *War Against the People*, 217.

57. Halper, 213–26. On weapons trade and Israel–European Union relations, see David Cronin, *Europe's Alliance with Israel: Aiding the Occupation* (London: Pluto Press, 2011), 86–135.

58. Loewenstein, *Palestine Laboratory,* 150.

59. Weizman, *Hollow Land,* 150.

60. State comptroller, quoted in Shir Hever, *The Privatization of Israeli Security* (London: Pluto Press, 2018), 126, emphasis added.

61. For detailed reports on the growth of Israel's private security industry, see Hever, *Privatization of Israeli Security;* Who Profits, *Private Security Companies and the Israeli Occupation* (Tel Aviv: Who Profits, 2016), https://www.whoprofits.org//writable/uploads/publications/1668628693_c198e9ad5a8d7a69ef3b.pdf.

62. Hever, *Privatization of Israeli Security.*

63. See note 6 of this chapter.

64. See Muhammad Khalidi, "'The Most Moral Army in the World': The New 'Ethical Code' of the Israeli Military and the War on Gaza," *Journal of Palestine Studies* 39, no. 3 (2010): 6–23.

65. Shira Havkin, "Outsourcing the Checkpoints: When Military Occupation Encounters Neoliberalism," in *Israelis and Palestinians in the Shadows of the Wall,* ed. S. Abdallah and C. Parizot (Farnham, U.K.: Ashgate, 2015), 36.

66. E.g., in 2005, Modi'in Ezrachi was ordered to return millions of shekels it owed to more than a thousand security guards in unpaid benefits and wages. In 2007, following an audit by the Accountant General's Office, it was found that the company systematically violated the rights of the security guards and owed NIS 15 million, and in separate cases in 2008 and 2017, Modi'in Ezrachi was challenged by former employees for payment deductions and intimidating behavior among management. See "The Ministry of Finance Threatened, and the Security Company 'Civil Intelligence' Will Return Millions of Shekels to the Workers" (in Hebrew), *Marker,* December 18, 2006, https://www.themarker.com/career/2006-12-18/ty-article/0000017f-e998-df2c-a1ff-ffd966530000; "Workers Sue Security Company Modi'in Ezrachi: 'We Didn't Receive Compensation Because We Refused to Harm a Competing Company'" (in Hebrew), *Marker,* December 24, 2008, https://www.themarker.com/law/2008-12-24/ty-article/0000017f-db41-db22-a17f-fff1032c0000.

67. Ir Amim, *Shady Dealings in Silwan* (Jerusalem: Ir Amim, 2009), https://www.ir-amim.org.il/sites/default/files/Silwanreporteng.pdf.

68. For reports of the incidents, see "Deaf Palestinian Shot by Israeli Forces at Checkpoint," *Al Jazeera,* August 17, 2020, https://www.aljazeera.com/news/2020/8/17/deaf-palestinian-shot-by-israeli-forces-at-checkpoint; Einav Halabi and Corinne Elbaz-Aloush, "An Unusual Incident at the Checkpoint near Bethlehem: Security Guards Shot at a Motorcyclist, Who Fled" (in Hebrew), *Ynet,* December 21, 2022, https://www.ynet.co.il/news/article/rksfzsxti; Antony Loewenstein and Matt

Kennard, "How Israel Privatized Its Occupation of Palestine," *Nation,* October 27, 2016, https://www.thenation.com/article/archive/how -israel-privatized-its-occupation-of-palestine/.

69. Erella Grassiani, *Soldiering under Occupation: Processes of Numbing among Israeli Soldiers in the al-Aqsa Intifada* (Oxford: Berghahn Books, 2013), 53.

70. Yesh Din, *The Lawless Zone: The Transfer of Policing and Security Powers to the Civilian Security Coordinators in the Settlements and Outposts* (Tel Aviv: Yesh Din, 2014), 4, http://files.yesh-din.org/userfiles/file /Yesh%20Din_The%20Lawless%20Zone_Web_EN%20(1).pdf.

71. Quoted in Loewenstein and Kennard, "How Israel Privatized Its Occupation of Palestine."

72. See Marya Farah and Maha Abdallah, "Security, Business and Human Rights in the Occupied Palestinian Territory," *Business and Human Rights Journal* 4, no. 1 (2019): 7–31.

73. See International Institute for Nonviolent Action, *The Invisible Force* (Paris: International Institute for Nonviolent Action, 2016), https://www .iraqicivilsociety.org/wp-content/uploads/2016/08/NOVACT_THE_ INVISIBLE_FORCE_2016.pdf.

74. The URL is no longer accessible.

75. Andy Clarno, *Neoliberal Apartheid: Palestine/Israel and South Africa after 1994* (Chicago: University of Chicago Press, 2017), 104.

76. Nahla Abdo, *Women in Israel: Race, Gender and Citizenship* (London: Zed Books, 2013).

77. Klein, *Shock Doctrine,* 430.

78. Clarno, *Neoliberal Apartheid,* 37–43.

79. The report is no longer available.

80. Sarah Willen, "Toward a Critical Phenomenology of 'Illegality': State Power, Criminalization, and Abjectivity among Undocumented Migrant Workers in Tel Aviv, Israel," *International Migration* 45, no. 3 (2007): 16.

81. Rebeca Raijman and Adriana Kemp, "The Institutionalization of Labor Migration in Israel," *ARBOR* 192, no. 777 (2016): 16. See also Sai Englert, "Settlers, Workers, and the Logic of Accumulation by Disposses- sion," *Antipode* 52, no. 6 (2020): 1662.

82. "Thai Workers in Israel Tell of Harrowing Conditions," BBC News, November 23, 2018, https://www.bbc.co.uk/news/av/world-middle-east -46311922; Human Rights Watch, *A Raw Deal: Abuse of Thai Workers in Israel's Agricultural Sector* (New York: Human Rights Watch, 2015), https:// www.hrw.org/report/2015/01/21/raw-deal/abuse-thai-workers-israels -agricultural-sector.

83. Human Rights Watch, *A Raw Deal,* 39.

84. Human Rights Watch, 40.

85. BBC News, "Thai Workers in Israel."

86. Penchan Charoensuthipan, "Govt Allays Israel Labour Pact Fears," *Bangkok Post,* February 9, 2020, https://www.bangkokpost.com/thailand /general/1853464/govt-allays-israel-labour-pact-fears; Matan Kaminer, "Saving the Face of the Arabah: Thai Migrant Workers and the Asymmetries of Community in an Israeli Agricultural Settlement," *American Ethnologist* 49, no. 1 (2022): 118–31.

87. Works that take this approach and inform the analysis in this chapter are Clarno, *Neoliberal Apartheid,* and Mark Griffiths and Andrew Brooks, "A Relational Comparison: The Gendered Effects of Cross-Border Work in Palestine within a Global Frame," *Annals of the American Association of Geographers* 112, no. 6 (2022): 1761–76.

88. Uri Blau, "The Settler Behind Shadowy Purchases of Palestinian Land in the West Bank," *Haaretz,* June 8, 2012, https://tinyurl.com /3dam4shb.

89. One company name used for the purchase and established by Mamo was Al Wattan ("the homeland" in Arabic). Al Wattan was registered with the Civil Administration (not the Registrar of Companies in Israel) and thus eligible to complete real estate transactions in the West Bank and able to pose as an Arab purchaser.

90. Blau, "Settler Behind Shadowy Purchases."

91. Brenna Bhandar, *Colonial Lives of Property: Law, Land, and Racial Regimes of Ownership* (Durham, N.C.: Duke University Press, 2018); Gary Fields, *Enclosure: Palestinian Landscapes in a Historical Mirror* (Berkeley: University of California Press, 2017).

92. Rashid Khalidi, *The Hundred Years' War on Palestine: A History of Settler Colonial Conquest and Resistance* (London: Profile Books, 2020); Gershon Shafir, "Theorising Zionist Settler Colonialism in Palestine," in *The Routledge Handbook of the History of Settler Colonialism,* ed. Edward Cavanagh and Lorenzo Veracini, 335–52 (London: Routledge, 2017).

93. This is based on a U.S. Internal Revenue Service submission dated 2017 that is publicly available at https://tinyurl.com/3rv3wdud.

94. https://www.jgive.com/new/en/gbp/donation-targets/110687 /about.

95. https://www.gofundme.com/f/rachel039s-tomb-project.

96. https://www.bruriah.org/copy-of-message-from-our-principal.

97. https://www.keverrachelheritagefund.org/.

98. Edward Said, "Dreams and Delusions," *Al-Ahram Weekly,* August 30, 2003.

99. See Mark Griffiths and Kali Rubaii, "Late Modern War and the Geos: The Ecological 'Beforemaths' of Advanced Military Technologies," *Security Dialogue* 56, no. 1 (2025): 38–57.

100. See Patrice Sutton and Robert Gould, "Nuclear Weapons," in *War and Public Health,* ed. Barry S. Levy and Victor W. Sidel (Oxford: Oxford University Press, 2008), 163–64.

101. Reuters, "Israel Reports Record $12.5 Billion Defence Exports, 24% of Them to Arab Partners," June 13, 2023, https://www.reuters.com/business/aerospace-defense/israel-reports-record-125-bln-defence-exports-24-them-arab-partners-2023-06-13/.

102. See, e.g., Abdo, *Women in Israel*; Pappé, *Idea of Israel.*

103. Ilan Pappé, "The Mukhabarat State of Israel: A State of Oppression Is Not a State of Exception," in *Thinking Palestine,* ed. Ronit Lentin, 120–32 (London: Zed Books, 2008); Oren Yiftachel, "(Un)settling Colonial Presents," *Political Geography* 27, no. 3 (2008): 364–70.

104. Eylon Etshtein, quoted in Ziv, "This Israeli Face-Recognition Startup."

105. Rhys Machold, "Reconsidering the Laboratory Thesis: Palestine/Israel and the Geopolitics of Representation," *Political Geography* 65 (2018): 91.

106. For clear accounts of this shared know-how, see Kaplan, *Our American Israel*; Massad, *Persistence of the Palestinian Question*; Steven Salaita, *Inter/nationalism: Decolonizing Native America and Palestine* (Minneapolis: University of Minnesota Press, 2016).

107. Massey, *For Space,* 9, 10.

6. RE/MAKING COLONIAL SPACE

1. https://darjacir.com/About-Us.

2. See a profile in the *New York Times*: Aruna D'Souza, "At a Cultural Hub in Bethlehem, Art Thrives in the Fray," July 15, 2021, https://www.nytimes.com/2021/07/15/arts/design/bethlehem-culture-center-.html. This article is also the source of the Aline Khoury quote in the chapter's epigraph.

3. Quoted in an *Art Newspaper* profile: Charlotte Jansen, "As Israel Is Rocked by Protests, a West Bank Cultural Centre Seeks to 'Represent the Palestinian Struggle,'" June 5, 2023, https://www.theartnewspaper.com/2023/06/05/as-israel-is-rocked-by-protests-a-west-bank-cultural-centre-seeks-to-represent-the-palestinian-struggle.

4. D'Souza, "At a Cultural Hub in Bethlehem."

5. On the uneven distribution of water in Palestine, see Hannah Boast, *Hydrofictions: Water, Power and Politics in Israeli and Palestinian Literature* (Edinburgh: Edinburgh University Press, 2020), and Jan Selby, *Water, Power and Politics in the Middle East* (London: I. B. Tauris, 2003).

6. These quotes are from a profile published by Xinhua News Agency

(the state news agency of China) titled "Palestinian Blacksmith Turns Tear Gas Canisters into Artworks," https://english.news.cn/20230320/4573bc 08bd9048bfb6fe6c74901b1c80/c.html, and the Palestinian Safa news agency. The full article is now deleted, but a summary is available: https://www.all4palestine.org/ModelDetails.aspx?gid=13&mid=120733.

7. https://www.alaslah.org/; https://aeicenter.org/.

8. Jenny Kelly, *Invited to Witness: Solidarity Tourism across Occupied Palestine* (Durham, N.C.: Duke University Press, 2022), 76–77.

9. Kelly, 2.

10. https://aeicenter.org/wallposters-2/.

11. Dana Hasan and Sahera Bleibleh, "The Everyday Art of Resistance: Interpreting 'Resistancescapes' against Urban Violence in Palestine," *Political Geography* 101 (2023): 1–11.

12. Tamara Nassar, "Banksy's 'Walled Off Hotel' Is a Form of Gentrification," *Mondoweiss*, March 2017, http://mondoweiss.net/2017/03/banksys -walled-gentrification/#sthash.RZC5LgIp.dpuf.

13. Ibrahim Fraihat and Hamid Dabashi, "Resisting Subjugation: Palestinian Graffiti on the Israeli Apartheid Wall," *Ethnic and Racial Studies* 47, no. 13 (2023): 2719.

14. Quoted in Bahira Amin, "Apartheid Art: The Stories Behind Striking Palestinian Graffiti," *Scene Now*, October 23, 2023, https://scenenow.com /ArtsAndCulture/Apartheid-Art-The-Stories-Behind-Striking-Palestinian -Graffiti.

15. Connie Gagliardi, "Palestine Is Not a Drawing Board: Defacing the Street Art on the Israeli Separation Wall," *Visual Anthropology* 33, no. 5 (2020): 448.

16. This quote is from an *Al Jazeera* video published on Facebook: "The Man Selling Coffee at Checkpoint 300 for More Than a Decade," https://www.facebook.com/watch/?v=347523819266707.

17. BBC, "Menu Written on West Bank Barrier," September 25, 2008, http://news.bbc.co.uk/1/hi/world/middle_east/7635585.stm.

18. Tawil-Souri, "Qalandia Checkpoint," 22.

19. Tawil-Souri, "New Palestinian Centers," 232.

20. Rema Hammami, "On the Importance of Thugs/The Moral Economy of a Checkpoint," *Jerusalem Quarterly* 22–23 (2005): 26.

21. Hammami.

22. Hammami, 28.

23. Hammami, "On (Not) Suffering at the Checkpoint."

24. Hammami, 1.

25. Nadera Shalhoub-Kevorkian, "Negotiating the Present, Historicizing the Future: Palestinian Children Speak about the Israeli Separation Wall," *American Behavioral Scientist* 49, no. 8 (2006): 1114.

26. Shalhoub-Kevorkian, *Militarization and Violence,* 188–89.

27. Shalhoub-Kevorkian, 197. Connected work on "checkpoint knowledge" and the manifold tactics used by Palestinians to maintain mobilities through checkpoints includes Amahl Bishara, "Driving While Palestinian in Israel and the West Bank: The Politics of Disorientation and the Routes of a Subaltern Knowledge," *American Ethnologist* 42, no. 1 (2015): 33–54, and Alexandra Rijke, "Checkpoint Knowledge: Navigating the Tunnels and Al Walaja Checkpoints in the Occupied Palestinian Territories," *Geopolitics* 26, no. 5 (2021): 1586–1607.

28. Tawil-Souri, "New Palestinian Centers," 230. On the Tora Bora method, see also Rema Hammami, "Qalandiya: Jerusalem's Tora Bora and the Frontiers of Global Inequality," *Jerusalem Quarterly* 41 (2010): 29–51 (quoted as this chapter's epigraph).

29. On settler colonialism, recognition, and integration, see Glen Coulthard, *Red Skin, White Masks: Rejecting the Colonial Politics of Recognition* (Minneapolis: University of Minnesota Press, 2014).

30. Agamben, *Homo Sacer*; Agamben, *State of Exception.*

31. Achille Mbembe, "Necropolitics," *Public Culture* 15, no. 1 (2003): 11–40; Mbembe, *Necropolitics* (Durham, N.C.: Duke University Press, 2019).

32. Foucault, *Society Must Be Defended.*

33. Agamben, *State of Exception,* 2.

34. Agamben, *Homo Sacer,* 8.

35. See, e.g., Neve Gordon, *Israel's Occupation* (Berkeley: University of California Press, 2008); Derek Gregory, *The Colonial Present: Afghanistan, Palestine, Iraq* (Oxford: Blackwell, 2004).

36. Honaida Ghanim, "Thanatopolitics: The Case of the Colonial Occupation in Palestine," in Lentin, *Thinking Palestine,* 67.

37. Camillo Boano and Ricardo Martén, "Agamben's Urbanism of Exception: Jerusalem's Border Mechanics and Biopolitical Strongholds," *Cities* 34 (2013): 16.

38. See Mathew Abbott, "No Life Is Bare, the Ordinary Is Exceptional: Giorgio Agamben and the Question of Political Ontology," *Parrhesia* 14 (2012): 23–36. For a longer discussion on necro-/thanatopolitics and Palestine, see Griffiths, "Thanato-geographies of Palestine."

39. Tawil-Souri, "Qalandia Checkpoint," 23.

40. Hammami, "On (Not) Suffering at the Checkpoint."

41. For work that engages with Foucault's work on power as it relates to space, see Stephen Legg's articles "Subject to Truth" and "Subjects of Truth: Resisting Governmentality in Foucault's 1980s," *Environment and Planning D* 37, no. 1 (2019): 27–45.

42. Foucault, *History of Sexuality, Volume 1,* 95–96.

43. Foucault, 143.

44. Agamben, *Homo Sacer,* 6–9.

45. Foucault, *Punitive Society,* 228.

46. See Zeina Ghandour, *A Discourse on Domination in Mandate Palestine: Imperialism, Property and Insurgency* (London: Routledge, 2009); Rosemary Hollis, "Palestine and the Palestinians in British Political Elite Discourse: From 'the Palestine Problem' to 'the Two-State Solution,'" *International Relations* 30, no. 1 (2016): 3–28.

47. Quoted in Bernard Regan, *The Balfour Declaration: Empire, the Mandate and Resistance in Palestine* (London: Verso, 2017), 79.

48. Quoted in Edward Said, *Covering Islam: How the Media and the Experts Determine How We See the Rest of the World* (London: Vintage, 1981), 26–27.

49. Article 22 of the Covenant of the League of Nations, which addresses Mandate territories.

50. Israel Ministry of Foreign Affairs, "Security Fence," 2019 (no longer available).

51. Edward Said, preface to *Dreams of a Nation: On Palestinian Cinema,* ed. Hamid Dabashi (London: Verso, 2006), 3.

52. Giorgio Agamben, *The Omnibus Homo Sacer* (Stanford, Calif.: Stanford University Press, 2017), 108.

53. Giorgio Agamben, *"What Is an Apparatus?" and Other Essays* (Stanford, Calif.: Stanford University Press, 2009), 24, emphasis added.

54. Agamben, *Omnibus Homo Sacer,* 108, emphasis added.

55. Griffiths and Joronen, "Ungovernability and Ungovernable Life"; Mikko Joronen and Mitch Rose, "Vulnerability and Its Politics: Precarity and the Woundedness of Power," *Progress in Human Geography* 45, no. 6 (2021): 1402–18.

56. Agamben, *Homo Sacer,* 45–67.

57. Edward Said, "Permission to Narrate," *Journal of Palestine Studies* 13, no. 3 (1984): 27–48.

58. E.g., in the fields of development and refugee studies, Christine Sylvester, "Bare Life as a Development/Postcolonial Problematic," *Geographical Journal* 172, no. 1 (2006): 66–77; Adam Ramadan, "Spatialising the Refugee Camp," *Transactions of the Institute of British Geographers* 38, no. 1 (2013): 65–77.

59. See, e.g., Jemima Repo, "Thanatopolitics or Biopolitics? Diagnosing the Racial and Sexual Politics of the European Far Right," *Contemporary Political Theory* 15, no. 1 (2016): 110–18; Weheliye, *Habeas Viscus.*

60. Ngugi wa Thiong'o, *Decolonising the Mind: The Politics of Language in African Literature* (Nairobi: East African, 1986).

61. Eve Tuck and Wayne Yang, "Decolonization Is Not a Metaphor," *Decolonization: Indigeneity, Education, and Society* 1, no. 1 (2012): 1–40.

62. Edward Said, *Orientalism* (London: Penguin Books, 1978), 44.

CONCLUSION

1. Segal and Weizman, *A Civilian Occupation,* 19. See also Weizman, *Hollow Land,* 179–81.

2. Tawil-Souri, "New Palestinian Centers"; Tawil-Souri, "Qalandia Checkpoint"; Tawil-Souri, "Checkpoint Time."

3. See texts referenced in chapter 1, which each includes excerpts from conversations and interviews: *Al Jazeera,* "A Gruelling Life for Palestinian Workers in Israel"; Ashly, "Israel's Checkpoint 300"; Booth and Taha, "A Palestinian's Commute"; Ross, *Stone Men.*

4. *Israelism* is a term used by filmmakers Erin Axelman and Sam Eilertsen to explore the ways that some "young American Jews . . . are raised to defend Israel at all costs." See https://www.israelismfilm.com/.

5. In a *Guardian* report on American settlers in the West Bank, Chris McGreal writes, "Many of the estimated 60,000 Americans living in the West Bank outside of occupied East Jerusalem moved to settlements for the lifestyle and have little to do with the Palestinians on whose land they live. But a core of ideologically driven US citizens were at the forefront of building religious settlements on land expropriated from Palestinians while others have led the rise of what has been described as 'settler terrorism.'" McGreal, "How American Citizens Are Leading Rise of 'Settler Violence' on Palestinian Lands," *Guardian,* December 15, 2023, https://www.theguardian.com/world/2023/dec/15/biden-extremist-jewish-settlers-travel-ban-loophole.

6. Massey, *For Space,* 9.

7. Mezzadra and Neilson, *Border as Method,* 8.

8. Balibar, *Politics and the Other Scene,* 78.

9. See, e.g., Kristen Biehl's account of refugee processing in Turkey or Javier Auyero's ethnography of waiting for documentation in Argentina. Biehl, "Governing through Uncertainty: Experiences of Being a Refugee in Turkey as a Country for Temporary Asylum," *Social Analysis* 59, no. 1 (2015): 57–75; Auyero, *Patients of the State: The Politics of Waiting in Argentina* (Durham, N.C.: Duke University Press, 2012). For Palestine-focused writing on uncertainty and bureaucracy, see Griffiths and Joronen, "Governmentalizing Palestinian Futures," and Joronen, "Spaces of Waiting."

10. Gloria Anzaldúa, *Borderlands: La Frontera* (San Francisco: Aunt Lute Books, 1987), 2–3.

11. This is a point made in chapter 2 but that bears repeating here: there is a large amount of Palestinian writing on checkpoints as a "quintessential Palestinian experience." Khalidi, *Palestinian Identity*, 1. Helga Tawil-Souri writes, "Given their ubiquity, their increasing centrality in Palestinian social and economic life, their symbolic significance, and their manifestations of Israeli power over Palestinian time-space, checkpoints ought to be adopted as the new Palestinian icon." Tawil-Souri, "Qalandia Checkpoint," 23. See also Abourahme, "Spatial Collisions"; Amiry, *Nothing to Lose but Your Life*; Barghouti, *I Saw Ramallah*.

12. Anzaldúa, *Borderlands*, 3.

13. Pain and Staeheli, "Introduction," 345.

14. Hyndman, "Feminist Geopolitics Revisited," 36.

15. Chris Harker's work on the family and Israeli colonialism in Palestine is essential to this reading and many other points made in the book. Harker, "Geopolitics and Family in Palestine," *Geoforum* 42, no. 3 (2011): 306–15; Harker, "Precariousness, Precarity, and Family"; Harker, *Spacing Debt: Obligations, Violence, and Endurance in Ramallah, Palestine* (Durham, N.C.: Duke University Press, 2020).

16. Saree Makdisi, *Palestine Inside Out: An Everyday Occupation* (New York: W. W. Norton, 2010), 268.

17. Joronen and Griffiths, "Affective Politics of Precarity."

18. Craig Jones, *The War Lawyers: The United States, Israel, and Juridical Warfare* (Oxford: Oxford University Press, 2020).

19. Peteet, *Space and Mobility in Palestine*, 85.

20. Mikko Joronen and Jouni Häkli, "Politicizing Ontology," *Progress in Human Geography* 41, no. 5 (2017): 572.

21. J. K. Gibson-Graham, "Diverse Economies: Performative Practices for 'Other Worlds,'" *Progress in Human Geography* 32, no. 5 (2008): 620.

22. John Law and John Urry, "Enacting the Social," *Economy and Society* 33, no. 3 (2004): 390–410.

23. Said, "Permission to Narrate."

24. Tuck and Yang, "Decolonization Is Not a Metaphor," 7.

25. Walter Mignolo and Catherine Walsh, *On Decoloniality* (Durham, N.C.: Duke University Press, 2018), 5.

26. Leanne Betasamosake Simpson, "Land as Pedagogy: Nishnaabeg Intelligence and Rebellious Transformation," *Decolonization: Indigeneity, Education, and Society* 3, no. 3 (2014): 16.

27. Texts that challenge such normalizations include Paulo Freire, *The Politics of Education: Culture, Power, and Liberation* (Westport, Conn.: Greenwood, 1985); Wa Thiong'o, *Decolonising the Mind*; and Sylvia Wynter, *We Must Learn to Sit Down Together and Talk About a Little Culture: Decolonizing Essays, 1967–1984* (Leeds, U.K.: Peepal Tree Press, 2022).

28. Tuck and Yang, "Decolonization Is Not a Metaphor."

29. James Esson, Patricia Noxolo, Richard Baxter, Patricia Daley, and Margaret Byron, "The 2017 RGS-IBG Chair's Theme: Decolonising Geographical Knowledges, or Reproducing Coloniality?," *Area* 49, no. 3 (2017): 385.

30. Frantz Fanon, *The Wretched of the Earth* (New York: Grove Weidenfeld, 1963), 36.

Index

able-bodied, 20, 38
Abourahme, Nasser, 24, 32
Abraham, 2, 105; burial site of, 83
Abu Akleh, Shireen, 158
Abu Ismail, Maram Saleh, 139
Abu Sheira, Abed, 27, 161
ACLU, 127
activism, 18, 156, 157, 166, 171, 174
ADEX, 126
AEI. *See* Arab Educational Institute
Agamben, Giorgio, 34, 116, 168, 170,
    175; colonialism and, 172; gov-
    erning and, 173; thanatopolitics
    and, 167
agency: Palestinian, 151, 152, 167,
    175; political, 39, 169, 170, 176,
    181
agriculture, 144, 153, 180, 184; guest
    workers for, 142
agri-resistance, as political act, 153
Aida Camp, 103, 106, 124, 130, 152,
    153, 160 (fig.); death row of, 98;
    raids on, 132
al-Amarin, Saleh, 98
al-Aqsa Mosque, 16, 45, 87
al-Arrub refugee camp, 27
al-Jaafari, Wajdi, 33
Al Jazeera, 27, 219n16
al-Najjar, Rouzan, 158
al-Walaja Checkpoint, 14, 51, 71,
    82, 88, 144, 178, 179, 184, 211n5;
    waiting in, 72
al-Walaja Women's Group, 14, 44, 45,
    46, 47, 49, 60, 62, 68, 70, 80–81;

furniture-making business and,
    63; working with, 66
al-Wa'ra, Akram, 153, 154
Al Wattan, 217n89
American Friends of Beit Orot, 145
American Friends of Yeshivat Bnei
    Rachel, 146
Amir, Merav, 31
Amiry, Suad, 65
Amoore, Louise, 135
Anastas family, 84, 94, 96, 161
Anastas house, 87 (fig.), 96, 112
Anastas Walled-In guesthouse, 96,
    154
anger, 26, 42, 56, 66, 75, 77–78,
    78–79, 80
anticolonialism, 52, 96, 118, 121, 129,
    156
anti-Semitism, 8, 158, 183
anxiety, 26, 27, 39, 56, 58–59, 60, 63,
    77, 79
AnyVision/Oosto, 119, 122, 125,
    129, 137, 148, 149, 212n18; Israel
    Defense Prize for, 126–27
Anzaldúa, Gloria, 185
apartheid, 86, 176, 197n18
Arab Educational Institute (AEI), 97,
    154, 158; Wall Museum of, 157
Arafah, Ayed, 153
Arafat, Yasser, 85, 106, 207n8
architecture, 22; security, 85–86,
    104, 120, 173, 183, 190
Area A, 85, 99, 99 (fig.), 102, 106,
    124, 152, 153, 161

Area C, 1, 17, 84, 85, 93, 98, 99, 99
  (fig.), 101, 102, 115, 124, 152, 153,
  154, 158, 161
Armistice Agreements (1949),
  195n1, 207n4
Armoured Dove (Banksy), 98
artworks, 87, 102, 158, 159; military
  medals used for, 154; politicized,
  152
Ashkenazi Western Jewish
  Community, 105
Awwad family, 93, 94, 95 (fig.)
Axelman, Erin, 222n4
Azza Camp, 84, 98, 99, 106

baby-changing rooms, 24, 54, 122
Baha, 14, 82, 157 (fig.)
Bahamas Seafood Restaurant, 161
Balfour, Arthur, 96, 172
Balfour Declaration (1917), 8, 81, 96
Balloons Pizza, 91 (fig.), 92, 108
Banksy (artist), 158, 159
Banksy Guest House, 94, 96, 98
bare life, 34, 116, 168, 170, 175
Basel System, 126
BBC, 143, 161
Beersheba, 177
Beit Alpha Technologies, 124, 126
Beit Hanoun, 10, 186
Beit Jala, 88, 167, 177, 179 (fig.),
  211n5
Beit Lechem, 110
Beit Orot, 145
Beit Safafa, 88, 92, 188, 207n7
Beit Sahour, 83, 88, 166, 167
Beit Shemesh, 134
Belfast Telegraph, 22
Ben Gurion Airport, 10
Berda, Yael, 60
Berlant, Lauren, 39
Bethlehem, 1, 2, 5, 12, 13, 14, 17, 44,
  45, 49, 60, 69, 81, 83, 87, 88, 90,
92, 96, 97; artworks/graffiti in,
  158; Checkpoint 300 and, 15;
  colonialism and, 208n11; colonial
  rule in, 141; colonial space in, 183;
  death row of, 98; Hebron Road
  and, 177; historic Palestine and,
  3; holy sites of, 21; incursion into,
  145; Jewish settlement of, 146;
  municipal government of, 187;
  Rachel's Tomb and, 108; raids on,
  132; spatial effects of, 114, 169;
  tourism in, 154, 156; visiting, 11;
  watchtower over, 84, 85 (fig.)
Bethlehem Governorate, Advisory
  Council of, 93
Bethlehem Municipality, 93, 101, 124
Better Tomorrow, 126, 127
Bilal bin Rabah Mosque, 2, 98, 104,
  105, 157
bin Laden, Osama, 165
biometrics, 7, 17, 22, 30, 119, 120,
  122, 126, 132, 154, 156
biopolitics, 20, 35, 36, 37–38, 42,
  167–68, 188; feminist interventions on, 41
Bissell, David, 26
blacklists, 1, 20, 32, 182
Black Lives Matter, 158
Bnei Brak, 134
Bnei Rachel (Sons of Rachel), 87
  (fig.), 110, 112, 146, 147, 182;
  complex, 113 (fig.), 145
Bnei Rachel Yeshiva, 113 (fig.), 146
Boer War, 130
Bolsonaro, Jair, 149
Booking.com, 94
border crossing, 15, 21, 25, 54, 61,
  188; children and, 47; exclusions
  from, 33; experience of, 58, 67,
  75; illegal, 38; men and, 68; route
  of, 51; smooth, 48; women and,
  47, 58–59

borderlands, 15, 86, 181, 186; spatial reach of, 185
Bosch, 127
Bourdieu, Pierre, 73
BP, 129
British Mandate for Palestine, 2, 8, 91, 105, 172
British Parliament, Palestine Problem and, 171
Bruriah High School, 146
B'Tselem, 26
bureaucracy, 20, 32, 45, 48, 59, 61, 62, 171, 183, 187–88, 202n60, 205n31; paper wall of, 46, 188; slow-motion, 46
Butler, Judith, 116

cameras, 12, 19, 25, 96, 126
Campaign against Arms Trade, 211n3
capital, 131; ideologized, 17; movement of, 120
capitalism, 150; labor, 82; reproduction of, 35
car barriers, 6 (fig.)
care, 49; gendered roles of, 180; guest workers and, 142; politics of, 44
Caritas Road, 84, 96
Carlyle Group, 131
carob tree checkpoint, 4, 6 (fig.)
Cave of the Patriarchs, 84
CCTV, 21, 96
cemeteries, Muslim, 98, 102–3, 104, 106, 109, 130
Césaire, Aimé, 134, 214n45
Chearland, 145
check booths, 19, 121, 172
checkpoint(s): avoiding, 62; beyond the checkpoint, 63; building, 40; children and, 56–57, 59, 61–62; conditions at, 75; crossing, 26, 30, 42, 58–59, 81–82, 182; dysfunction of, 24; experiences at, 42, 79; fear at, 58; female-friendly, 34; flying, 4; global patterns at, 149; materialities of, 43; modification of, 162; network of, 165; number of, 5; overthrowing, 162; passing through, 55 (fig.); physical design of, 20; private, 166; regulation and, 16; sexualized attention at, 34; state-controlled, 35; sudden, 92; temporalities of, 16, 71–72; understanding, 63, 119, 151; women and, 41, 44, 45, 49, 50, 52–53, 59
Checkpoint Watch, 46
children: border crossing with, 57–58; care for, 56–57; checkpoints and, 77–78; relationships with, 77–78, 79
choke points, 86, 114, 161, 178
Christmas Restaurant, 92, 161
Church of the Nativity, 2, 87, 100
Civil Administration (COGAT), 5, 45, 46, 47, 203n4, 211n6, 217n89
civil society, 45, 48, 102, 179
COGAT. See Civil Administration
colonial control, 1, 66, 69, 121, 137, 140, 144, 151; Israeli, 152; spaces of, 37
colonialism, 8, 80, 115, 138, 146, 162, 176, 186; actionable knowledge of, 18, 189; contemporary, 184; dynamics of, 11; formation of, 181; Israeli, 9, 18, 114, 121, 147, 149, 150, 154, 167, 168, 172, 182; reproduction of, 35; waiting and, 73. See also settler colonialism
Colonial Office, 130; Palestine Problem and, 171
colonial power, 11, 17, 33, 164, 167, 174, 189; failure of, 171; Israeli,

41, 72; logics of, 40; space and, 81, 167

colonial restrictions, 4 (fig.); map of, 3 (fig.)

colonial space, 8, 15–16, 41, 67, 134, 151, 167, 177–78, 181, 183, 184; formation of, 12, 121; geography of, 190; key aspects of, 18; maintaining, 147; re/making, 17–18, 150; understandings of, 189

colonial state, 72, 120, 121, 176, 180, 185, 188; Israeli, 149

colonized, 80, 135, 171, 189

colonizers, 11, 135, 166, 171

Colt, 126

Combined Systems, 124, 125, 148, 213n30; tear gas cannister, 128 (fig.); tear gas from, 130–31

commuting, 23, 182; enduring, 69; punitive, 63

concrete blocks, 99, 99 (fig.)

Connolly, William, 37

control, 116, 174, 188; designs on, 169; domestic, 129, 134; economic, 36; impact of, 43; imposing, 140–41; Indigenous, 175; mechanism of, 27, 30, 60, 79, 120; spatial, 19, 166, 182, 185–86; state, 170. *See also* colonial control

Coole, Diana, 37, 39

Corporate Occupation, 211n3

corridors, 1, 11, 15, 19, 23, 26, 28 (fig.), 29 (fig.), 31, 38, 39, 67; caged, 21–22; children and, 54; women in, 51

Covid-19 pandemic, 102

Cultural Heritage Center, 98

cultural life, 45, 48, 152, 173, 182; Palestinian, 97; preservation of, 175

culture: border, 185; Indigenous, 175; Palestinian, 101, 103; third country, 185

Dabash, Hamid, 159

Darajah, Ahmed, 19, 33

Dar Jacir, 152, 153, 161, 167

Dayan, Moshe, 106

DCLs. *See* district liaison offices

death, politics of. *See* thanatopolitics

decolonization, 18, 152, 174, 175, 176, 189, 190

de-development, 18, 114, 181

defense contracts, 136, 148

delays, 1, 7, 8, 22, 25–26, 38, 45, 66, 68, 71, 72, 74–75, 76, 82

denial: possibility of, 48, 50, 62; threats of, 1, 32, 47

deterrence, 59, 62, 187

differently abled, 20, 182

dispossession, 40, 157, 162, 180, 187

district liaison offices (DCLs), 203n4

DJI Matrice 600 drone, 131

documentation, crossing without, 38–39

domestic life, 41, 44, 70, 138, 178

drones, 120, 124, 126, 132; tear gas from, 131

Duangdeegaew, Wicha, 143

East Jerusalem, 5, 45, 126, 132, 138, 142; ring settlements in, 88; tear gas in, 130

ecocide, 162

economic growth, 105–6, 145

economic life, 45, 114, 173, 223n11; gray zones of, 17; preservation of, 175; women and, 16

Economic Stabilization Plan (1985), 8, 141

education, 81, 102

Egyptian Border Guard, 10
Egyptian Central Security Forces, 131
Eilertsen, Sam, 222n4
Elbit Systems, 121, 124, 125, 126, 131–34, 137, 148, 149; Rotem-Reut border management database of, 122
Elbit Systems of America, 132, 133
el-Haddad, Laila, on waiting, 73
Elisra, 132
Elite KL, 133
Elon, Benny, 145
Erez Checkpoint, 10, 186
Eshkol, Levi, 106
ethics, 24, 173, 182, 188
Etshtein, Eylon, 127, 129
Etzion DCO, 46, 203n6
exhaustion, 8, 42, 46, 49, 50, 51, 59, 67, 72–73, 75–76, 77, 79, 82

facial recognition, 31, 120, 121, 125, 137
fear, 27, 42, 56, 57, 58, 66
feminism, Second Wave, 80
Floyd, George, 158
foreign aid, U.S., 136
Foucault, Michel, 39, 61, 220n41; biopolitics and, 36, 167–68; power and, 170
Fraihat, Ibrahim, 159
Francis, Pope, 34, 122, 208n16
Freeman, Morgan, 159
fruit/vegetable stands, 162 (fig.)

Gagliardi, Connie, 159
Garrett, 122, 125
Gate of the Patriarchs, 84, 85 (fig.), 87, 94, 98, 99, 124
Gaza, 8, 11, 96, 97, 131, 132, 133, 134, 146, 185; bombardments of, 20; crisis in, 9–10, 185; march in, 158; violence in, 186

gender, 63, 79, 182; delimiting, 62; dynamics, 51; effects, 33–34; maintaining of, 80; progressive policies on, 71; relations, 43, 81; roles, 70, 71; security and, 202n1; social organization of, 80
genocide, warnings of, 9
geopolitics, 11, 79, 136–37, 184; feminist, 18, 186; neorealist, 80, 186; security and, 80
George, David Lloyd, 171
Ghanim, Honaida, 168
Ghawanma, Yousef Jum'a, 27
Gibson-Graham, J. K., 188
Gilo Checkpoint, 15, 88, 90
globalization, 142, 148, 149, 150, 181; geometries of, 120, 121, 124
Golden State Warriors, 129
Google Ayosh, 127
governing, 60–61, 170, 173; analytic of, 61; attempts at, 169; biopolitical modes of, 41; colonial, 171; conception of, 167; condition of, 171; slow-motion, 26
graffiti, 158, 159
Graham, Stephen, 116
gray zones, 17, 86, 176
Great March of Return, 158
Green Line, 2, 88, 90, 188, 202n61; described, 195n1
grenade launchers, 126, 132
guest workers, 17, 119–20, 138, 142, 144, 186
Gush Etzion, 46, 177

Haaretz, 102, 145
Haddad, Iyad, 140
Hage, Ghassan, 73
Haies, Evelyn, 145
Häkli, Jouni, 188
Halabi Building, 100, 124
Hall, Alexandra, 134

Hallaq, Iyad, 158
Halper, Jeff, 136
Hamas, 9
Hammami, Rema, 59, 60, 135, 151, 162, 164, 170
Harb Building, 87 (fig.), 102, 103 (fig.), 108, 112, 115, 124
hardware, 12, 120, 121, 124, 125, 137, 211n7; military, 186; security, 134, 150, 152
Har Gilo, 90, 177, 179 (fig.)
Har Homa, 88
Harker, Chris, 80, 223n15
Hazboun, Joseph, 161
Hebron, 2, 5, 27, 69, 83, 98, 100, 154, 177; spatial designations of, 196n6
Hebron Governorate, 22
Hebron Hotel, 97
Hebron Road, 2, 6 (fig.), 15, 17, 21, 22, 32, 82–88, 85 (fig.), 87 (fig.), 89 (fig.), 93, 96, 100, 107 (fig.), 108, 109, 124, 125, 130; area of/ description, 114; Bethlehem and, 177; character of, 92; as commercial center, 105–6; control on, 121, 169; global wares/capital and, 120; light rail along, 90; as nonplace, 117–18; Palestinian life on, 112; soldiers on, 98; surveillance along, 132; tear gas on, 131; transformation of, 117–18; as urban battle space, 123 (fig.); urban warfare on, 115, 132; vibrancy of, 114–15; wall along, 102
Hertz, 141
Hewlett-Packard, 126
Hilo, Ala', 14
Homebred III, 145
homo sacer, 168, 169, 170, 175
house demolitions, 158, 180, 183, 187

Houston Texans, 129
HRW. See Human Rights Watch
humanitarianism, 10, 54, 187
humanitarian lane, 21, 33, 52, 121
human rights, 46, 63, 127, 140
human rights organizations, 24, 127, 143, 198n3, 203n6
Human Rights Watch (HRW), 143, 198n3
humiliation, 22, 26, 42, 43, 44, 53, 54, 61, 66, 156; daily, 62; gendered, 180
Hyndman, Jennifer, 186

Ibrahimi Mosque (al-Haram al-Ibrahimi), 83–84
ID cards, 4, 22, 30, 31, 156, 195n2, 207n7; black marks on, 38; blue/green, 92; checking, 5, 7, 13, 140; Jerusalem, 208n11; Palestinians and, 195n2; West Bank, 188
IDF. See Israel Defense Forces
inequality: gendered, 81; racial/ spatial, 156
infrastructure: checkpoint, 138; control, 67, 79; military, 154; security, 12, 38, 41, 44, 58, 61, 69, 78, 117, 120, 150, 166
Instro Precision Ltd., 133
International Monetary Fund, 141
Intifada: First, 3, 81, 130, 142; Second, 3, 108
intimidation, 4, 43–44, 46, 51, 53, 57, 60, 61, 62, 187, 203n6, 215n66
ISPRA Cyclone Anti-Riot Drone System, 124, 126, 131
Israel Defense Forces (IDF), 40, 84, 101, 102, 110–11, 112, 115, 116, 126, 131, 132; morality narrative of, 139; raids by, 98; slogan of,

127; T&M Israel and, 141; weapons for, 140

Israel Homeland Security, announcement by, 128 (fig.)

Israeli Air Force, 131

Israeli Border Police, 87, 124, 115

Israeli Business Initiative, 132–33

Israeli Military Industries, 124

Israeli Ministry of Defense, 45, 122, 126, 141, 211n6

Israeli Ministry of Finance, 211n6

Israeli Ministry of Foreign Affairs, 40, 172

Israeli Ministry of Interior, 132, 213n30

Israelism, 183, 222n4

Israeli Tourist Board, 124

Israel Police: checkpoint operations and, 122; guidelines from, 139; morality narrative of, 139

Israel Weapons Industries (IWI), 124, 126, 132

Issa, 97, 158

IWI. *See* Israel Weapons Industries

Jacir, Emily, 153

Jacir Palace, 87 (fig.), 99 (fig.), 100, 102, 104 (fig.), 109, 112, 123 (fig.), 124

Jaffa Gate (Bab al-Khalil), 83, 84

Jerusalem, 2, 5, 20, 26, 31, 45, 47, 48, 49, 54, 57, 59, 60, 74, 84, 87, 88; border crossing upgrades in, 122; entering, 7; ID card for, 92; infrastructure around, 138; struggles in, 185. *See also* East Jerusalem

Jerusalem Central Bus Station, 88

Jerusalem Light Rail, 90

Jerusalem Municipality, 88, 106, 207n7

Jesus, 2, 83

Jewish Voice for Peace, 127

Jordan River/Valley, 8, 180, 184, 195n1

Joronen, Mikko, 188

Kalman Katz Yaron Katz (firm), 210n36

Kando, 112

Kando gas station, 97

Kelly, Jenny, 154

Kever Rachel Fund Inc., 147

Kever Rahel. *See* Rachel's Tomb keys, on parking lot attendant's desk, 163 (fig.)

Khaled, Leila, 158

Khalidi, Rashid, 19, 32

Khalil. *See* Hebron

Khoury, Aline, 151, 218n2

kollel, 110, 146

Kotef, Hagar, 30

Kuwait, Iraqi invasion of, 8–9

labor, 39, 54; agreements, 142; agricultural, 81; checkpoint, 139; conditions, 138, 144; cross-border, 141, 144, 188; distribution of, 66; domestic, 7, 16, 60, 67, 70, 186; gendered divisions of, 35, 40, 47–48, 63, 67, 70, 71, 74; geographies of, 141; importing/deporting, 142–43; laws, 143; Palestinian, 20, 21, 120, 121, 198n3; physical/emotional, 67, 180; privatizing, 140; racialized, 138; reproduction of, 66; security, 139; waged, 60, 182, 186

labor market, 61, 70, 120, 138, 139; global, 144; Israeli, 44

Lachrymatory Generators, 130

Lancet, The, 129

land: designations, 184; Indigenous, 189; ordering of, 189–90; stewardship of, 189
"Land of Creation" campaign, 124
lateness: prospect of, 26, 27, 30; threats of, 32
League of Nations, 172
liberal democracy, 148, 149, 179
Likud party, 149
Loewenstein, Anthony, 134, 136
Louis Vuitton, 141
Lucy's furniture store, 90, 91 (fig.), 92
Lushsux, 159, 168

Machold, Rhys, 149
Machsomwatch, 203n6
Makdisi, Saree, 187
Manchester Airport Group, 125
Mandela, Nelson, 159
Manger Square, 100
Manger Street, 2, 84, 85 (fig.), 98, 100, 124
MAN Group, 124, 126
Mar Elias monastery, 92
marginalization, 80, 138, 142, 144, 169, 180, 182
Massey, Doreen, 120, 150, 184
Massumi, Brian, 27
Mauge, Nadir, 14, 86
Mbembe, Achille, 167
McGreal, Chris, 222n5
Memories (bar), 92, 108
Mercedes-Benz, 129
metal detectors, 19, 53–54, 121, 125
Mezzadra, Sandro, 184
MGM, 129
Microsoft, 127
Micro-Tavor, 124
Milipol, 126
militarism, 8, 148
Minca, Claudio, 135

Mitchell, Timothy, 40
Mizrahi Jews, 142
mobility, 45, 48, 49, 57, 114, 173, 180; economy of, 87–88; Palestinian, 166; restricted, 4, 62, 182
Modi, Narendra, 136, 149
Modi'in Ezrachi, 138, 139, 215n66
Mondoweiss, 159
Montefiore, Moses, 105
MR Hunter, 125–26, 131
M12, 127
M203 grenade launcher, 126
Mujahidin, 165
Musallam Building, 109, 110, 112, 113 (fig.), 124, 144, 145, 146, 157
My Tomb, Your Tomb, Rachel's Tomb (film), 14, 86

Nablus, 2, 5
Nakba, 8, 81, 96, 195n1
Naqab (Negev), 180, 184
Nassar, Tamara, 159
Nasser house, 94, 95 (fig.)
NATO, 125
Natsheh, Tawfeek, 109
Nazareth, 2, 177
NBC, 127, 129
necropolitics, 167, 188. See also thanatopolitics
Neilson, Brett, 184
nervousness, 77, 78–79
Netanyahu, Benjamin, 136, 149
New York Times, 153
No Safe Space: Health Consequences of Tear Gas Exposure among Palestine Refugees (Human Rights Center), 130
Nothing to Lose but Your Life: An 18-Hour Journey with Murad (Amiry), 65
NSO group, 136

Obeidallah, Abed al-Rahman Shadi, 98
occupation, 81, 158, 185; civilian, 90; justifying, 175; waiting and, 74
OCHA, 47
Odortec, 124
Olmert, Ehud, 108, 177
Organisation for Economic Co-operation and Development, 142
Orthodox Jews, 110, 145; anti-Zionist, 134
OSI Systems, 125
Oslo Accords (1995), 81, 85, 96, 102, 106, 108, 148, 153; construction boom following, 142
Oslo II Agreement, Rachel's Tomb and, 108
OSSA, 178

Pain, Rachel, 186
Palestine Action, 133
"Palestine is not a drawing board," 160 (fig.)
Palestine Laboratory, 134
Palestine Liberation Organization, 8
Palestinian Authority, 83
Palestinian Bureau of Statistics, 198n1
Palestinian Heritage Center, 153
Palestinian Identity: The Construction of Modern National Consciousness (Khalidi), 19
Palestinian life, 175; communal, 115; dismissing, 40, 176; persistence of, 167; regulation of, 38
Palestinians: conditions for, 10, 175; degradation of, 199n10; displacement of, 8; fissures between, 25; im/mobility of, 139; Indigenous, 148; mistreatment of, 35, 139; punishment of, 11; regulating movement of, 2

parenting, 70; limits on, 77–78
parking lot, 161, 163 (fig.)
Passover, 87
patriarchy: colonial, 44, 52; Palestinian, 81; struggles against, 81
Pegasus phone-hacking tool, 136
PENN ARMS, 131
permit system, 1, 16, 22, 38, 43, 45, 51, 54, 59, 61, 66, 70, 180, 182; depoliticizing, 66; described, 20; discriminatory, 67; gender, 67; wage labor and, 67
Peteet, Julie, 46, 72, 81
philanthropy, Zionist, 181, 184
physical harm, 76; increase in, 26–27
piety, 49, 50, 180
PINI Group, 178
planning: gray zone of, 17; regulations, 86; urban, 116
Plasan, 124, 125
Point Lookout Capital Partners, 131
political life, 1, 35, 40, 45, 82, 168; Palestinian, 97, 152, 169; preservation of, 175
politics, 43, 81, 152, 167; decolonial, 174, 176, 189; Israeli, 136; Palestinian, 188; possibility of, 151, 176; state control and, 170; women and, 16
Porush, Menachem, 106
positionality, 44, 52, 68, 182, 188, 192
power, 37, 41, 174, 189; defining, 170–71; dynamics of, 54, 56, 72, 138; microphysics of, 36; questions of, 32; relations, 35, 73, 79–80, 114, 172, 173, 188; space and, 114; state, 129, 168; tension and, 170; totalizing, 170. See also colonial power

precarity, 120, 121, 185; exposures to, 80; notion of, 116
production, machinery of, 36, 39, 41

Qabr Rāhīl. *See* Rachel's Tomb
Qalandia Checkpoint, 2, 5, 31, 74, 139, 140, 165, 180
"Qalandia Checkpoint as Space and Nonplace" (Tawil-Souri), 119
"Qalandiya: Jerusalem's Tora Bora and Frontiers of Global Inequality" (Hammami), 151
Qualcomm Ventures, 127
Queen's University Belfast, 137
queues, 22, 23, 23 (fig.), 26, 30, 65, 68, 69, 187; anxiety at, 77; described, 8, 157–58; disadvantages in, 51–52; waiting in, 73–74
Qumran Caves, 97

Rabin, Yikzhak, 85, 106
Rachel, 84, 105, 106, 109, 112; burial place of, 209n25; death of, 110, 206n1; legacy of, 147
Rachel's Children Reclamation Foundation, 147
Rachel's Tomb, 4 (fig.), 17, 85, 87 (fig.), 97, 98, 103, 104, 105, 107 (fig.), 110, 111 (fig.), 112, 113 (fig.), 118, 121, 124, 130, 131; annexation of, 106, 108, 109; artworks/graffiti near, 158; checkpoint and, 2, 4, 15, 122; colonialism and, 146; enclosing/fortifying, 120, 144, 209–10n31; Israeli presence at, 115–16, 146; Muslim cemetery at, 109; renovation of, 210n36; visiting, 147
Rafah crossing, 10, 186, 197n17
Ramadan, 16, 45, 47, 48, 49, 87, 164
Ramah, 206n1, 209n25
Ramallah, 2, 74, 162, 209n25

Rapiscan, 122, 125, 135
Red Crescent/Red Cross, 117
Repo, Jemima, 14
resistance, 4, 157, 159, 165, 171; domination and, 174; national, 151
responsibilities, 78; housework, 76; political, 120; pressure/stress from, 79; sharing, 71
Reuters, 129
Rijke, Alexandra, 135
Road of the Patriarchs, 2. *See also* Hebron Road
Rosh Hashanah, 109
Ross, Andrew, 20–21, 198n1, 202n60
Rotem-Reut, border management database, 122, 125, 132, 133
Rothschild, Jonathan, 133
Route 60, 176, 178, 179
Royal Melbourne Institute of Technology, 133
Russian Jews, arrival of, 142

Sabatin, Taqieddin, 158
Saca Cultural Heritage Center, 97
Saca family, 98
Said, Edward, 147, 172, 173, 195n3
Saleh, Mohammed, 152
Salsa, Wisam, 96
Sansour, Leila, 153
Sansur, Shibli, 100
Sansur Building, 84, 87 (fig.), 100, 102, 112, 154, 155 (fig.)
scanners, 5, 12, 17, 22, 119, 120, 121, 122, 135, 156
secret garden, 153, 155 (fig.), 161
security, 22, 34, 46, 61, 120, 172, 186; battle-tested, 125; domestic, 17, 119; environments, 119, 129; gender and, 202n1; geopolitics and, 80; global, 135; homeland, 133,

196n13; masculine logics of, 44;
military, 141; privatized, 139, 140,
141; regimes, 137, 156; strategies,
48; threats, 20, 69
Security Cabinet: Decision 64/B,
109; meeting of, 108–9
security checks, 30, 49, 54, 58, 59;
Israeli, 22; passing through, 57
Security Envelope, 108
security fences, 15, 172
security industry, 14, 120, 138,
203n10, 215n61
security staff, 22, 25, 35, 42, 44, 45,
121, 122, 132, 134–35, 138–39,
140, 215n66; harassment by, 16;
Israeli, 52, 53; shortages of, 69;
violence of, 67
security technologies, 19, 51, 121,
131; international networks of,
119; proliferation of, 138
Seesukha, Praiwan, 143
Segal, Rafi, 178
segregation, 7, 46, 138, 141, 144;
economic, 44; logics of, 188
self-governing, 61, 62, 204n27
separation barriers, 1, 15
Sephardic Oriental Jewish
Community, 105
September 11th, 9, 134
settlements, 146; legal ambiguity of,
21, 31; ring, 88
settler colonialism, 11, 15, 92, 133,
145, 147, 178, 185, 188, 197n18.
See also colonialism
7amleh, 127
Shalhoub-Kevorkian, Nadera,
59, 164–65; on children/
checkpoints, 61–62
Shamrad Electronics, 125
Shas Party, 108, 109
Sheleg Lavan, 211n5
#ShutDownElbit campaign, 133, 148

Simpson, Leanne Betasamosake, 189
Six Day War (1967), 96, 106
skunk water, 98, 102, 116, 124,
125–26; announcement about,
128 (fig.)
smart gates, 7, 22, 30, 122, 123 (fig.),
126
social life, 1, 35, 43, 81, 82, 103, 178;
Palestinian, 138, 169; women
and, 16
social organization, 44, 80
social reproduction, 42, 71, 74, 144
Soltam Systems, 132
Sons of Rachel. See Bnei Rachel
sovereignty, 54, 116, 175, 185
Soviet Union, breakup of, 142
space, 34, 82, 86, 168, 188; affective,
41; anxiety-inducing, 63; bare,
170; checkpoint, 2, 37, 38, 39,
42, 82; decolonial, 174, 186;
disciplinary, 37, 41; domestic,
143; economic, 180; gendered,
42, 44; geometric, 182; lived, 170;
militarized, 165; Palestinian, 34,
115, 152, 161, 164; place and, 115;
power and, 114; residential, 180;
security, 26, 122, 136; sovereign,
35, 165; thanatopolitical, 116. See
also colonial space
space-making, 144, 152, 167; colonial, 152, 164
spacio-cide, 18, 92, 93, 114, 115, 121,
162, 167, 169, 181
spatiality, 26, 34, 41, 60, 61, 66, 67,
81–82, 165, 167, 176, 180; border,
33; checkpoint, 33; geopolitical,
186; women and, 72
Speed Venture Partners, 127
Srouji, Dima, 153
Staeheli, Lynn, 186
State of Israel, 146, 148; declaration
of, 8; Palestinian society and, 179

"Status Quo in the Holy Places" policy, 105
St. Michael's Hotel, 112
Stock (bar), 100, 209n22
Stockholm International Peace Research, 136
stress, 22, 26, 27, 39, 42, 56, 66, 80; levels of, 38; pressure and, 78; responsibilities and, 79
subjectivity, 19, 41, 51, 172, 185
Superbus, 88
Surda Checkpoint, 162, 164
surveillance, 7, 22, 129, 132, 154, 137, 172, 173, 208n16; automated, 120; contracts, 127; drone, 184; hardware of, 12; mass, 149; proliferation of, 118; systems, 119, 136

Taavura Holdings, 131
Tadiran, 132
Talpiot Road, 88
Tamimi, Ahed, 158
Tana, Ibrahim Saleh, 139
T&M Israel, 122, 138–39, 141
T&M Protection Resources LLC (T&M USA), 122, 141
Tariq al-Khalil. See Hebron Road
Tavor TAR-21, 126
Tavor X95 assault rifle, 124, 132
Tawil-Souri, Helga, 32, 39, 119, 164, 165, 180; checkpoint economy and, 86; checkpoint time and, 74; colonial struggle and, 162; on Qalandia Checkpoint, 31; on waiting, 73
tear gas, 98, 102, 116, 119, 121, 124, 125, 126, 129–31, 151; attacks with, 130; boomerang effect of, 129, 134; cannister, 128 (fig.); deaths from, 131; exposure to,

129, 130; launchers, 130, 213n30; production of, 130, 137; suppliers of, 130–31
technologies, 25, 67, 125, 178; battle-tested, 119, 129, 132, 137; boomerang, 129, 134; checkpoint, 34, 39–40, 135; colonial, 42; political, 36; renovating, 122; weapon, 118. See also security technologies
Tech Parks Arizona, 132
Tel Aviv, 11, 126, 127
temporalities, 60, 67, 72, 74
terrorism, 40, 172, 222n5
Thai–Israel Cooperation on the Placement of Workers (2011/2020), 143
thanatopolitics, 34, 35, 116, 152, 167, 170, 172, 175, 188; logic of, 168
Tohono O'odham, 132
toilets, 34, 46, 54, 101, 122
Tora Bora method, 165
tourism, 32, 159; birthright, 183; political, 156; religious, 112; solidarity, 154, 156
transportation, 11, 26, 112, 188
Tuck, Eve, 175
Tunnels Highway, 176, 178, 179, 179 (fig.), 211n5
turnstiles, 1, 11, 12, 13 (fig.), 15, 19, 21, 22, 25, 26, 27, 30, 31, 38, 39, 49, 51, 55 (fig.), 67; children and, 54; remote-controlled, 122; women in, 51
T-walls, 109

UAV Tactical Systems, 133
UK Customs, 125
Umm Tuba, 88
ungovernability, 18, 40, 152, 164, 170, 171, 172, 173, 174

unionists, 20, 33, 38, 143
United Nations, 5, 9, 136, 207n3;
    Security Council resolutions, 8,
    196n11
University of Arizona, Elbit and, 132
University of California, Berkeley
    Human Rights Center, 130
urban battle space, 118, 123 (fig.),
    124, 181
urban warfare, 102, 115, 116, 132
USAID, 197n18
U.S. Central Command, 196n13
U.S. Customs and Border Protection,
    132
U.S. Department of Defense, 125
U.S. Department of Homeland
    Security, 125
U.S. Embassy, 90
U.S. European Command Area of
    Responsibility, 196n13
U.S. Internal Revenue Service,
    217n93

VENOM tear gas launchers, 131,
    213n30
violence, 11, 42, 67, 80, 94, 116, 117,
    171, 186; checkpoint, 31; colonial,
    38, 134, 157, 187; emergence
    of, 54; gendered, 180; military,
    7, 100, 117, 173; monopoly on,
    139; political, 164; sovereign,
    60; state, 35, 139, 140; threats of,
    22, 38

waiting, 23, 26, 42, 46, 48, 52, 72, 87;
    colonialism and, 73; corporeality
    of, 27; "disjunctive temporality"
    of, 73; in queues, 73–74
wall, 40, 158; construction of, 5, 111
    (fig.)
wall crawling, 24, 24 (fig.), 52

Walled Off Hotel, 96, 97, 112, 154,
    159
Wall Museum, 151
Waqf Ministry of Religious Affairs,
    97, 108, 112
War on Terror, 9
Washington Post, 24, 202n60
watchtowers, 85 (fig.), 98, 100, 113
    (fig.), 117, 208n16
Wauchope, Sir Arthur, 130
weapons, 118, 140, 148; crowd
    control, 17; international ex-
    change of, 138; non/lethal, 120;
    standard-issue, 178
weapons industry, 96, 136, 137
Weizman, Eyal, 25, 178
Weizmann, Chaim, 172
West Bank, 5, 11, 12, 20, 45, 46, 48,
    69, 74, 83, 84, 93, 96, 97, 100,
    114, 119; Americans in, 222n5;
    attacks on, 153; checkpoints in,
    1; holy sites in, 106; ID card for,
    92; Jordanian rule of, 105; Jordan
    River and, 8; settlers in, 183; sur-
    veillance in, 127; tear gas in, 130;
    tourism in, 159; tunnel in, 177;
    unemployment in, 7
West Bank Palestinians, 2, 21, 84, 86,
    115, 141, 152, 177, 178; im/mobil-
    ity of, 137; permits for, 20
Whistleblowers, Activists and
    Communities Alliance, 133
Who Profits, 14, 213n30
Wi'am Building, 102, 112, 115, 154
women: colonized, 49, 71, 72;
    controlling, 16–17, 56, 58, 61,
    63; embarrassment for, 33–34;
    experiences of, 58–59, 79; hu-
    manitarian land and, 52; mobility
    of, 49; power dynamics and, 72;
    secondary role for, 70–71; social

acceptability for, 52; visibility of, 48
women's rights movement, 63
World Bank, 141

X-ray inspections, 22, 30

Yang, Wayne, 175
yeshiva, 112, 145, 146, 154, 182

Yishai, Eli, 109
Yom Kippur, 87

Zionism, 8, 96, 105, 127, 144, 145, 146, 147, 171–72, 181, 184
Zionist National Regulations Party, 108
Zionist Organization, 171
Zion Towers, 88

Mark Griffiths is reader in political geography at Newcastle University. He is coeditor of *Encountering Palestine: Un/making Spaces of Colonial Violence.*